GENDER, CRIME & JUSTICE
CRITICAL AND FEMINIST PERSPECTIVES

First Edition

By Rosalva Resendiz
University of Texas - Pan American

Bassim Hamadeh, CEO and Publisher
Michael Simpson, Vice President of Acquisitions
Jamie Giganti, Managing Editor
Miguel Macias, Graphic Designer
Marissa Applegate, Acquisitions Editor
Gem Rabanera, Project Editor
Alexa Lucido, Licensing Coordinator
Mandy Licata, Interior Designer

ISBN: 978-1-62661-827-5 (pbk) / 978-1-62661-828-2 (br)

www.cognella.com   800-200-3908

CONTENTS

INTRODUCTION

Gender, Crime, and Justice: Feminist Sexual Politics

By Rosalva Resendiz

I n selecting the articles for this reader, I had to consider how to engage the student with the topic of gender, crime and justice through a critical feminist lens, which would aid the student in understanding how gender has been utilized to socially control an individual's body. It has been my goal to create a reader that would intersect gender and crime in a discourse of feminist sexual politics.

Hence, the reader addresses four main topics surrounding gender: socialization, human rights, violence, and crime. The reader introduces the student to feminist perspectives and the concepts associated with gender, from equality to violence, by exploring the socialization of girls and boys. And in the second half of the reader, the student has a more in-depth look into crimes of sex and the discourses surrounding sexual autonomy.

The reader is intended to explore the concept of gender and sex as a means of social control, which has subjected, subjugated, dominated, and oppressed females, as well as males—in particular, those who do not conform to gender stereotypes of femininity and masculinity. The social control of gender, sex, and sexuality is addressed through an exploration of patriarchal values which endorse sexual violence and sex crimes.

The reader explores the socio-historical treatment of women, but also includes issues associated with masculinity. We tend to focus on women only when we speak of gender, but the concept of gender is not mutually exclusive. To understand and discuss gender, it must be inclusive. In the selections, the discourse on gender explores the various ways in which it affects females and males in a society that values heteronormative masculinity.

The reader begins with an introduction of feminist criminology, including a definition of feminism, highlighting that there must be a "recognition that gender is a cultural organizing principle of social life" in which male domination upholds a patriarchal system that values men over women, masculinity over femininity (Renzetti, 2012, p. 129).

Feminism is a pedagogical tool used to deconstruct the binary. Feminism seeks to explore the multiple inequalities that intersect to form a hierarchy of domination, subjugation, oppression, and victimization. By exploring the inequality in our socio-legal system, we are able to begin to eradicate many of the social problems associated with gender and sex. As such, feminism is a tool for social change and engages in body politics, making the personal, also a political issue (hooks, 1984).

The second reading explores the links between masculinity and crime (Messerschmidt & Tomsen, 2012). Not only are women and girls subjected to patriarchal notions of masculinity; boys and males are also victims to this socialization. Hegemonic masculinity, or the hierarchy of male/masculine/heterosexual superiority, has been reproduced historically through socio-legal mechanisms, as well as through violence and crime. Hegemonic masculinity is exerted in various forms: through language, sex, and violence. Hegemonic masculinity plays its part in sexual assault, rape culture, hate crimes, and organized crime.

The reader proceeds to explore how girls and adolescents have historically been controlled to conform to gender stereotypes, by focusing on their sexuality and sexual reputation (Banks, 2013). Patriarchal values have been endorsed by institutions in subjecting the feminine and the female, while promoting violence against nonconformist individuals. Although there are violent female offenders, their pathways to delinquency and crime are complicated by victimization and abuse. Female offenders are both subjects and agents in delinquency and crime. The victimization and abuse that children, men, and women suffer are based on traditional patriarchal values which emphasize power and control over other bodies.

The fourth reading, "A Gendered View of Violence," addresses the roots of feminist perspectives on women and violence (Paquette Boots & Wareham, 2013). Various theories are provided on the socialization of gender as it pertains to offending and victimization. Females are involved in various types of violence as offenders and as victims, from homicide to intimate partner violence to gang involvement. The next reading specifically explores the links between patriarchy and violence against women (York, 2011). Patriarchy promotes a culture of male dominance, gender-based inequality, and exploitation. Violence is encouraged and normalized in order to preserve patriarchal traditions. This reading allows the student to see beyond their socialization and explore the various ways in which society has inculcated gender inequality as normal.

In addressing the socialization process of inequality, the reader includes two discussions on the autonomy of the body: "Women's Human Right to Health" and "Women's Human Rights to Reproduction and Sexuality" (Mertus & Flowers, 2008a, 2008b). It is imperative that students understand basic human rights of bodily autonomy. The discourse on autonomy is subverted by paternalistic notions of protection, but the reality is that these notions harm women and children. A woman has a right to health, reproduction and sexuality. Every individual has the right to make decisions about his or her own body. Hence, human rights become sexual body politics. These two articles provide exercises that will help students facilitate their understanding of issues surrounding women's health and choice.

The second half of the text focuses on crimes associated with sex: rape, human trafficking, and prostitution. Reading #8, "Rape and Child Molestation" (Flora & Keohane, 2008), lists the numerous types of sexual crimes, as well as types of offenders. Women, men, and children have been subjected to sexual violence, and only recently has the definition of rape included both men and women. The next two readings discuss the politics of rape (Jervis 2008; Filipovic 2008). Although rape is considered a crime, patriarchy has contested the reality of the crime by blaming women. Hegemonic masculinity has promoted a rape culture in which women are sexual objects that can be taken at any time. And in this rape culture, men are not always held accountable for their behavior.

Sexual violence against women and children has grown into a criminal enterprise of human trafficking, in violation of fundamental human rights. Those who are trafficked are forced into labor, marriage, and/or prostitution. Burke (2013) provides an overview of the various forms of human trafficking, as well as the international conventions that fight against modern slavery, in addition to U.S. efforts. Individuals who are trafficked face well-organized syndicates, which work in cooperation with corrupt governments. The second reading on human trafficking focuses on the extent of sex trafficking (Samarasinghe, 2007). The illicit nature of human smuggling and human trafficking make it difficult to truly grasp the seriousness of the problem. Samarasinghe addresses the reasons why these types of crimes persist today and enumerates the various efforts taken by the United Nations.

Many of the victims of sexual violence are immigrant women, who suffer at the hands of smugglers and/or traffickers. Perez (2008) discusses that the victimization of immigrants is complicated by racist and classist U.S. immigration policies. Immigrant women not only face sexual violence by their captors, but suffer institutional violence as well.

The final two readings look at female and male prostitution. In "Prostitution: The Gendered Crime," the authors point out that these crimes persist because of the high demand for women and girls as sexual commodities (Raphael & Ellison, 2013). Many of the prostitutes in the United States have suffered physical and sexual abuse as children and entered prostitution before the age of 18. Some of these children have been prostituted by their families, while others have been recruited by pimps. Violence and addictions are associated with a life of a prostitute, yet prostitution has been normalized in our culture through legalization. It is clear that children and adolescents are victims of prostitution/trafficking, but it becomes complicated when adults are sex workers. For some feminists, the ability to choose sex work can be a source of empowerment, yet the circumstances in which these women are forced to choose, framed by a sexist society that treats women as sexual objects, makes prostitution exploitive.

The final reading by Weitzer (2011) notes that male and transgender prostitution has been ignored in the literature. Weitzer indicates that the female and male prostitutes have similar hierarchies, placing street walkers at the bottom, while escorts have high status. And in the same way that adolescent female runaways engage in "survival sex," young males on the streets will do the same. Weitzer also finds differences beyond the economic reasons. Males may engage in prostitution for sexual adventure, are less likely to be coerced, have greater control over their working conditions, and have diverse sexual orientations.

It has been my goal to provide the student with the necessary intellectual tools to understand the complexity of inequality and oppression and to empower the student with an understanding of his or her agency and subjectivity in society. Each of the readings was selected by thinking about the discourse of body politics and sexual politics, while intersecting issues of justice. The discourse serves to deconstruct critically the multiple ways in which gender impacts our society. With this in mind, I hope that students will see beyond their socialization and truly learn social justice.

REFERENCES

Banks, C. (2013). Gender and juvenile justice. In C. Banks (Ed.), *Youth, crime & justice* (pp. 75–102). New York: Routledge.

Burke, M. C. (2013). Introduction to human trafficking: Definitions and prevalence. In M. Burke (Ed.), *Human trafficking: Interdisciplinary perspectives* (pp. 3–23). New York: Routledge.

Filipovic, J. (2008). Offensive feminism: The conservative gender norms that perpetuate rape culture and how feminists can fight back. In J. Valenti & J. Friedman (Eds.), *Yes means yes* (pp. 13–27). Berkeley, CA: Seal Press.

Flora, R., and Keohane, M. L. (2008). Rape and child molestation. In R. Flora & M. L. Keohane (Eds.), *How to work with sex offenders: A handbook for criminal justice, human service & mental health professionals* (pp. 146–161). New York: Routledge.

Jervis, L. (2008). An old enemy in a new outfit: How date rape became a gray rape and why it matters. In J. Valenti & J. Friedman (Eds.), *Yes means yes* (pp. 163–170). Berkeley, CA: Seal Press.

hooks, b. (1984). *Feminist theory: From margin to center*. Boston, MA: South End Press.

Mertus, J. A., & Flowers, N. (2008a). Women's human rights to reproduction and sexuality. In J. A. Mertus & N. Flowers (Eds.), *Local action/global change: A handbook on women's rights* (pp. 127–146). Boulder, CO: Paradigm.

Mertus, J. A., & Flowers, N. (2008b). Women's human right to health. In J. A. Mertus & N. Flowers (Eds.), *Local action/global change: A handbook on women's rights* (pp. 112–126). Boulder, CO: Paradigm.

Messerschmidt, J. W., and Tomsen, S. (2012). Masculinities. In W. E. Dekeseredy & M. Dragiewicz (Eds.), *Handbook of critical criminology* (pp. 172–185). New York: Routledge.

Paquette Boots, D., & Wareham, J. (2013). A gendered view of violence. In C. M. Renzetti, S. L. Miller, & A. R. Gover (Eds.), International handbook of crime & gender studies (pp. 163–176). New York: Routledge.

Perez, M. Z. (2008). When sexual autonomy isn't enough: Sexual violence against immigrant women in the United States. In J. Valenti & J. Friedman (Eds.), *Yes means yes* (pp. 141–150). Berkeley, CA: Seal Press.

Raphael, J., & Ellison, M. C. (2013). Prostitution: The gendered crime. In C. M. Renzetti, S. L. Miller, & A. R. Gover (Eds.), *International handbook of crime & gender studies* (pp. 141–157). New York: Routledge.

Renzetti, C. M. (2012). Feminist perspectives in criminology. In W. E. Dekeseredy & M. Dragiewicz (Eds.), *Handbook of critical criminology* (pp. 129–137). New York: Routledge.

Samarasinghe, V. (2007). Female sex trafficking: Defining the nature and size of the problem. In V. Samarasinghe (Ed.), *Female sex trafficking in Asia* (pp. 1–9). New York: Routledge.

Weitzer, R. (2011). Male prostitution. In C. D. Bryant (Ed.), *The handbook of deviant behavior* (pp. 378–382). New York: Routledge.

York, M. (2011). The influence of patriarchy and traditional gender role attitudes on violence against women. In M. York (Ed.), *Gender attitudes and violence against women* (pp. 13–28). El Paso, TX: LFB Scholarly Publishing.

CHAPTER ONE

Feminist Perspectives in Criminology

By Claire M. Renzetti

INTRODUCTION: WHAT IS FEMINIST CRIMINOLOGY?

In recent interviews with social activists working to address the problem of sex trafficking worldwide, I have posed the question, "Do you consider yourself a feminist?" The common reply from interviewees goes something like this: "No, I wouldn't say I'm a feminist; I think all people should be treated equally and respectfully." Before answering the question, "What is feminist *criminology*?," then, it would be useful to first answer the question, "What is *feminism*?," for there appears to be some confusion as to the meaning of this term. And it is undeniably a label that nowadays is loaded with social and political baggage.

The emergence of contemporary feminism is typically dated in the 1960s. At that time in the United States, Canada, Britain, and Europe, various social movements developed in response to widespread social injustice, including racial and ethnic inequality, colonialism, and the Vietnam War. Women were active participants in these movements, but quickly (and correctly) perceived that they frequently were not treated as equals by male participants. At the same time, women in what may be considered more mainstream social venues—for example government, business, and education—grew increasingly dissatisfied with how little genuine equality they enjoyed despite their formal legal rights. Not surprisingly, university campuses were often at the center of this social and political activism, and many academics—mostly, but not solely, women—began to take a careful look at their respective disciplines to learn how these might be actively or implicitly reproducing social inequalities, including gender inequality. Criminology was no exception.

From this introspection, a number of different perspectives emerged, all of which may be labeled feminist. There are several core principles, though, that feminist theories share. First, at the heart of feminism is the recognition that *gender* is a central organizing principle of social life. Gender may be defined as the *socially constructed* expectations or norms governing female and male behavior and attitudes that are usually organized dichotomously as *femininity* and *masculinity* and are reproduced and transmitted through socialization. Of course, biology influences the development of gender, too, but, although feminist perspectives recognize the complex interaction between biology and environment, feminism emphasizes the socially constructed, rather than innately determined, aspects of gender.

If gender is constructed dichotomously, then membership in gender categories is exclusive. In other words, a person is *either* feminine *or* masculine. Setting aside for the moment the problematic aspects of conceptualizing gender this way, an issue to which we will return later in the chapter, consider first the fact that the genders are not equally valued in the vast majority of societies. A second core principle of feminism, therefore, is that most societies, both on a macro (structural/institutional) level and on a micro (interpersonal) level, are characterized by *sexism*, that is, the differential valuing of one gender over the other. In most societies, this sexism is a built-in feature of a *patriarchal* social system in which men dominate women and what is considered masculine is more highly valued than what is considered feminine.

The academic disciplines exist within the patriarchal social system, so it is hardly surprising that women have been systematically excluded from many fields, including criminology, which are not considered "feminine" or appropriate for women. Moreover, women and girls have been systematically excluded from the studies conducted by members of male-dominated fields under the assumption that what women do, think, or say is unimportant or uninteresting (Lorber, 2009). Similar to other disciplines, beginning in the 1970s feminist criminologists highlighted the gender biases in widely used criminological theories and how women and girls have historically been overlooked in studies of crime and criminal justice (Chesney-Lind, 2006; Jurik, 1999). Consequently, another core principle of feminism is the inclusion of female experiences and perspectives in theorizing and research. This is not to say that male experiences and perspectives should be excluded; rather, feminists emphasize the critical importance of ensuring that female voices are heard, given that they have typically been silenced or simply ignored. A major goal of feminist research and theorizing is to uncover and explain similarities and differences in women's and men's behaviors, attitudes and experiences, which arise from their different locations in—and differentially imposed valuing by—the social structure. Although their different social locations constrain their responses or resistance to their relative circumstances, the ways that women and men choose to respond or resist—the ways they exercise *agency*—are, like all other aspects of social life, gendered.

The focus on gender, and not solely on women, is a critically important point because many people, as indicated by my interviewees' responses, think of feminism as "only" about women or "women's issues." It is certainly the case that feminist theorists and researchers have prioritized the study of women's attitudes, behaviors, and experiences because these have largely been neglected and excluded. Nevertheless, feminist perspectives include research and theorizing about both masculinities and femininities. Indeed, in studying women's *and* men's lives over the past four decades, feminist researchers have shown that not all groups of men benefit equally or in the same ways from gender privilege. As feminism has developed and matured, therefore, another significant principle to which many feminist theorists adhere is the necessity of analyzing how gender inequality *intersects* with multiple inequalities, including racism, classism, heterosexism, ageism, and ableism, to form an interlocking system of oppression that impacts women's and men's everyday lives, including their risk of criminal victimization and offending and their treatment as "clients" or employees of the criminal justice system (Burgess-Proctor, 2006; Risman, 2004).

Unlike other perspectives, feminism is not solely a set of theories; it is also a *social movement* informed by a theoretical framework with the goal of collective action to eliminate sexism and promote gender equity in all areas of social life. In conducting research and explaining their findings, feminist social scientists, including feminist criminologists, are engaged in what sociologist Joann Miller (2011) has called *purpose-driven research*: research that raises public awareness, in this case of gendered inequalities, and which produces usable knowledge that contributes to the social reconstruction of gender and gender relations so they are more equitable. Feminist researchers strive to acquire scientific knowledge through the research process that empowers individuals and groups to act to change behaviors and conditions which are harmful or oppressive.

This goal has important implications for how feminist research is conducted. Examples of feminist research will be discussed throughout this chapter, but suffice it to say here that, in general, feminist researchers reject the traditional model of science "as establishing mastery over subjects, as demanding the absence of feeling, and as enforcing separateness of the knower from the known, all under the guise of 'objectivity'" (Hess & Ferree, 1987, p. 13; see also Naples, 2003; Reinharz, 1992). Instead, feminist research is often characterized by *reciprocity* between the researcher and the research participants; rather than establishing relational distance from the research participants, the researcher engages in self-disclosure and may offer resources and helpful information, recognizing that research participants are frequently revealing private, sometimes traumatic aspects of their lives to a stranger and that they may, in fact, need assistance that the researcher can provide. Feminist researchers also try to take an *empathic stance* toward the participants in their studies; instead of imposing their own ideas or categories of response on their participants, they give participants a more active role in guiding the direction of the research and attempt to understand the phenomena they are studying from the participants' viewpoints.

This approach to research reflects another core principle of feminist perspectives: the research process is *dualistic*; that is, it has both subjective and objective dimensions. Feminists emphasize that no research is completely unbiased or value-free. No matter how objective researchers like to believe they are, they cannot help but be influenced by values, personal preferences, and aspects of the cultural setting and institutional structures in which they live. That said, research is not totally subjective either. Although a researcher may be influenced by values (i.e. judgments or appraisals), her or his goal is the collection of facts (i.e. phenomena that can be observed or empirically verified). Feminists challenge researchers to explicitly acknowledge the assumptions, beliefs, sympathies, and potential biases that may influence their work. They question not only the possibility, but also the desirability, of value-free science; however, although they reject this notion, they do not reject scientific standards in their research (Reinharz, 1992). And although the ideals of reciprocity and an empathic stance imply an emphasis on qualitative methods, such as ethnography and in-depth interviewing, many feminist researchers, including feminist criminologists as we will see shortly, conduct quantitative studies using sophisticated statistical techniques to analyze their data, or mixed approaches that incorporate both quantitative and qualitative methods (see, for example, Campbell, 2011a,b).

So to return to the question that opened this chapter: "What is feminist criminology?" The short answer is that feminist criminology is a paradigm that studies and explains criminal offending and victimization as well as institutionalized responses to these problems as fundamentally gendered and which emphasizes the importance of using the scientific knowledge we acquire from our study of these issues to influence the creation and implementation of public policy that will alleviate oppression and contribute to more equitable social relations and social structures. Like many short answers, however, this one is inadequate and unsatisfying. As was noted at the outset, there is no single, unitary feminist perspective, but rather a diversity of feminist perspectives, each with variations on the core principles presented. Let us turn, then, to a discussion of some of the major feminist perspectives in criminology.

FEMINIST CRIMINOLOGIES

A number of typologies have been offered in an attempt to classify the many feminist perspectives currently being applied to the study of social life (see, for example, Lorber, 2009). Within criminology, it is argued that there are at least 12 distinct feminist theories (Maidment, 2006). Space constraints preclude a review of every theoretical perspective that may be considered feminist, so a select few— what I consider to be the major feminist criminological theories—will be discussed in this chapter. That said, it must be acknowledged that not all feminist criminologists agree on which theories to label "major"; some readers, therefore, will likely disagree with my selection, perhaps considering it too "conventional," and would choose other theories to highlight instead. Keep in mind, too, that the presentation of these theories is not chronological. Although some theories preceded others temporally and new perspectives built on these initial or early approaches, several theories were being developed and tested simultaneously, as is typically the case in criminology and other disciplines.

Liberal Feminist Criminology

In general, liberal feminism may be described as an "equal rights" approach in that the focus is largely on securing the same legal rights for women that men enjoy. Liberal feminists consider the major cause of gender inequality to be blocked opportunities, so the primary goal of their social activism has been dismantling gender discrimination in employment, education, government, and other social institutions. In addition, as women and men are taught specific—and unequal—gender roles, liberal feminists have sought to change traditional gender socialization practices so that men and women learn to be more alike in terms of their attitudes and behaviors.

Liberal feminism influenced several feminist criminological theories, particularly early in the development of feminist criminology. For example, emancipation theories of female offending (Adler, 1975; Simon, 1975) are rooted in liberal feminism. Emancipation theorists sought to explain what they perceived to be dramatic increases in female offending during the late 1960s and early 1970s. They attributed these changes to newly opened opportunities for women and girls, thanks to the women's liberation movement. In short, these theories argue that, just as legitimate opportunities opened for women and girls, so too did illegitimate or criminal opportunities. And because females were being encouraged to behave more like males, it should be no surprise that this would lead them to do so in less than positive ways as well, such as being more violent and committing more property crimes.

The value of any theory, of course, depends on how well it stands up to empirical testing. Emancipation theories were shown to be seriously flawed through research that demonstrated that, in fact, the gender gap in the crime rate was not closing as much as emancipation theorists believed, and that females were not becoming more like males in terms of the types of crimes they were committing. To be sure, women and girls were being arrested and imprisoned more frequently than in the past—and this trend has continued—but to a large extent this change reflected their greater likelihood of committing the property crimes for which they were traditionally charged (e.g. larceny, fraud) and drug offenses. Some feminist critics of the emancipation perspective have also argued that females' elevated arrest and incarceration rates are the result of policy and practice changes in the criminal justice system. More specifically, critics argue that the 1980s "war on crime" essentially became in practice a war on women and racial minorities, especially blacks, and that rising arrest and incarceration rates of women represent "equality with a vengeance" (Chesney-Lind, 2006). The question of whether females, or some groups of females, are treated more or less leniently by the criminal justice system continues to be debated and researched by feminist criminologists (see, for example, Spohn & Brennan, forthcoming), but empirical evidence clearly does not support the notion that a "downside" of the women's liberation movement is that it motivated women and girls to commit more crimes or to act "more like men."

Another liberal feminist theory is power-control theory (Hagan, 1989; McCarthy, Hagan, & Woodward, 1999). Power-control theory looks at how social class, as a mediating factor in gender socialization, may result in different rates of female and male offending, especially juvenile delinquency. In families characterized by patriarchal control—that is, families with a traditional gendered division of labor in which the husband/father is in the paid labor force and the wife/mother remains at home to care for the household and socialize the children—girls are socialized to be like their mothers (domestic, subdued, and, therefore, unlikely to take risks), whereas boys have considerably more freedom and more opportunities for risk-taking, including crime. Power-control theory posits that this arrangement is more common among working-class families. In families that are more egalitarian or "balanced" in terms of the gendered division of labor, in which both husbands/fathers and wives/mothers are in the paid labor force, girls and boys are treated more alike. Mothers in these families are still seen as primarily responsible for the gender socialization of their children and, the theory maintains, they less tightly control their daughters' opportunities and behavior and increase their control over their sons, such that the girls' and boys' behavior is likely to be more similar, including in terms of risk-taking and delinquency. Power-control theory sees this arrangement as more common among middle-class families.

Empirical support for power-control theory has been mixed at best (see, for example, Heimer & DeCoster, 1999; Morash & Chesney-Lind, 1991). The theory has also been critiqued for its simplistic conceptualization of social class and the gendered division of labor in the home and workplace, and for its lack of attention to racial/ethnic differences in gender socialization and to single-parent families, most of which are headed by women. Another significant weakness in power-control theory is its limited definition of patriarchal control, which is reduced to parental supervision (Chesney-Lind, 1997; Chesney-Lind & Sheldon, 1992). Patriarchal control, however, is far more complex and may take a variety of forms, ranging on a continuum from severe, brutal violence at one extreme, to what has been called "chivalry" or "benevolent sexism" at the other extreme. Let us consider, then, additional feminist criminological perspectives that recognize the importance and complexity of patriarchy and patriarchal control.

Radical Feminist, Marxist Feminist, and Socialist Feminist Criminology

One theoretical approach that broadens the scope of patriarchal control is radical feminist criminology. Radical feminism maintains that gender inequality or sexism is the most fundamental form of oppression and that it is females who are oppressed. Indeed, radical feminists argue that, throughout the world, females are the most oppressed group and that, regardless of race, ethnicity, or social class, men enjoy gender privilege, which includes the subordination and control of women. Patriarchal social structures, including the criminal justice system, serve to preserve male power and ensure female subordination, and one of the primary ways that this is accomplished is through the threat or actual use of violence. Radical feminist criminologists, then, have pioneered the study of women as crime victims, particularly as victims of violent crimes perpetrated by men, and the failure of the criminal justice system to protect women from men's violence.

Victimization by violent crime is gendered. Although males are more likely than females to be the victim of a violent crime, research by radical feminist criminologists and others consistently documents the alarming frequency of violence against women throughout the world and the multitude of forms it takes, including sexual harassment, sexual assault and rape, battering, and homicide (see Renzetti, Edleson, & Bergen, 2010). This research also shows that, ironically, although we advise girls not to talk to strangers, they are significantly more likely to be harmed by someone they know; in 70 percent of violent crimes committed against women, the victim knew her assailant, whereas in only 45 percent of violent crimes committed against men did the victim know his assailant (Truman & Rand, 2010; see also Kruttschnitt, 2001). According to radical feminist criminologists, however, despite these data the police, courts, and criminologists themselves have been preoccupied with male street crime, and the criminal justice system has been overwhelmingly ineffective in keeping women and girls safe, and holding men and boys accountable for the violence they perpetrate against them.

Work by radical feminist criminologists laid the foundation for the burgeoning research on violence against women that continues at present. Nevertheless, critics of radical feminist criminology maintain that this perspective still portrays the criminal justice system too negatively. Significant legislative and enforcement reforms have occurred over the past several decades (e.g. changes in rape laws designed to shift the focus of blame from the behavior of the victim to the behavior of the assailant, harsher penalties for batterers). Although some feminist researchers have identified gaps between these laws on paper and how they are actually implemented (e.g. Caringella, 2008), it cannot be denied that they have been beneficial to women.

Another criticism of radical feminist criminology is that it characterizes all men as oppressors, equally likely to harass, rape, or abuse women, even though it is the case that the majority of men do not violently victimize women and some profeminist men actively work to prevent and respond to such victimization. Moreover, this perspective overlooks women's violent offending, a point to which we will return shortly. And finally, by fore-grounding gender as the paramount oppression, radical feminist criminologists inaccurately universalize the categories of "female" and "male," while overlooking the reality that gender inequality intersects with other types of inequality, particularly racism and social class inequality (Burgess-Proctor, 2006).

Marxist feminist criminologists differ from radical feminist criminologists in that they prioritize social class inequality over gender inequality. Marxist feminist criminologists maintain that societies with less social class inequality also have less gender inequality, because male dominance, like other types of discrimination, grows largely out of unequal economic conditions, specifically the exploitative class relations inherent in capitalism. Thus, from this perspective, if capitalism is replaced with a more egalitarian mode of production, this egalitarianism will be reflected in other spheres of social life, including gender relations.

However, some feminist criminologists see Marxist feminism as making an error similar to radical feminism: one form of inequality does not take precedence over another form of inequality. Oppression is not linear. Instead, in their everyday lives people *simultaneously* experience the effects of *multiple inequalities*, just as they also experience different forms and degrees of *privilege*. Socialist feminist criminology is one theoretical perspective that recognizes the importance of examining how the interaction of gender and social class inequalities influences criminal opportunities, victimization experiences, and responses by the criminal justice system to both offenders and victims. Messerschmidt (1993), for example, argues that the crimes individuals commit reflect both their social class position and their socialized conceptions of masculinity and femininity.

Socialist feminist criminologists were also the first to draw attention to the fact that the traditional criminological construction of offenders and victims as two distinct or dichotomous groups is largely inaccurate when gender is also taken into account (Jurik, 1999). Research shows that violent victimization, especially during childhood, is often a pathway to subsequent involvement in crime, more so for girls than for boys. For instance, Widom and Maxfield (2001) found a significant increase in arrest for violent crime among girls who were neglected and abused compared with girls who had not been neglected and abused, but this relationship did not hold for boys (see also Siegel & Williams, 2003). This pattern is found in studies of adult offenders as well (English, Widom, & Brandford, 2001; Morash, 2006).

However, although socialist feminist criminology attends to the dual importance and interactive effects of sexism and social class inequality, and highlights the salience of victimization in understanding pathways to criminal offending, particularly by women and girls, this perspective has been criticized nevertheless for depicting women and men as relatively homogeneous social categories, distinguishable only by social class differences. More recent feminist theories have drawn attention to the need to examine how race and ethnicity intersect with gender, social class, and other locations of inequality in order to understand both criminal offending and victimization, and the responses of the criminal justice system. It is to these theories that we turn to conclude this chapter.

CONTEMPORARY AND FUTURE DIRECTIONS IN FEMINIST CRIMINOLOGICAL PERSPECTIVES

As noted in the chapter introduction, gender is typically conceptualized in dichotomous terms: a person is *either* feminine *or* masculine. Recently, however, some feminist criminologists have adopted the reconceptualization of gender as *situated action* or *situated accomplishment* (West & Fenstermaker, 1995; West & Zimmerman, 1987); that is, gender is something one *does* in response to contextualized norms. From this perspective, males and females "do gender" in various situations, and make choices—albeit choices constrained by structural conditions and normative expectations—about how they will establish their masculinity and femininity respectively. Gender, then, is in flux; it changes over time, and from situation to situation, in response to normative demands and an individual's resources and perceptions of others' evaluations of him or her. This perspective also takes into account intersecting locations of inequality, such that individuals also simultaneously do race/ethnicity, social class, sexuality, and age, thereby producing multiple masculinities and femininities, "each shaped by structural positioning" (Miller, 2002, p. 435). Consequently, some feminist criminologists are theorizing that crime is a means for accomplishing gender in certain contexts, and these efforts to do gender also affect who is victimized. Consider, for instance, the recent studies of hate crime conducted by Bufkin (1999) and Perry (2001). In their analyses of the characteristics of hate crime perpetrators and their victims, as well as the characteristics of the crimes themselves (e.g. language used by perpetrators, the group nature of most hate crimes, use of alcohol by perpetrators), these feminist criminologists theorize that committing a hate crime is a means of accomplishing a particular type of masculinity, *hegemonic masculinity*, which is described as white, Christian, able-bodied, and heterosexual.

Other feminist criminologists call for even greater attention to the intersection of gender, social class, and race/ethnicity as well as other inequalities, emphasizing their interlocking nature in a "matrix of domination" (Collins, 2000). For example, black feminist criminology builds on both critical race feminist theory and black feminist theory more generally. This theoretical perspective is often referred to as a "standpoint theory," in that it focuses on the lived experiences of black women, recognizing their multiple intersecting identities and analyzing their oppression both within the black community and in the larger society, as well as their resistance to these forms of oppression. Potter (2006) identifies four themes in black feminist criminology—social structural oppression, interactions in the black community, intimate and familial relations, and the black woman as individual—and applies them in an analysis of intimate partner violence in the lives of black women to show how black women's intertwined racialized and gendered identities produce experiences of intimate partner violence that are different from the experiences of other groups of women and, therefore, require different responses. Even more broadly, Burgess-Proctor (2006) challenges feminist criminologists to embrace multiracial feminism in their work, emphasizing the critical importance of considering the *interactive* rather than additive effects of race, gender, class, age, sexuality, and other social locators on offending, victimization, and criminal justice processes. She offers numerous examples of criminological studies that demonstrate how the intersection of these factors affect the "production of crime," the relationship between victimization and offending, and criminal justice outcomes such as sentencing disparities.

A brief chapter such as this one can hardly do justice to the diversity of feminist perspectives within criminology, and I have overlooked many, such as pragmatic feminism (McDermott, 2002) and postmodern and poststructural feminism (Howe, 2000; Wonders, 1999). Nevertheless, this overview offers perhaps a sampling of some of the most influential and most promising feminist theoretical perspectives in criminology today. Undoubtedly, the work of feminists of color and also that of Third World feminists in non-Western or economically developing societies in Africa, Asia, and Latin America will enrich feminist criminology—and criminology as a discipline—in the years to come.

REFERENCES

Adler, F. (1975). *Sisters in crime.* New York: McGraw-Hill.

Bufkin, J. (1999). Bias crime as gendered behavior. *Social Justice, 26*, 155–176.

Burgess-Proctor, A. (2006). Intersections of race, class, gender, and crime: Future directions for feminist criminology. *Feminist Criminology, 1*, 27–47.

Campbell, R. (Ed.). (2011a). Special issue: Methodological advances in recruitment and assessment. *Violence against Women, 17*(2), 159–162.

Campbell, R. (Ed.). (2011b). Special issue: Methodological advances in analytic techniques for longitudinal designs and evaluations of community interventions. *Violence against Women, 17*(3), 291–294.

Caringella, S. (2008). *Addressing rape reform in law and practice.* New York: Columbia University Press.

Chesney-Lind, M. (1997). *The female offender.* Thousand Oaks, CA: Sage.

Chesney-Lind, M. (2006). Patriarchy, crime, and justice: Feminist criminology in an era of backlash. *Feminist Criminology, 1,* 6–26.

Chesney-Lind, M., & Sheldon, R. G. (1992). *Girls' delinquency and juvenile justice.* Pacific Grove, CA: Brooks/Cole.

Collins, P. H. (2000). *Black feminist thought* (2nd edn.). New York: Routledge.

English, D. J., Widom, C. S., & Brandford, C. B. (2001). *Childhood victimization and delinquency, adult criminality, and violent criminal behavior: A replication and extension.* Final report. Washington, DC: U.S. Department of Justice, National Institute of Justice.

Hagan, J. (1989). *Structural criminology.* New Brunswick, NJ: Rutgers University Press.

Heimer, K., & DeCoster, S. (1999). The gendering of violent delinquency. *Criminology, 37,* 277–318.

Hess, B. B., & Ferree, M. M. (1987). Introduction. In B. B. Hess & M. M. Ferree (Eds.), *Analyzing gender* (pp. 9–30). Newbury Park, CA: Sage.

Howe, A. (2000). Postmodern criminology and its feminist discontents. *Australian and New Zealand Journal of Criminology, 33,* 221–236.

Jurik, N. C. (1999). Socialist feminist criminology and social justice. In B. A. Arrigo (Ed.), *Social justice, criminal justice* (pp. 30–50). Belmont, CA: Wadsworth.

Kruttschnitt, C. (2001). Gender and violence. In C. M. Renzetti & L. Goodstein (Eds.), *Women, crime and criminal justice* (pp. 77–92). Los Angeles: Roxbury.

Lorber, J. (2009). *Gender inequality: Feminist theory and politics.* New York: Oxford University Press.

Maidment, M. R. (2006). Transgressing boundaries: Feminist perspectives in criminology. In W. S. DeKeseredy & B. Perry (Eds.), *Advancing critical criminology: Theory and application* (pp. 43–62). Landham, MD: Lexington Books.

McCarthy, B., Hagan, J., & Woodward, T. S. (1999). In the company of women: Structure and agency in a revised power-control theory of gender and delinquency. *Criminology, 37,* 761–788.

McDermott, M. J. (2002). On moral enterprises, pragmatism, and feminist criminology. *Crime & Delinquency, 48,* 283–299.

Messerschmidt, J. W. (1993). *Masculinities and crime.* Lanham, MD: Rowman & Littlefield.

Miller, J. (2002). The strengths and limits of "doing gender" for understanding street crime. *Theoretical Criminology, 6,* 433–460.

Miller, J. A. (2011). Social justice work: Purpose-driven social science. *Social Problems, 58,* 1–20.

Morash, M. (2006). *Understanding gender, crime and justice.* Thousand Oaks, CA: Sage.

Morash, M., & Chesney-Lind, M. (1991). A re-formulation and partial test of power-control theory. *Justice Quarterly, 8,* 347–377.

Naples, N. A. (2003). *Feminism and method.* New York: Routledge.

Perry, B. (2001). *In the name of hate: Understanding hate crime.* New York: Routledge.

Potter, H. (2006). An argument for black feminist criminology: Understanding African American women's experiences with intimate partner abuse using an integrated approach. *Feminist Criminology, 1,* 106–124.

Reinharz, S. (1992). *Feminist methods in social research.* New York: Oxford University Press.

Renzetti, C. M., Edleson, J. L., & Bergen, R. K. (Eds.) (2010). *Sourcebook on violence against women* (2nd edn.). Thousand Oaks, CA: Sage.

Risman, B. J. (2004). Gender as social structure. *Gender & Society, 18,* 429–450.

Siegel, J. A., & Williams, L. M. (2003). The relationship between child sexual abuse and female delinquency and crime: A prospective study. *Journal of Research in Crime and Delinquency, 40,* 71–94.

Simon, R. J. (1975). *Women and crime.* Washington, DC: Government Printing Office.

Spohn, C., & Brennan, P. (forthcoming). Sentencing and punishment. In C. M. Renzetti, S. L. Miller, & A. Gover (Eds.), *Handbook of gender and crime studies*. London: Routledge.

Truman, J. L., & Rand, M. R. (2010). *Criminal victimization, 2009*. Washington, DC: U.S. Department of Justice, Bureau of Justice Statistics.

West, C., & Fenstermaker, S. (1995). Doing difference. *Gender & Society, 9*, 8–37.

West, C., & Zimmerman, D. H. (1987). Doing gender. *Gender & Society, 1*, 125–151.

Widom, C. S., & Maxfield, M. G. (2001). *An update on the "cycle of violence."* Washington, DC: U.S. Department of Justice, National Institute of Justice.

Wonders, N. A. (1999). Postmodern feminist criminology and social justice. In B. A. Arrigo (Ed.), *Social justice, criminal justice* (pp. 109–128). Belmont, CA: Wadsworth.

CHAPTER TWO

Masculinities

By James W. Messerschmidt and Stephen Tomsen

INTRODUCTION

Since the early 1990s, criminological scholars have examined the relationship between masculinities and crime, resulting in numerous individually authored books (Collier, 1998; Messerschmidt, 1993, 1997, 2000, 2004, 2010; Mullins, 2006; Polk, 1994; Tomsen, 2009; Winlow, 2001), edited volumes (Bowker, 1998; Newburn & Stanko, 1994; Tomsen, 2008), special academic journal issues (Carlen & Jefferson, 1996), and a variety of scholarly articles (e.g. Cohen & Harvey, 2006; Hearn & Whitehead, 2006; Peralta & Cruz, 2006; Whitehead, 2005). This chapter provides an overview of certain key features of this relatively recent criminological literature regarding masculinity and crime, as well as some of the more significant empirical studies in this new field. It describes the evident strengths of the emerging "masculinities" paradigm in criminology. But it also notes the pitfalls of any gender-centric analysis of criminality, which could overlook a skewed criminalization process that frequently targets, criminalizes, and punishes men and boys from disadvantaged and marginal social settings.

Male offenders commit the great majority of crimes. Arrest, self-report, and victimization data reflect that men and boys perpetrate more conventional crimes—and the more serious of these crimes—than do women and girls. And men have a virtual monopoly on the commission of syndicated, corporate, and political crime (Beirne & Messerschmidt, 2010). Criminologists have consistently advanced gender as the strongest predictor of criminal involvement and, consequently, studying men and boys provides insights into understanding the highly gendered ratio of crime in industrialized societies. Historically, the reasons for this highly gendered ratio of crime have puzzled researchers, officials, and commentators. Although criminal justice agencies focus heavily on detecting, prosecuting, and punishing the working-class, poor, and minority male offenders, it is apparent that high levels of recorded and reported offending reflect a real and pervasive social phenomenon of disproportionate male criminality. Since its origins at the end of the 1800s, criminology has experienced difficulty explaining the link between masculinity and crime, and research has often disregarded the link between criminal offending and maleness.

Much traditional criminological discourse closely concerned the study and control of "dangerous" forms of masculinity, particularly working-class male delinquency, but did not address the relation between criminality and the socially varied attainment of masculine status and power. Criminologists studied crime from a "male norm" perspective, and never developed a sufficiently critical view of its link to gender, especially to non-pathological and widespread forms of masculine identity that are tied to offending. The result has been a tendency to naturalize male offending and reversion to gender essentialism by explaining male wrongdoing as an inherent and pre-social phenomenon to which men are drawn.

The earliest criminologists—such as Edwin Sutherland (1956 [1942]) and Albert Cohen (1955)—relied ultimately upon an essentialist "sex-role" framework to explain the relationship between masculinity and crime. That is, the presumption was that a "natural" distinction existed between men and women, a distinction that led ineluctably to masculine men and feminine women. Accordingly, what united these criminologists was that their theoretical frameworks ultimately ascribed to individuals certain innate characteristics that formed the basis of gendered social conditions—the male and female sex roles—which led to specific sexed patterns of crime. In other words, biogenic criteria allegedly established differences between men and women, and society culturally elaborated the distinctions through the socialization of sex roles. These sex roles, in turn, determined the types and amounts of crime committed by men and women, and by boys and girls. Thus, for these early criminologists, the body entered criminological theory cryptically as biological differences between men and women (Messerschmidt, 1993).

Notwithstanding, early criminologists such as Sutherland and Cohen can be credited for putting masculinity on the criminological agenda. These scholars perceived the theoretical importance of gender and its relation to crime, and they acted upon that awareness. However, their conclusions demonstrate the limitations that one would expect from any pre-feminist criminological work. Gender essentialism was the accepted doctrine of the day; it took modern feminism to dismantle that powerful "commonsense" understanding of gender. Rather than being gender blind, then, Sutherland and Cohen simply had a different conception of gender from what exists among critical criminologists today. The social and historical context in which they wrote embodied (1) a relative absence of feminist theorizing and politics and (2) an assumed "natural" difference between men and women. Accordingly, it should not be surprising that they advanced the types of theories they advanced.

This focus on biology by early criminologists also often viewed crime as a reflection of *defective* male and female bodies/identities (Gould, 1981). A range of subsequent accounts similarly disregarded the social link between crime and masculinity. These have included Marxist and left accounts that focused on class differences to explain crime, and they either relied on biological sex differences to explain the gendered pattern of most criminal offending or they simply ignored it (Bonger, 2003 [1916]; Taylor, Walton, & Young, 1973).

This legacy has been challenged by contemporary research on the social construction of masculinities and the "everyday" qualities of their aggressive and destructive forms. Since the 1980s, this shift has been a response to the wider reflection on gender and identity born of social movements including feminism, gay and lesbian activism, and sections of "the men's movement." In particular, research on violence against women has stressed the relationship between offending and everyday, often legitimized constructions of manhood. In the academy, there has been a growth in research on male violence and a general expansion of research on masculinity or "men's studies" (see Connell, Kimmel, & Hearn, 2005; Kimmel, 1987; Segal, 1990).

MASCULINITY THEORY

This new field also owes much of its inspiration to the theoretical contributions by the well-known Australian sociologist Raewyn Connell (1987, 1995), who developed a key explanatory model of different forms of masculinity. Connell's concept of *hegemonic masculinity* has been defined not as a particular character type, but as an entire complex of historically evolving and varied social practices in societies that either legitimize, or attempt to guarantee, the shoring up of patriarchy and male domination of women. Hegemonic masculinities, then, are those forms of masculinity in particular social settings that structure gender relations hierarchically between men and women and among men. This relational character is central, in that it embodies a particular form of masculinity in hierarchical *relation* to a certain form of femininity and to various non-hegemonic masculinities. Arguably, hegemonic masculinity has no meaning outside its *relationship* to femininity—and non-hegemonic masculinities—or to those forms of femininity that are practiced in a complementary, compliant, and accommodating subordinate relationship with hegemonic masculinity. It is the legitimization of this relationship of superordination and subordination whereby the meaning and essence of hegemonic masculinity is revealed. Moreover, any attainment or approximation of this empowered hegemonic form by individual men is highly contingent on the uneven levels of real social power in different men's lives.

A key marginalized form is "protest masculinity" (Connell, 1995, p. 109). This is a concept that has been used before by criminologists and it appropriates the psychoanalytic description of "masculine protest." It describes a gender identity that is characteristic of men in a marginal social location with the masculine claim on power contradicted by economic and social weakness. Protest masculinity may be reflected in hypermasculine aggressive display, as well as in anti-social, violent, and criminal behavior. Frequently, it exhibits a juxtaposition of overt misogyny, compulsory heterosexuality, and homophobia.

This model of "hegemonic" and other masculinities has been quite influential but also much contested in the social sciences, including criminology. For some liberal critics, this model may seem too closely tied to Marxist ideas about an overarching dominant ideology as a ruling set of oppressive masculine beliefs. Yet much of the critique has come from the left and post-modern camps. Some critics have suggested that this model downplays social class and reflects a degrading view of working-class men as inherently violent and destructive (Hall, 2002). Jefferson (2002) suggests that this model results in a narrow view of true masculinity as a wholly negative set of personal attributes. Collier (1998) argues that the model offers an imprecise notion that "masculinity" comprises whatever men do. He rejects the gender/masculinities approach for a particular focus on the male body that may overstate gender differences and struggle to explain the diversity, contradictions, and subtleties of social forms of masculinities.

MASCULINITIES AND CONTEMPORARY CRIMINOLOGY

The above-discussed criticisms have been soundly challenged (Connell, 2002; Connell & Messerschmidt, 2005; Messerschmidt, 1999a); consequently, the notion of hegemonic and marginalized masculinities has been displayed in a rich and widening range of criminological studies that examine the full spectrum of masculine offending. The fundamental feature of the concept of hegemonic masculinity remains the combination of the plurality of masculinities and the hierarchy among hegemonic masculinities and femininities, as well as non-hegemonic masculinities. This basic idea has well withstood over 22 years of research experience. Moreover, multiple patterns of masculinity have been identified in numerous studies, in a variety of countries, and in different institutional and cultural settings. And it is a widespread research finding that certain masculinities are hegemonic, necessarily in *relation* to femininities and non-hegemonic masculinities. That the concept of hegemonic masculinity presumes the subordination of femininities and non-hegemonic masculinities is a process that has been well documented in many international settings (Connell & Messerschmidt, 2005).

Critical work in criminology has emphasized that masculinity is linked to more than just violent crime by less powerful men, and relates widely to such matters as motor vehicle offenses, theft, drug use and dealing, white-collar crime, and political crime. In the "new masculinities" approach there is an emphasis on the relations between different masculinities, the causes and patterns of most criminal offending and victimization, and the broader workings of the wider criminal justice system of public and private policing, criminal courts, corrections, and prisons (Newburn & Stanko, 1994).

These scholars share the view that masculinities are plural, socially constructed, reproduced in the collective social practices of different men, and embedded in institutional and occupational settings. Furthermore, masculinities are linked intricately with struggles for social power that occur between men and women and among different men. They vary and intersect importantly with other dimensions of inequality. Messerschmidt's (1993, 1997, 2000, 2004) influential accounts of crimes as "doing masculinity"—to be understood within a structured action framework—incorporate differences of class, race/ethnicity, age, sexuality, and bodies, and the common concern with power. As there are different forms of masculinity that are differently linked to the attainment of social power, crime itself is a means or social resource/practice to construct masculinity, and analyses must balance consideration of structural forces and human agency.

Differences in masculinity that shape violence against women are a frequent topic of interest. For example, Kersten (1996) details cross-cultural evidence to illustrate an underlying link between masculine domination and a wide range of reported and unreported rapes, forms of sexual harassment, and coercion from both male strangers and acquaintances. Additionally, he stresses the national differences in gender relations and evolving masculinities to argue that, although these assaults are related to a range of social and historical factors, their incidence is higher in Australia (than Germany or Japan) because of its overtly aggressive public masculine culture. Such violence is viewed as a means of asserting or seeking a male identity that is increasingly under threat of change from new social forces. Likewise, the important work of DeKeseredy and Schwartz (2005) has shown that, for a variety of forms of male physical and sexual violence against women, the intent of the perpetrator often is to deploy violence as a means of presenting a particular type of dominating masculine image to himself, to the victim, and to his peer group. The work of Cruz (2003) shows similar masculine dynamics among gay men involved in domestic violence.

A key analysis of the 1990s concluded that the typical "masculine scenarios" of most killings are disputes between men regarding insults and slights to personal honor or assaults directed at controlling female spouses and domestic partners (Polk, 1994). A detailed discussion of many incidents reflects the masculine and everyday forms of most fatal interpersonal violence. It appears the criminal defenses (particularly provocation) that are invoked by many accused have been generally unavailable to women who kill, which suggests a link with notions of masculine violence and a degree of respect in the criminal justice system and wider culture.

Research on anti-homosexual killings has also suggested a masculine pattern in much of this violence and the official criminal justice system response to it (Tomsen, 2009). Anti-homosexual killings occur within two general masculine scenarios. Typically they comprise fatal attacks in public space that are perpetrated by groups of young males concerned with establishing a manly self-image, and in more private disputes with allegations of an unwanted homosexual advance by a perpetrator protecting a masculine sense of honor and bodily integrity through retaliatory violence. Thus, many hate crimes (racist attacks as well as violence directed at gay men, lesbians, and transgender people) are not a form of offending that is wholly distinct from other masculine violence (Tomsen, 2001).

In probably the best study to date on masculinities and street violence, Mullins (2006) presents an important account of how and why a specific form of hegemonic masculinity is embedded in the street life of St. Louis, Missouri. His analysis not only supports previous theoretical work on masculinity and street crime, but also extends that work by demonstrating that street-life hegemonic masculinity can be understood only in its relationship to subordinated "punk" masculinities—masculinities that likewise are constructed in the same street-life culture—and in relation to particular femininities in that street culture. Mullins's exposition of street violence is solid, confirming previous theoretical work that considerable violence among men in public settings results from masculinity challenges (Messerschmidt, 2000). Mullins explores how men within specific social situations come to view certain practices of other men as a threat to their masculinity, a threat that requires a culturally supported masculine response: physical violence. Moreover, he clarifies how such masculinity challenges can subsequently escalate, resulting all too often in the death of one or more of the male interactants.

Mullins' analysis adds two new and intriguing dimensions to our understanding of men involved in street violence. First, he presents an incisive discussion of interaction among street men and the various women in their lives. Previous work on masculinities and street crime unaccountably ignores this salient component of gender relations. Mullins, however, uniquely explicates that such men tend to construct *hegemonic* masculinities—or those masculinities that fashion power relations between men and women and among men—over women on the street and/or over those sharing domestic households. Second, Mullins examines one of the most under-explored areas of research on masculinities in general—the contradictions involved in masculine constructions. The author lucidly illustrates how the men in his study vacillated among multiple meanings of masculinity according to their interactional needs.

Until quite recently, there has been scant analysis of masculine attitudes toward subjection to violence beyond the general finding that men as a group tend to be less fearful in relation to crime. Australian and European research within the new masculinities approach has studied the experience of confrontational violence by tracing the role of victimization in establishing power relations between men and the mixed effects on victims that both undermine and reinforce conventional ideas of masculinity (Stanko & Hobdell, 1993; Tomsen, 2005).

The narrow view that masculine crime solely comprises acts of physical violence has been balanced by accounts of gendered patterns of theft, economic, corporate, and political offending. An important early example of this view was an analysis of the particular masculine attractions that motor-vehicle offending and thefts hold for many working-class boys (Cunneen, 1985; see also Cunneen & White, 1996). The broad potential of this explanation of non-violent offending has been recognized in international studies; for example, an important interview study provides further understanding of the motivations and processes involved in the masculine magnetism to a range of non-violent offending by exploring the group interactions and exchanges that precede collective offending—including robbery, burglary, and vehicle theft by groups of young risk-taking males (Copes & Hochstetler, 2003).

In an interesting examination of how masculinity is tied to social class through economic fraud committed by socially privileged men, the authors did not attempt to uncover the causes of the criminal behavior but, rather, analyzed how the offenders subsequently explained and justified their actions (Willott, Griffin, & Torrance, 2008). Specifically, during the interviews the sample of privileged men drew on particular masculine discourses to present a cohesive and plausible account of their offending behavior. For example, these men stated that they used the male breadwinner discourse (he is the economic "provider" for the family) but extended this notion to include employees and their families. That is, they described themselves as "normal men" who engaged in financial fraud unpretentiously to provide for their families and to protect their employees and their employees' families from economic ruin. In this sense, then, these professional men constructed themselves in a specific middle-class masculine way: they must shoulder more responsibility than working-class men, who are simply providers for their families but not protectors of others.

The masculine seductions of criminal risk at higher levels of social class and privilege are apparent in a classic account of the 1985 *Challenger* disaster that seriously undermined confidence in the U.S. Space Shuttle program. The fatal decision to launch against strong evidence of equipment failure and the resulting crew deaths reflected the dominance of a particular managerial masculinity that valued risk and decisiveness and discounted human consequences (Messerschmidt, 1995).

Institutional crime by collective decision-making or oversight does not fit the classic liberal notion of a single-reasoning (presumptive male) criminal actor. These insights into the masculinity of corporate and economic crime might well inform the recent criminological interest in state crime. There is a range of major public institutional offending of concern to critical criminology—including internal and external official violence, paramilitary activity, and warfare—that also is deeply masculine, yet remains a fertile but mostly untouched field for researchers of this ilk. Destructive military masculinities have been of particular concern in recent discussions about the potential success of international peacekeeping efforts in a range of post-war settings (Breines, Connell, & Eide, 2000). Messerschmidt's (2010) newest work—*Hegemonic Masculinities and Camouflaged Politics: Unmasking the Bush Dynasty and Its War against Iraq*—investigates the orchestration of regional and global hegemonic masculinities through the speeches of the two U.S. Bush presidents—George H. W. Bush and George W. Bush—that contrast forms of communicative social action to "sell" the long-standing war against Iraq. The study makes the case for a multiplicity of hegemonic masculinities, and outlines how state leaders may appeal to particular hegemonic masculinities in their attempts to "sell" wars and thereby camouflage salient political and criminal practices that subsequently and significantly violate international law.

CULTURE, ETHNOGRAPHY, AND LIFE HISTORIES

The new crime and masculinities research also has examined the discursive analysis of cultural representations and has included a variety of ethnographic studies that seek out the viewpoints that inform masculine social action in relation to crime and criminal justice. The significance of a general vicarious masculine interest in violence, crime, and wrongdoing is evident from contributions made by researchers exploring the status of cultural meanings in a wide range of societies. Sparks (1996) has explained how popular Hollywood depictions of male heroism as a critical aspect of policing and law enforcement—in such films as *Dirty Harry, Lethal Weapon,* and *Total Recall*—shape and skew public understanding of crime and the law. Cavender (1999) has shown how masculine models were constructed differently in Hollywood feature films of the 1940s from those of the 1980s. This is not just a matter of the characters written into the scripts. Practice at the local level—that is, the actual faceto-face interaction of shooting the film *as an actor*—ultimately constructs masculine fantasy models (in this case "detectives") at the society-wide or regional level.

The tension between individual agency and objective factors in masculine criminal activity and the value of an insider understanding of that tension are evident in the fully ethnographic picture drawn by Bourgois's (2002) study of New York crack dealers from a deprived Puerto Rican neighborhood. The men studied by Bourgois struggled for masculine respect through their wrongdoing. Drug-dealing, violence, and sexual assaults provided a distorted mirror of the limited empowerment that was won by male forebears in a traditional rural patriarchy, in which protection and provision for women and families were vital aspects of gender dominance. Graphic snapshots of brutality, gang rapes, and other crimes and cultural detail gathered by painstaking and dangerous fieldwork fleshed out the racialized, criminal masculinities assumed by these young men.

The theme of masculine crime in deindustrialized settings has been pursued by Australian and British ethnographic researchers studying night-time leisure and related offending and policing (Hobbs, Hadfield, Lister, & Winlow, 2003; Tomsen, 1997; Winlow, 2001). There are sensual attractions in the liminal "night-time" economy for its many young participants, and an allied official ambivalence toward the male aggression and disorder that characterize it. In Monaghan's (2002) insider account of "bouncing" in a study of private security officers working in nightclubs and pubs in city centers in southwest Britain, physicality and violent potential are transformed into a workplace skill built on the importance of forceful bodies. The mixed official response to the economic benefits and social costs of the expanding night economy that fosters drunkenness, male conflicts, and disorder problems is evident also in the discomfort with, and reliance on, the aggressive masculinity of security officers instructed to maintain a semblance of public order.

The danger of this work generates hierarchies of male physical ability within private policing, especially reflected in the masculine contrasts between "hardmen," "shopboys" working security in retail stores, and "glass-collector types" who are less physically imposing and are unable to deal with the risks of violent encounters. The same masculine hierarchy inflects the positioning of the minority of women working in this occupation; they are either denigrated as unmasculine and physically incapable or, in fewer cases, given a marginal position in a masculine hierarchy.

This hierarchy is a specific form of masculinity that has global manifestations and corresponds with images from a general culture. It also seems to involve a form of private policing that is laxly regulated and which reproduces forms of masculine identity that are close to the original aggressive physicality of traditional, unreformed public policing. Given the fine line between legitimate force and actual assault, bouncing itself encapsulates a gendered identity at the edge of protest and official masculinities that criminal justice systems often express as tensions and convergence.

In a North American study, Anderson, Daly, and Rapp (2009) explored the relationship between masculinities and crime within the hip-hop and electronic dance music nightclub scenes. The authors found that respondents who revealed they contextually constructed masculinity "upward" through excessive alcohol use, heightened sexuality, competitiveness, and commercialization were the most frequently involved in nightclub crime. These males defined "clubbing" as a status-oriented and hedonistic endeavor in which "they must toughen or macho up to navigate," thereby constructing a masculine performance that often simultaneously leads to crime.

The importance of life-histories research to studies of crime and masculinity that seek out insider perspectives on offending has appeared in a range of recent accounts. Jefferson (1997) argued that researchers in this field should not ignore the unconscious and contradictory personal aspects of any criminal masculine identity. Obviously, he had in mind the lessons of his own life-history account of Mike Tyson, which traces the evolution of a socially vulnerable boy into a champion athlete and convicted rapist, and reveals the links between racial marginality and hypermasculine violence. Similarly, in one of Messerschmidt's recent studies, a dynamic interplay of hegemonic and other masculinities is demonstrated through discussion of the lives of youth assaultive and sexual offenders from working-class neighborhoods. This interplay occurs against the backdrop of different relations between the body and achievable masculinities, as social understandings of the body shape offending in two different criminal pathways (Messerschmidt, 1996b, 2000).

Despite a recent attempt to challenge the notion that some girls/women under specific situations construct masculinities through criminal practices (Irwin and Chesney-Lind, 2008), the fact that gender is not determined biologically surely leads scholars to identify and examine possible *masculinities by women and girls* (and femininities by men and boys) and their relation to crime. There remains a necessity in the new masculinities criminological research to uncover girls' and women's relations to crime and violence, and to determine whether or not such social action constructs masculinity or femininity.

Jody Miller's (2001, 2002) work is unique in this regard, as her important book, *One of the Guys*, shows that certain gang girls identify with the boys in their gangs and describe such gangs as "masculinist enterprises": "To be sure, 'one of the guys' is only one part of a complex tapestry of gender beliefs and identities held by the gang girls I spoke with—and is rarely matched by gendered actions—but it remains significant nonetheless" (Miller, 2002, p. 442). Pointing out that gender inequality was rampant in the mixed-gender gangs of which these girls were members—such as male leadership, a double standard with regard to sexual activities, the sexual exploitation of some girls, and most girls' exclusion from serious gang crime—certain girls differentiated themselves from other girls through a construction of "one of the guys." In other words, the notion "one of the guys" is not fashioned by being *similar* to boys (because of inequalities) but, rather, certain girls are *different* from other girls because they embrace a masculine identity. Miller's research contributes to the process of discovering differences among gang girls, especially regarding how the distribution of male and female members within particular gangs may impact gender construction. Moreover, her work helps point scholars in an important direction for discovering these differences and demonstrates how certain girls, like certain boys, can construct a masculine self through involvement in crime.

Similarly, in his book *Flesh and Blood*, Messerschmidt (2004) demonstrated through a study of adolescent assaultive violence that numerous gender constructions by violent girls were prevalent, and that some girls "do" masculinity by in part displaying themselves in a masculine way, by engaging primarily in what they and others in their milieu consider to be authentically masculine behavior, and by outright rejecting of most aspects of femininity.

In addition to eschewing possible masculinities by girls and women and femininities by boys and men, most writing on crime and masculinity concentrates on the *mind* while ignoring the *body*. Messerschmidt's work, however, just discussed, highlighted how violent boys *and* girls interact with and through their body. The interview data in his study demonstrated that the body is not neutral in "doing masculinity" (or femininity) but, rather, is an agent of social practice: often the body initially constrained, yet eventually facilitated, gendered social action; it mediated and influenced future social practices. Given the social context, bodies could do certain things but not others—the bodies of these youth are "lived" in terms of what they can "do." Consequently, for these youth "doing masculinity" (or femininity) is experienced in and through the body: eventually they literally construct a different body and, thus, a new gendered self through their embodied violent practices.

The life-histories approach has also been deployed to offer clues about questions raised by non-offenders. As crime is a ready resource for attaining masculinity, particularly among socially marginal or highly competitive groups of men, researchers wonder what this means for the masculinity of non-offenders. Accordingly, British researchers have explored the subjective significance of "desistance" for male working-class offenders (Gadd & Farrell, 2004). Ending criminal offending and criminal careers is a puzzle for conventional criminology that the masculinities approach may help to unravel. By following the signposts in Jefferson's analysis of violence and the masculine unconscious and by balancing individual agency with structural determination (of the sort stressed in research on risk factors and life-course stages), these researchers conclude that desistance is a complex gendered process (Gadd & Farrell, 2004). A detailed discussion of life circumstances reveals the contradictory nature of this desistance. An apparent ending to criminality is shaped around heroic male discourses of redemption and protectiveness and the uncertain possibilities of male renunciation of actual or fantasized violence, the latter being more widespread and commonly shared by offenders and other males alike.

An additional value of insider understanding in accounts of masculine offending and non-offending is signalled by a study of young Australian men and security officers involved in regular episodes of drinking violence and disorder (Tomsen, 2005). The point is that, although the link between masculinity and criminality has been newly emphasized, researchers have minimal understanding of the means by which withdrawal from violence fits with a socially respected masculine identity. "Disengagement" is understood here as a process of situational decision-making and withdrawal from conflicts and offending that may characterize a broad population of non-criminal men, rather than as any full "desistance" from a set criminal pathway and identity. Involvements in drinking-related public violence are tied to matters of male group status, the protection of honor in episodes involving insults and slights that must be addressed, and the collective pleasure of carnival-like rule-breaking in public disorder. Yet an awareness of danger and a disengagement from occasions of conflict can fit with rational and restrained models of a masculine self. This may even be cultivated by public safety campaigns that provide an exaggerated belief that individual agency always prevails in avoiding violence.

THE MASCULINITY AND CRIMINALIZATION CONUNDRUM

A growing number of studies in this new field explore the ties between masculinity and elements of the justice system: policing, courts, prisons, and probation. A close look at these studies suggests the contradictory relations that exist between criminal "protest" masculinities and "official" state masculinities in this sphere. Any full understanding of this evidence must consider the ways in which criminalized masculinities are produced in tension with the official forms of masculinity inscribed in policing and criminal justice systems. As Connell (1995) has suggested, dynamic relationships exist between hegemonic and other subordinated or marginalized forms of masculinity that produce different masculinities and gender politics within masculinity. The criminological implication is that social forms of masculinity linked to violence and offending are both produced and policed by aspects of the criminal justice system and state institutions.

In this sense, Hall's critique of hegemonic masculinity does usefully draw attention to the interrelation of different masculinities, and how problematic conceiving the differences between hegemonic and potentially criminal protest masculinities has become for criminologists with an elastic use of these terms in some discussions of male criminality. Furthermore, the commentator hypocrisy in this field to which he refers suggests that there remains an insufficient understanding of the condoning and cultivation of violent forms of masculinity by capitalist, imperial, and contemporary post-colonial nation-states. Moreover, masculine violence is deployed internally and externally in a range of state forms, and both legitimized and denounced in different historical and social circumstances (however, see the earlier discussion of Messerschmidt's (2010) newest book as it begins to fill this research void).

The paradox of regulating criminalized masculinities with the formally law-abiding though sexist and aggressive official masculinities of criminal justice systems is reflected in research on policing (Prokos & Padavic, 2002). For example, Nolan (2009, p. 250) recently discussed the existence in policing of an "idiosyncratic construct of masculinity that privileges tacit conspiracies of silence," thereby validating heterosexuality, hierarchical regimentation, homosocial bonding, homophobia, and paternalistic misogyny among North American male police officers. Responses to criminal justice intervention that foster and reproduce masculinities with a direct or indirect relation to criminality are uncovered in other contemporary studies. Most notably, the general failure of prisons to deter crime or to rehabilitate inmates with any certainty is now informed by accounts of inmate masculinity, illustrating the sharp struggles over male power and status and the masculine hierarchies that characterize prison subcultures and the lives of incarcerated men.

An interview study with British prisoners suggests that a specific form of masculinity which is hard, aggressive, bullying, and conformist is a usual adaptation to prison (Jewkes, 2005). Prisons have a dehumanizing impact that threatens personal identity through a climate of "mortification and brutality." This impact engenders a hard masculine social performance among inmates. Jewkes' analysis and related work on prison masculinities cogently suggest that aspects of the intervention process itself affirm destructive forms of male identity, to which criminal justice systems ostensibly are opposed (Sabo, Kupers, & London, 2001; Whitehead, 2000, 2005).

This contradiction leads to a major conceptual problem for the new crime and masculinities paradigm, as a critical analysis of masculine offending necessitates an understanding of the historically shifting and fluid way that destructive masculinities have been either condoned or denounced by policing and criminal justice systems. Moreover, this problem results in dilemmas for programs of punishment, correction, and crime prevention that may appear to both treat and foster male criminality (Holland & Scourfield, 2000).

Feminists have been critical of the way in which male violence against women has been simultaneously denounced yet condoned or ignored in the wider culture and in traditional "hands off" police responses. Further examples of the mixed official reaction to male violence from the new literature on masculinity and crime concern the shifting historical responses to public violence and various forms of hate crime (Tomsen, 2001). In many of these cases, discouraged reporting, lax policing, and lenient sentences signal support for the generation of an aggressive masculinity in relation to public leisure and spaces. Male on male violence that results from this may be regarded as a minor public nuisance or an inevitable aspect of the social reproduction of appropriate masculinities.

Furthermore, violence and criminal offending by groups of men can also signal resistance against social hierarchy. Historical and cross-cultural scholarship has convincingly demonstrated that much male violence is an ambiguous form of protest or rebellion against social hierarchies based on social class, caste, and racial/ethnic differences. This research includes studies of disorder, unruly leisure, festivals, carnivals, and more direct acts of insubordination, including rallies and riots, as means of symbolic protest and collective cultural resistance to the moral values of ruling groups (Rude, 1995; Scott, 1985; Tilly, 2003). In fact, official and police concerns over collective male disorder that refer to a compelling need to protect the broader public are driven also by anxiety about the symbolic challenge to state, class, and racial authority that this disorder can comprise.

These different examples reflect the complexities of official reactions and the criminalization process in relation to different crimes and masculinities. Male crime is gendered crime; yet when commentators on the masculinity–crime nexus cannot acknowledge the link between the bulk of male offending and such other factors as social class and race, they risk inadvertently naturalizing male offending. This shortsighted view reinforces a widespread public belief in a commonsense opinion of masculinity as a force inevitably leading millions of men to involvement in crime and violence.

The dilemmas of problematic-gendered male offending and an overlapping criminalization process are evidenced in the debate raised by certain key examples of contentious crimes and their policing. Among these are the controversies surrounding acts of public disorder perpetrated by young "Middle Eastern" men in south-western Sydney, Australia, and the trials and imprisonment of key offenders given heavy sentences in a series of group rape cases (Poynting, Noble, & Tabar, 2003; Warner, 2004). More recently, the ongoing concern in Australia over how to deal progressively with the issue of domestic and sexual assaults in indigenous communities has become increasingly public (HEREOC, 2006). In such cases, different forms of violence are related to particular racialized protest masculinities that reflect distinct histories of marginality due to the effects of migration and racial dispossession in a white Anglo-dominated culture.

CONCLUSION

Research findings affirm the overall value in acknowledging the link between crime and masculinities for criminological understanding. It is now incumbent upon critical criminology to move beyond the impasse generated by explanations of crime that either downplay male offending or focus on it to the exclusion of evidence of criminalization and other social factors. Criminalization is a common strategy in a contemporary era of post-left-new-social movement activism toward crime that may dovetail with punitive law and order politics (Snider, 1998). This strategy can encourage a major expansion of police and prisons, and the imposition of longer and often mandatory sentences, which erodes any commitment to alternative punishments. Such harsh penalties will have the pernicious effect of net widening, mass incarceration, and punishment for vengeance sake, rather than reform or rehabilitation. And, of course, this strategy specifically targets and brutalizes poor, black, and indigenous men, causing further divisive and negative impacts on their fragile communities.

Masculine crime may appear to be inevitable, even abhorrent. Yet there is scant progressive gain in simple essentialist understandings of male offending, a denial of human agency, or a cynical dismissal of substantial efforts to educate and promote diverse and non-violent masculinities among marginalized boys and men. To be critically aware of the extent and effects of the criminalization process and its secondary effects in racist and class-divided societies requires a constant reflexivity in analyzing the masculinity–crime nexus.

REFERENCES

Anderson, T., Daly, K., & Rapp, L. (2009). Clubbing masculinities and crime: A qualitative study of Philadelphia nightclub scenes. *Feminist Criminology, 4*(4), 302–332.

Beirne, P., & Messerschmidt, J. W. (2010). *Criminology: A sociological approach*. New York: Oxford.

Bonger, W. (2003 [1916]). Criminality and economic conditions. In E. McLaughlin, J. Muncie, & G. Hughes (Eds.), *Criminological perspectives: Essential readings*. London/Thousand Oaks: Sage.

Bourgois, P. (2002). In search of respect: Selling crack in El Barrio. New York: Cambridge University Press.

Bowker, L. (Ed.). (1998). *Masculinities and violence*. Thousand Oaks, CA: Sage.

Breines, I., Connell, R. W., & Eide, I. (Eds.). (2000). *Male roles: Masculinities and violence: A culture of peace perspective*. Paris: UNESCO.

Carlen, P., & Jefferson, T. (Eds.) (1996). Masculinities and crime. Special issue of the *British Journal of Criminology, 33*(6).

Cavender, G. (1999). Detecting masculinity. In J. Ferrell & N. Websdale (Eds.), *Making trouble: Cultural constructions of crime, deviance and control*. New York: Aldine de Gruyter.

Cohen, A. (1955). *Delinquent boys: The culture of the gang*. New York: Free Press.

Cohen, J. W., & Harvey, P. J. (2006). Misconceptions of gender: Sex, masculinity, and the measurement of crime. *Journal of Men's Studies, 14*(2), 223–233.

Collier, R. (1998). *Masculinities, crime and criminology: Men, heterosexuality and the criminal(ised) Other*. London: Sage.

Connell, R. W. (1987). *Gender and power*. Sydney: Allen and Unwin.

Connell, R. W. (1995). *Masculinities*. St. Leonards, NSW: Allen and Unwin.

Connell, R. W. (2002). On hegemonic masculinity and violence: Response to Jefferson and Hall. *Theoretical Criminology, 6*(1), 89–99.

Connell, R. W., Kimmel, M., & Hearn, J. (Eds.). (2005). *Handbook of studies on men and masculinities*. Thousand Oaks, CA: Sage.

Connell, R. W., & Messerschmidt, J. (2005). Hegemonic masculinity: Rethinking the concept. *Gender and Society, 19*(6), 829–859.

Copes, H., & Hochstetler, A. (2003). Situational construction of masculinity among male street thieves. *Journal of Contemporary Ethnography, 32*(3), 279–304.

Cruz, M. (2003). "Why doesn't he just leave?" Gay male domestic violence and reasons victims stay. *Journal of Men's Studies, 11*(3), 309–323.

Cunneen, C. (1985). Working class boys and crime: Theorising the class/gender mix. In P. Patton & R. Poole (Eds.), *War/masculinity.* Sydney: Intervention Publications.

Cunneen, C., & White, R. (1996). Masculinity and juvenile justice. *Australian and New Zealand Journal of Criminology, 29*(1), 69–73.

DeKeseredy, W., & Schwartz, M. (2005). Masculinities and interpersonal violence. In R. W. Connell, M. Kimmel, & J. Hearn (Eds.), *Handbook of studies on men and masculinities.* Thousand Oaks, CA: Sage.

Gadd, D., & Farrall, S. (2004). Criminal careers, desistance and subjectivity: Interpreting men's narratives of change. *Theoretical Criminology, 8*(2), 123–156.

Gould, S. (1981). The ape in some of us: Criminal anthropology. In *The mismeasure of man.* New York: W. W. Norton.

Hall, S. (2002). Daubing the drudges of fury: Men, violence and the piety of the "hegemonic masculinity" thesis. *Theoretical Criminology, 6*(1), 35–61.

Hearn, J., & Whitehead, A. (2006). Collateral damage: Men's "domestic" violence to women seen through men's relation with men. *Probation Journal, 53*(1), 38–56.

HEREOC. (2006). Ending family violence and abuse in aboriginal and Torres Strait islander communities: Key issues. Australian Human Rights and Equal Opportunity Commission, June, 2006.

Hobbs, D., Hadfield, P., Lister, S., & Winlow, S. (2003). *Bouncers: Violence and governance in the nighttime economy.* Oxford: Oxford University Press.

Holland, S., & Scourfield, J. B. (2000). Managing marginalised masculinities: Men and probation. *Journal of Gender Studies, 9*(2), 199–211.

Irwin, K., & Chesney-Lind, M. (2008). Girls' violence: Beyond dangerous masculinity. *Sociological Compass, 2*(3), 837–855.

Jefferson, T. (1997). Masculinities and crime. In M. Maguire, R. Morgan, & R. Reiner (Eds.), *The Oxford handbook of criminology.* Oxford: Clarendon Press.

Jefferson, T. (2002). Subordinating hegemonic masculinity. *Theoretical Criminology, 6*(1), 63–88.

Jewkes, Y. (2005). Men behind bars: "Doing" masculinity as an adaptation to imprisonment. *Men and Masculinities, 8*(1), 44–63.

Kersten, J. (1996). Culture, masculinities and violence against women. *British Journal of Criminology, 36*(3), 381–395.

Kimmel, M. S. (Ed.). (1987). *Changing men: New directions in research on men and masculinity.* Newbury Park, CA: Sage.

Messerschmidt, J. W. (1993). *Masculinities and crime: Critique and reconceptualization of theory.* Lanham, MD: Rowman & Littlefield.

Messerschmidt, J. W. (1995). Managing to kill: Masculinities and the space shuttle *Challenger* explosion. *Masculinities, 3*(4), 1–22.

Messerschmidt, J. W. (1997). *Crime as structured action: Gender, race, class, and crime in the making.* Thousand Oaks, CA: Sage.

Messerschmidt, J. W. (1999a). Review of: *Masculinities, crime and criminology: Men, heterosexuality and the criminal(ised) Other* by R. Collier. Thousand Oaks, CA: Sage, 1998. *Theoretical Criminology, 3*(2), 246–249.

Messerschmidt, J. W. (1999b). Making bodies matter: Adolescent masculinities, the body, and varieties of violence. *Theoretical Criminology, 3*(2), 197–220.

Messerschmidt, J. W. (2000). *Nine lives: Adolescent masculinities, the body, and violence.* Boulder, CO: Westview Press.

Messerschmidt, J. W. (2004). *Flesh and blood: Adolescent gender diversity and violence.* Lanham, MD: Rowman & Littlefield.

Messerschmidt, J. W. (2010). *Hegemonic masculinities and camouflaged politics: Unmasking the Bush dynasty and its war against Iraq.* Boulder, CO: Paradigm.

Miller, J. (2001). *One of the guys: Girls, gangs, and gender.* New York: Oxford University Press.

Miller, J. (2002). The strengths and limits of "doing gender" for understanding street crime. *Theoretical Criminology, 6*(4), 433–460.

Monaghan, L. F. (2002). Hard men, shop boys and others: Embodying competence in a masculinist occupation. *Sociological Review, 50*(3), 334–355.

Mullins, C. (2006). *Holding your square: Masculinities, streetlife, and violence.* Portland, OR: Willan.

Newburn, T., & Stanko, E. (Eds.) (1994). *Just boys doing business? Men, masculinities and crime.* London: Routledge.

Nolan, T. (2009). Behind the blue wall of silence. *Men and Masculinities, 12*(2), 250–257.

Peralta, R., & Cruz, M. (2006). Conferring meaning onto alcohol-related violence: An analysis of alcohol use and gender in a sample of college youth. *Journal of Men's Studies, 14*(1), 109–125.

Polk, K. (1994). *When men kill: Scenarios of masculine violence.* Melbourne: Cambridge University Press.

Polk, K. (1998). Violence, masculinity and evolution: A comment on Wilson and Daly. *Theoretical Criminology, 2*(4), 461–469.

Poynting, S., Noble, G., & Tabar, P. (2003). Protest masculinity and Lebanese youth in western Sydney: An ethnographic study. In S. Tomsen & M. Donaldson (Eds.), *Male trouble: Looking at Australian masculinities.* Melbourne: Pluto Press.

Prokos, A., & Padavic, I. (2002). "There oughtta be a law against bitches": Masculinity lessons in police academy training. *Gender, Work and Organizations, 9*(4), 439–459.

Rude, G. (1995). *The crowd in history.* London: Serif.

Sabo, D., Kupers, T., & London, W. (Eds.). (2001). *Prison masculinities.* Philadelphia: Temple University Press.

Scott, J. (1985). *Weapons of the weak: Everyday forms of peasant resistance.* New Haven, CT: Yale University Press.

Segal, L. (1990). *Slow motion: Changing masculinities, changing men.* London: Virago.

Snider, L. (1998). Towards safer societies: Punishment, masculinities and violence against women. *British Journal of Criminology, 38*(1), 1–39.

Sparks, R. (1996). Masculinity and heroism in the Hollywood "blockbuster": The culture industry and contemporary images of crime and law enforcement. *British Journal of Criminology, 36*(3), 348–360.

Stanko, E., & Hobdell, K. (1993). Assault on men: Masculinity and male victimization. *British Journal of Criminology, 33*(3), 400–415.

Sutherland, E. (1947). *Principles of criminology.* Philadelphia: Lippincott.

Sutherland, E. (1956 [1942]). Development of the theory. In A. Cohen, A. Lindesmith, & K. Schuessler (Eds.), *The Sutherland papers.* Bloomington: Indiana University Press.

Taylor, I., Walton, P., & Young, J. (1973). *The new criminology: For a social theory of deviance.* London: Routledge and Kegan Paul.

Tilly, C. (2003). *The politics of collective violence.* Cambridge: Cambridge University Press.

Tomsen, S. (1997). A top night: Social protest, masculinity and the culture of drinking violence. *British Journal of Criminology, 37*(1), 90–103.

Tomsen, S. (2001). Hate crimes and masculine offending. *Gay and Lesbian Law Journal, 10*, 26–42.

Tomsen, S. (2005). "Boozers and bouncers": Masculine conflict, disengagement and the contemporary governance of drinking-related violence and disorder. *Australian and New Zealand Journal of Criminology, 38*(3), 283–297.

Tomsen, S. (Ed.). (2008). *Crime, criminal justice, and masculinities*. Burlington, VT: Ashgate.

Tomsen, S. (2009). *Violence, prejudice and sexuality*. New York: Routledge.

Warner, K. (2004). Gang rape in Sydney: Crime, the media, politics and sentencing. *Australian and New Zealand Journal of Criminology, 37*(3), 344–361.

Whitehead, A. (2000). Rethinking masculinity: A critical examination of the dynamics of masculinity in the context of an English prison. Ph.D. dissertation. University of Southampton, Southampton, UK.

Whitehead, A. (2005). Man to man violence: How masculinity may work as a dynamic risk factor. *Howard Journal of Criminal Justice, 44*(4), 411–422.

Willott, S., Griffin, C., & Torrance, M. (2008). Snakes and ladders: Upper middle class male offenders talk about economic crime. In S. Tomsen (Ed.), *Crime, criminal justice, and masculinities*. Burlington, VT: Ashgate.

Winlow, S. (2001). *Badfellas: Crime, tradition and new masculinities*. Oxford: Berg.

CHAPTER THREE

Gender and Juvenile Justice

By Cyndi Banks

Offenses committed by girls have always made up a minor component of the overall rate of crime committed in the U.S. and in other countries. In fact, so negligible has been their criminality that until quite recently girls were almost invisible in juvenile justice. The study of girls' criminality serves as a lens into how gender has shaped the lives of girls who come into contact with the law. Beginning with gendered laws that punished girls who violated expectations of proper conduct by, for example, running away from home because of ill-treatment or sexual abuse, the juvenile justice system created a framework of status offenses that empowered the court to control girls' sexuality. In seeking the causes and identifying the circumstances of girls' criminality, research into pathways and life course reveal that sexual and physical abuse have often been the determinants of the lives of girl offenders.

Gender stratification can be seen as the product of a patriarchal society in which gender relations are founded on the organizing principle of male superiority. As James Messerschmidt notes, "in most, (but clearly not all) situations, men are able to impose authority, control and coercion over women" (1993: 71). The reality of girls' lives reveals a sexual double standard and an expectation that they will adhere to a role considered appropriate for girls. In other words, social conformity is gendered. In North American cultures, for example, girls are socialized to be nice, non-aggressive and empathic, and to be concerned about others (see Zahn-Waxler (2000) for an in-depth discussion). Generally, gender distinctions arise out of different socialization practices; thus, gender is socially constructed. While socialization is accomplished through interaction with parents and teachers and within power relations, children themselves are not without agency. As Thorne (1993: 3) notes, theorists now contend that "children participate in their own socialization." There are stages in the gender socialization process which arguably begin by the age of 2. Katz (1979: 9) suggests that these comprise: learning the appropriate behavior for a male or female child; acquiring concepts about what is appropriate conduct for a female or male adult; and behaving in ways deemed appropriate for male and female adults during the life span.

Early and late adolescence are the periods when changes occur. For example, youth rely more on peers than on parents or teachers for information and opinions. It is when girls approach puberty that parental monitoring and supervision is enhanced, sometimes resulting in oppositional incidents. As Thorne (1993: 156) puts it, "parents in gestures that mix protection with punishment, often tighten control of girls when they become adolescents, and sexuality becomes a terrain of struggle between the generations." Parents begin to apply a sexual double standard that encourages males to explore their sexuality but sanctions female sexuality (Chesney-Lind and Irwin 2008: 75). It is at this time that adolescent subcultures and the media begin to significantly influence girls' sexuality, requiring that they be both sexually alluring and chaste as well as sexually responsible (Durham 1998: 385).

To explain delinquency among girls necessitates an examination of gender stratification and a critical mapping of the extent of social control exercised by the juvenile justice system, noting how that system continually reinforces female subordination by labeling and relabeling girls as deviant. Yet even before coming under the control of the juvenile justice system girls are controlled by multiple institutions and structures, and the daily scrutiny to which they are subjected is far more intense than that applied to boys (Cain 1989: 1). Feminists have suggested that informal controls over girls, especially the focus on sexuality and sexual reputation, are reproduced by the juvenile justice system. Thus, when girls are perceived as having violated the norms of behavior expected of them, they are seen as having violated the informal rules of femininity as well as the formal law (Brown 2005: 134).

Prevailing discourses propose rationales for the increased social control of girls, especially their sexuality. For example, the so-called "liberation hypothesis" has been advanced, contending that as an outcome of feminist advocacy and action, girls are becoming "mean girls" or are achieving equality with boys in committing acts of violence. This discourse has raised questions about whether researchers such as Prothrow-Stith and Spivak (2005: 44, 48) are correct in claiming that "girls are beginning to show up in a new role, a new behavior—the ones doing the killing."

These discourses can assume the form of a moral panic (see Chapter 7) where rational explanations are disregarded in favor of incarcerating "the new violent girl" (Chesney-Lind and Jones 2010: 4). Underlying these moral panics are the same gender stereotypes that have always condemned girls for alleged "immorality" now perhaps supplemented by racial fears because today four out of ten girls and young women under 25 years of age are of color—a visible indicator of social change (Males 2010: 15).

Possible explanations for apparent increases in girls' violence that pinpoint policy changes in policing domestic violence incidents, as well as changes in punishing girls for bullying in schools, are ignored in the interests of publishing sensationalist commentaries that feed fears and reinforce gender and racial stereotypes. As Worrall notes (2004: 44), more girls who offend are now brought within the control of the criminal justice system rather than by systems that provide welfare. Girls' bad behaviors are being redefined and relabeled as criminal and there has been a shift away from welfarism toward criminalization. The criminal justice system and the media appear to complement each other's roles in controlling women. As Chesney-Lind and Eliason (2006: 43) explain:

> Popular media masculinize and demonize a few women, effectively casting them out of the "protected" sphere of femininity, while celebrating the presumed passivity of the rest of

womanhood. The criminal justice system steps in, both ratifying and enforcing the gender order, along with the racial, sexual and class order, through its processing and punishment regimes.

When processed through the juvenile justice system, adjudicated delinquent and placed in custody for a status offense, delinquent girls suffer the inadequacies of poor or non-existent treatment and programming because institutional regimes of treatment fail to meet their specific needs. These and related topics will be explored in this chapter. Throughout, it will be seen that constructions of gender underpin all explanations, theories and propositions about girls' criminality.

CONTROLLING GIRLS: GENDER AND HISTORY

From the very beginnings of colonization, the family unit constituted the means of juvenile social control and imposed discipline and order upon children. Early laws even provided the penalty of death for children who disobeyed their parents. For example, the 1641 *Body of Liberties* of Massachusetts provided that children over 16 years of age who "curse or smite their natural father or mother" could suffer the death penalty, subject to various defenses (Krisberg 2005: 23, 24). As noted in Chapter 3 the establishment of Houses of Refuge enabled parents who could not control their children to commit them to custody, and *Ex parte Crouse* affirmed the right of Mary Crouse's mother to have her daughter committed even though she had committed no crime.

The "child savers" elevated the role and importance of the family and parental authority as well as of normative conduct (Platt 1977: 98). Middle-class women began to concern themselves with the morality of working-class girls and women while urban growth and industrialization brought about social change. Delinquent children and dependent children could be taken into custody for a variety of non-normative acts. For example, in Illinois in 1879, the Industrial School for Girls Law authorized any "responsible" resident to petition the courts to enquire into a girl's dependency and, if satisfied that her parents were not fit to have custody, to commit her to the school until she reached the age of 18. Dependency was defined by the law to include: begging and receiving alms for selling; wandering through streets and alleys or other public places; living with or associating with thieves; or being found in a house of ill repute or a poor house (p. 111). Parents who were unable to control their daughters applied to the court to restrain them. As Odem (1995: 5) suggests, contextually, it is helpful to envisage the court system in such cases as "a complex network of struggles and negotiations among working-class parents, teenage daughters, and court officials."

In the Progressive era, from the 1890s to the 1920s, female delinquency came to be seen as a serious social problem, female stereotypes flourished, and girls' "immorality" was broadly defined, especially in relation to immigrant girls who met with punitive punishment (Schlossman and Wallach 1978: 68). "Social purity" became the goal and, between 1910 and 1920, 23 girls' reformatories were opened, representing a dramatic increase in government intervention in girls' delinquency (p. 70). "Immorality" became designated as the catch-all charge for the social control of girls. The label did not mean that a girl had had sexual relations; rather, that she displayed signs of having had intercourse or was suspected of having a propensity to engage in sex in the near future. The acts regarded as evidence of such immorality included being away from home, coming home late at night, attending dance houses, masturbating, using obscene language and riding in vehicles without a chaperone (p. 72). Girls ran away from home for many reasons, including, for example, that a girl "was tired of restrictions placed on her by her parents and planned to leave home and seek employment and make her own way in the world" (*Oakland Tribune*, February 9, 1912 quoted in Odem 1995: 50).

During this period young women began to work outside the home in factories, offices and retail stores. While domestic service had previously been the principal means of employment for young women, the percentage of women employed as domestic servants fell dramatically. For example, between 1870 and 1910 it decreased from 61 percent to 26 percent (Odem 1995: 21). In the new workplaces young women met and interacted with young men, and from the 1880s onwards were able to enjoy the commercialized amusements available in the cities such as dance-halls, amusement parks and movie houses. These entertainments predominantly attracted the young and unmarried of both genders without chaperones (D'Emilio and Freedman 1988: 195). By the 1920s, this new order of pleasure was causing problems in working-class and immigrant families where demands that a girl's wages be handed over to her family, or that she always be chaperoned, were liable to provoke rebellion (D'Emilio and Freedman 1988: 199). Middle-class women reformers, believing their notion of sexual purity and innocence to be under challenge, sought to impose the ideals of middle-class morality on working-class girls. Thus, girls who flirted with men, attended dance-halls, wore makeup and fancy clothes or had sex outside marriage were considered "wayward" and in need of moral protection (Odem 1995: 25).

In the field of girls' delinquency, Knupfer (2001: 35) explains how the discourses of psychology and psychiatry promoted the "medicalization of heterosexuality" following the establishment of the first juvenile court in Chicago in 1899. Judges began to call for testing and diagnoses of the suspect behavioral problems of alleged delinquents. Interrogations and elicited confessions by professionals produced medical histories, case studies and records from which were built diagnoses and treatment plans for these delinquents. According to Knupfer (2001: 36), these accounts established norms of appropriate sexual conduct so that those who deviated from them were faced with technologies of control in the form of hospitals, industrial schools, clinics and reformatories.

Psychologists and psychiatrists investigated the etiology of immorality and explained it as an outcome of feeble-mindedness (immigrant and poor girls were most often classified in this way), or, where girls had aggressive personalities as evidenced by acts such as running away, destruction of property and bad habits of a sexual nature, as "psychopathic" (Knupfer 2001: 40). Psychopathic girls were described as suffering "mania, hallucinations, and insanity" as well as being "cunning" and stubborn (p. 40). Another category was constituted by "hysterical" girls who exhibited aggression and a set of associated symptoms that included delusions, stupor, amnesia and anxiety, believed to be the outcome of repressing sexual desires (p. 41). The notion that these girls may have been demonstrating independence rather than aggression was not entertained. Immorality in the juvenile court was heavily gendered. For example, in 1912, a three-year study revealed that 80 percent of girls were brought before the court on a charge of immorality as compared to only 2 percent for boys (p. 92). In its decision making the juvenile court followed a "maternalist ideology," and "motherhood, marriage and home" comprised its guiding precepts and reform program (p. 97).

Gender also figured in decisions about institutionalization. In 1912, Sophonisba Breckinridge and Edith Abbott, Directors of the Department of Social Investigation, Chicago School of Civics and Philanthropy, published *The Delinquent Child and the Home* (quoted in Odem 1995: 100). They contended that delinquency could be explained as the outcome of the harsh economic and social conditions of the working class (quoted in Odem 1995: 103). They, like other reformers, continued to promote the notion that delinquent girls had a greater need for institutionalization than delinquent boys owing to the relative seriousness of the girl's offense. As the authors explained it, the delinquent girl "is in a peril which threatens the ruin of her whole life, and the situation demands immediate action … the delinquent boy, on the other hand, is frequently only a troublesome nuisance who needs discipline but who, as the probation officer so often says is 'not really a bad boy'" (quoted in Odem 1995: 115). These reformers believed that removing a delinquent girl from her degrading family life and placing her in an institution was her only hope for the future.

In the immediate postwar period the female delinquent was viewed as challenging the authority of the family through acts of revolt, alienation and violation of the law. In the period from 1945 to 1965 the majority of girls' crimes continued to be status offenses, the dominant acts being "ungovernability," running away from home, sexual offenses and truancy (Devlin 1998: 88–89). It was thought that girls were becoming "tough," "hardened" and "vicious" while boys' delinquency could be dealt with by a firm hand and through the courts, embracing the "back to the woodsheds movement" (p. 93). On the other hand, girls' conflicts with the law were depicted as more difficult to control yet still requiring an authoritative approach (p. 93). Yet repression seemed not to be the solution to girls' delinquency. For example, the *Saturday Evening Post* ran a series on delinquency under the title "The Shame of America" which included the story of Florence, a case study against parental authoritarianism. Florence's father required her to be circumspect in her conduct; she was not permitted to attend dances, even high school-sponsored dances, and was not allowed to wear lipstick. In response, she ran away from home, became involved with several men and learned about "beer joints and narcotic peddlers," finally ending up in a state training school for girls as "incorrigible." The *Saturday Evening Post* argued that "heavy use of rod not only failed to keep Florence on the straight and narrow path but obviously had driven her from it" (quoted in Devlin 1998: 93).

Nowadays, youth can be policed proactively for antisocial behaviors because of the assumed risk that such behaviors can escalate into serious delinquency. Over the past two decades policing strategies have emphasized situational crime prevention and zero-tolerance tactics that target minor forms of criminality as a technique to deter serious crime. This strategy has involved making arrests or 'charging up,' in particular in relation to crimes of violence, meaning that charges laid are more serious than before. For example, domestic violence has come to be regarded as a public crime, and is no longer a private family affair. Violence, in all its forms, is seen as an act that will not be tolerated, and modes of behavior that were formerly regarded as merely antisocial are now perceived to be manifestations of violence and have been criminalized as such. These modes and techniques of crime control aim to reduce and manage risk and to collectively form a culture of crime control (Garland 2002; Steffensmeier et al. 2005: 363). In terms of gender, such strategies have resulted in an increased interest in girls' violence, especially within schools where a wide range of hidden criminality in the form of bullying and relational violence has been "revealed." Thus, expansive definitions of conduct seen as constituting violence have redefined disorderly behaviors and transformed them into simple assaults, and upgraded simple assaults to aggravated assaults. Given that girls tend to commit milder forms of violence, net-widening and charging-up techniques have impacted them adversely through heavier sanctions (Steffensmeier et al. 2005: 365).

The punitive attitude toward delinquent youth has included the readiness to treat girls as adults and to have them tried in adult courts and, when convicted, to be incarcerated in adult prisons. Accordingly, between 1992 and 1995, 41 states enacted laws that facilitated trying juveniles as adults and, as of June 30, 2007, 116 females under the age of 18 were in custody in state prisons (Sabol and Couture 2008: 9). However, little is known about this population. A study of 22 girls incarcerated in a women's prison in the southwest noted the absence of comparative research addressing the differences between juvenile institutions holding girls in custody and women's prisons (Gaarder and Belknap 2002). However, the researchers reported limited access to education, health professionals, vocational work and social activity, even relative to the adult women who were incarcerated there (p. 508).

GIRLS OFFENDING

Male offenders dominate the juvenile justice system. In 2003, the 14,590 female juvenile offenders in custody comprised only 15 percent of all offenders in custody. Of the 15 percent of female juveniles in custody, 14 percent had been adjudicated delinquent and 40 percent were in custody for status offenses (Snyder and Sickmund 2006: 206). However, the proportion of female offenders in custody varies between states, ranging from no more than 10 percent of those in custody in Colorado, Maryland, New Jersey and Rhode Island to at least 25 percent in Hawaii, Nebraska, North Dakota, South Dakota and Wyoming (p. 207). In 2003, female offenders were more likely than males to be in custody for simple assault, technical violations and status offenses, indicating that despite the rhetoric about violent girls, it is boys, not girls, who are detained for the serious violent offenses of aggravated assault, robbery and murder (p. 210).

Between 1991 and 2003 the detained population of juveniles increased for both males and females. Yet there is a striking contrast, because while among males the increase was 23 percent for those committed and 29 percent for those detained, among females the increases were 88 percent and 98 percent respectively (Snyder and Sickmund 2006: 208). Status offenders accounted for a large proportion of female offenders in custody in 2003 but the proportion of female offenders in custody for status offenses had fallen from 33 percent in 1991 to only 13 percent in 2003. In contrast, for males, the status offender proportion has remained steady at between 3 percent and 6 percent (p. 206). Running away from home and prostitution are the only two categories of conduct for which more girls than boys are arrested, although running away far outstrips prostitution in its incidence. In 2003, for example, almost 50,000 girls were taken into custody as runaways, while fewer than 1,000 were arrested for prostitution (Chesney-Lind and Irwin 2008: 80).

Girls are increasingly arrested for crimes of violence. The Ten Year Arrest Trend from 1997 to 2006 shows that girls' arrests for the category "other assaults" increased by 18.7 percent while boys' arrests for the same category of offense decreased by 4.3 percent over this period (FBI 2007: Table 33). For females the increase in "person offenses" cases from 1985 to 2002 was 202 percent. The juvenile female arrest rate for cases of "simple assault" for the period 1980 to 2003 far outpaced the increase for males—the rate for females increased by 269 percent compared to 102 percent for males (Snyder and Sickmund 2006: 142, 161). How are these apparent increases in cases involving female violence to be explained? Do they indicate that girls are becoming more violent, or can the data be explained in other ways?

As noted in Chapter 7 in the discussion of girl gangs and girl violence as moral panics, while the statistical data reveal a dramatic increase in girls' violence, accepting statistical evidence at face value is problematic because the statistics may not so much be depicting "facts" about criminality as indicating changes in policing practices and criminal justice policies (Alder and Worrall 2004: 3). Chesney-Lind argues that increases in girls' violence can be explained by changes in policy and practice involving arrests for incidents of domestic violence, and by an increased intolerance for violence in schools post-Columbine. These policies, she argues, have resulted in more referrals of girls to court for violations of zero-tolerance policies (Chesney-Lind 2010: 60). Her view is supported by the fact that self-report delinquency data reveal a trend of decreases in self-reported school-aged youth violence. Accordingly, the Centers for Disease Control (CDC) *Youth Risk Behavior Survey* conducted biannually reveals that while 34.4 percent of girls surveyed in 1991 reported having been in a physical fight in the preceding 12 months, in 2009, only 22.9 percent reported similarly for the previous year (CDC, 1991–2009). Victimization data reveal a similar trend, suggesting that the shifts in girls' arrests do not relate to actual changes in behavior and are not indicative of girls becoming more violent.

In relation to incidents of domestic violence, due to legislative changes, the police have implemented domestic violence policies that have resulted in increased arrests. While domestic violence laws were originally targeted to address the needs of female victims, legislation has since expanded the types of relationships included so that now the police are required to respond to heterosexual and same-sex relationships, and to take account of others in households including siblings, parents, teenagers and so on (Buzawa and Hirschel 2010: 33). Laws now authorize the police to arrest without warrant for misdemeanor charges in domestic violence incidents and to arrest on a presumptive basis (p. 34). Data reveal that other forms of family violence make up a large proportion of the incidents reported to the police. For example, over the past 25 years, surveys have shown that each year up to 33 million siblings violently assault their brothers and sisters, and over a million parents each year are victims of assaults by their children aged 15 to 17 (p. 35). Other studies tend to indicate that the proportion of non-adult partner violence being brought to police attention has been increasing (p. 35). Thus, overall, not only has there been an increase in the extent of domestic violence coming to the attention of the police, but there is an increased likelihood of being arrested as a result of a reported incident of domestic violence (p. 35).

Research has shown that juveniles involved in cases of domestic assault are more likely to be arrested than adults (Buzawa and Hirschel 2010: 36). Further research indicates that female juvenile offenders are more likely to be impacted by domestic violence policies and practices because their acts are likely to be classed as misdemeanors as compared to male acts of violence (p. 36). Chesney-Lind (2002) has suggested that in practice the police may often act to uphold the parents' authority where a domestic assault involves parent and child by making an arrest where previously they may have proceeded by way of a non-criminal status offense classifying the juvenile as an "incorrigible" or as a "person in need of supervision." Thus, it is argued that status offenses have, in effect, been revived and reclassified as assaults, imposing a greater degree of social control than previously existed. Consequently, the disproportionately increased arrest rates for female juvenile offenders may be explained, in part, by the dramatic increase in domestic violence arrest rates (Chesney-Lind 2002).[1]

According to Feld, the notion that females who would previously have been dealt with as status offenders are now subjected to "bootstrapping" and relabeling as delinquents may be credited to the deinstitutionalization mandates of the *Juvenile Justice and Delinquency Prevention Act* of 1974 (2009: 241). The 1974 Act banned states from confining status offenders with delinquents in secure facilities and withheld funds from states that took no action to remove them. The intention of the legislation was that programs within the community would be developed to take status offenders who would be diverted into those programs. However, a 1980 amendment to the Act, added at the request of the National Council of Juvenile and Family Court Judges, permitted states to confine status offenders for violating "valid court orders." This gave the judges the power to bootstrap status offenders under a delinquency label and to place them in custody for contempt of court for violating conditions of probation. The outcome of the deinstitutionalization policy was a substantial reduction in the number of status offenders held in custody in secure facilities but with no commensurate increase in community sanctions into which to divert status cases. In the absence of any incentive to offer community services, this in turn was an impetus to continue to confine status offenders by relabeling them as delinquents (Feld 2009: 244, 245). There is a considerable overlap between a status offense and a delinquent act because, for example, a runaway girl may also engage in delinquency, or the acts of an "unruly" girl may also constitute an assault. After analyzing the use of the contempt powers of the juvenile courts for violation of court orders, Bishop and Frazier (1992) found that differential treatment by gender as well as the bootstrapping of girls perpetuated gender bias. Thus, the courts and other actors in the juvenile justice system demonstrate their reluctance to give up their power to discipline "unruly" girls.

It is significant that the rate at which the police arrested girls for the offense of simple assault in 2005 was almost four times the arrest rate in 1980, yet by comparison arrests of juvenile males only doubled over the same period (Feld 2009: 250). After comparing arrest data covering boys and girls from the FBI Uniform Crime Reports with victim self-reports and juveniles' self-reports, no systematic changes in girls' rates or prevalence compared to that of boys were found, despite the dramatic increase in girls' arrests for violence (Steffensmeier et al. 2005). As Steffensmeier et al. (2005: 387–390) point out,

> the rise in girls' arrests for violent crime and the narrowing of the gender gap have less to do with underlying behavior and more to do with … net-widening changes in law and policing toward prosecuting less serious forms of violence … and less biased or more efficient responses to girls' physical or verbal aggression on the part of law enforcement, parents, teachers, and social workers.

In their review of all assault cases from 2,819 jurisdictions in 19 states for the year 2000, Buzawa and Hirschel (2010) examined whether age and gender had any effect on police responses to calls for assistance. They found that juveniles were more likely to be arrested than adults, with juvenile females having the highest arrest rates for aggravated and simple assault. Juveniles were far more likely to be arrested for assaulting adults, and adults were far less likely to be arrested for assaulting juveniles (p. 46). This research clearly raises questions about how the police determine the appropriate course of action when a juvenile is said to have assaulted an adult.

As is pointed out in Chapter 7, the discovery of girls' "relational" aggression and its relationship with the mix of behaviors that constitute bullying has resulted in increased monitoring and surveillance of girls' conduct in schools. This has been justified on the basis that relational aggression is a form of serious bullying. It is now argued that girls are as aggressive as boys when relational aggression is taken into account. The kinds of behaviors included within the relational mirror stereotypical labels that have been associated with women for centuries, namely the devious, cunning and manipulative female figure. Chesney-Lind and Jones (2010: 112) argue that this approach to girls' aggression provides "new ways to devalue and demonize girls" and suggests "the need to police their behavior even more assiduously." School zero-tolerance policies for bullying and all forms of aggression mean that girls are now more likely to be referred to law enforcement for incidents that would formerly have been dealt with internally. Schools are now being required to adopt anti-bullying prevention and education policies, and 32 states had introduced bills with such provisions as of May 2003 (p. 118).

Physical aggression has been shown to be normative in pre-school years and then as declining (Vaillancourt and Hymel 2004). Verbal and social modes of aggression emerge later and become increasingly normative with age. Studies have consistently shown that boys engage in greater levels of physical aggression than girls but gender differences in verbal forms of aggression have not been clearly established (p. 61). Thus, despite the claims now being made that girls are just as violent as boys, a number of studies have found no difference between boys' and girls' performance of relational aggression, and moreover, some studies have found boys to be more relationally aggressive than girls (Chesney-Lind and Jones 2010: 113). As well, research has failed to demonstrate a progression from relational aggression to actual violence (pp. 116, 117). As always, context is vital to explaining and understanding girls' behaviors in school where relational aggression is said to have occurred, and the circumstances and gender arrangements need to be fully examined in each case (p. 123).

PATHWAYS TO DELINQUENCY

Traditional theories of crime causation tend to be based on male models of crime and male conduct, and fail to explain the experiences of delinquent girls (Belknap 2001; Chesney-Lind and Shelden 2004). The "Life Course Development Model" contends that offending behavior is age associated and related to the various developmental stages of the life course (Laub and Lauritsen 1993: 235). The stage of adolescence is perceived as a time of risk for delinquent behavior owing to stresses such as peer pressure and puberty. While life-course approaches to delinquency do address concepts such as "poor family functioning," they fail to adequately account for childhood victimization such as neglect, and parental physical and sexual abuse, as well as for experiences of discrimination and oppression based on race and sex.

The "pathways to crime" approach to girls' offending seeks to identify the childhood experiences that place girls at risk of offending. Studies adopting the pathways approach indicate that childhood sexual and physical abuse and child neglect are often associated with the likelihood of criminality (Belknap and Holsinger 1998; Daly 1992: 11). The pathways perspective recognizes that girls' criminality is associated with their social conditions as well as with their role as females within a patriarchal society where the intersecting oppressions of gender, race, class and sexuality exist. The "blurred boundaries" theory of victimization and criminalization is a prominent feature of recent models of etiology of women's crime but it has also been critiqued because it may not capture the complexities and meanings of agency and responsibility involved in women's violations of the law (Daly 1992: 48). Of course, not all sexually or otherwise abused girls become delinquent and not all delinquent girls are survivors of sexual and other forms of abuse. However, there is no doubt that childhood abuse, in its various forms, is disproportionately represented in girls adjudicated as delinquent.

How does race influence girls' pathways to offending? Studies seem to suggest that black girls are more likely to engage in serious forms of delinquency than other racial groups (Holsinger and Holsinger 2005: 214). Research also indicates that black girls are socialized to become self-sufficient and to be more independent than white girls and consistent with this, black girls report more assertiveness and self-confidence than white girls and seek to project an image of power through their distinct style of dress (Holsinger and Holsinger 2005: 218). Based on samples of white and black girls, researchers found that black girls reported experiencing less abuse, less drug use and fewer incidents of suicide or self-injury than white girls. Even so, physical abuse was reported in 70 percent and sexual abuse in 46 percent of black girls sampled, compared to 90 percent and 62 percent for white girls (p. 227). For black girls in the study, correlates of delinquency were abuse, drug and alcohol use, family experience and antisocial personality (p. 232). For white girls, the strongest correlates were antisocial personality, mental health and drug use (p. 232). According to Holsinger and Holsinger, these differential pathways to violence and self-injurious conduct reflect racial differences in self-esteem and socialization, with black girls socialized to be self-reliant and therefore likely to act in more assertive ways, while white girls, raised to be dependent and accepting of traditional gender roles, are more likely to internalize problems, leading to self-criticism, low self-esteem and mental health issues (p. 236).

The association between childhood abuse and victimization and girls' delinquency has been confirmed in many studies. In most cases girls have been victims themselves before they offend (Girls Incorporated 1996). Substantial numbers of girls in the juvenile justice system report a history of victimization as children through physical or sexual abuse (Dembo et al. 1993). In examining the linkages between victimization and delinquency some argue that behaviors such as running away from home, prostitution and gang membership operate as strategies of resistance and coping mechanisms in girls' lives.

GIRLS' VIOLENCE: DEFINITIONS AND EXPLANATIONS

As Worrall puts it, "No longer 'at risk' and 'in moral danger' from the damaging behavior of men, 'violent girls' now exist as a category within penal discourse" (2004: 41). Violence and aggression are terms that carry different meanings for different people, and a range of competing discourses define and elaborate their meanings. Laws generally specify forms of violence on a scale of seriousness ranging from a simple assault to aggravated assault and finally to murder. However, when criminal files are examined to explore the actual events and conduct that constitute an offense, they sometimes appear not to meet the popular perceptions of that particular mode of criminality. For example, Chesney-Lind and Paramore (2001: 142) show that when the police reported an increase in juvenile robbery in the city and county of Honolulu over two separate periods of time, the acts that constituted robbery comprised a pattern of acts involving largely youthful victims, the majority of whom were at least casually acquainted with the offenders. The median value of items stolen from all victims in 1991 was US$10 and in the second period of robberies, in 1997, the median value dropped to only US$1.25 (p. 157). In the majority of robberies no weapon was involved and most robberies did not result in serious injuries to the victims. The robberies followed a similar pattern—they were characterized by slightly older youth bullying and hijacking younger youth for small amounts of cash and sometimes for jewelry. The authors suggest that there was no surge in robberies but rather that the redefinition of thefts that occurred within school grounds to "robbery" had a substantial effect on the increase in the number of arrests of juveniles for robbery (p. 162).

Definitions of what is considered violence are also subjective, and in deciding what amounts to aggression or violence it is important to know how juvenile girls themselves explain these terms. In this way we can share their knowledge of acceptable and non-acceptable behaviors. For example, among girls living in group homes owing to violent behaviors in Nova Scotia, Canada, all defined violence in terms of physical acts that involved striking another with some part of their body (Brown 2010). They did not include relational forms of violence within their definitions of this term. All the girls living in group homes had experienced violent behaviors as children, thus blurring the boundary between victimization and perpetrating violence, and all developed survival strategies of fighting back. As Brown (2010: 181) puts it:

> The girls did not cross a line one day, moving from victim to perpetrator. Their use of violence was not retold according to a catalyst event. The move was seamless, between being witness to and living in an environment of violence to using violence to protect or express oneself.

Thus the lived experience of girls adds a context to violence and to the "violent" girl, and expectations of appropriate feminine behaviors ought to take account of the different environments to which girls are subjected and in which they are brought up. Differing race and class backgrounds also function to define what is regarded as "violence." Thus, it has been suggested that the concept "violent girls" is merely a construct of white middle-class culture and that girls of color are constructed as always-already "violent," regardless of how they present themselves (Batacharya 2004: 61).

Girls' violence is often closely linked to their environments. Those who experience violence as part of their daily life in distressed inner cities must develop survival skills if they are not themselves to be subjected to gender-specific violence. The experience of violence for a black inner city girl will be different to that of a white middle-class girl living in the suburbs. As Nikki Jones (2010: 203) explains, black inner city girls develop "situated survival strategies" growing up in neighborhoods where the ruling ethic is "the code of the street" under which black men practice hegemonic masculinity, relying on physical domination in their daily interactions (p. 205). For black girls the challenge of growing up in such circumstances is a gendered challenge and they are assessed not only according to normative gender expectations that apply to all girls regardless of color, but also according to expectations of how black women and girls ought to behave (p. 206). These girls must navigate the streets and learn how to manage potential threats of violence at the risk of violating expectations of appropriate femininity that place considerable constraints on how they may act. For example, they are expected to avoid physical violence and employ forms of relational aggression but in the environment of the inner city "sometimes you do got to fight" and, if you do, you risk being judged as "street" or "ghetto" (p. 207). Naming girls as such adds a gendered dimension because good and decent girls are "young ladies" but "ghetto chicks" are young girls whose "behaviors, dress, communication and interaction styles" violate both mainstream and black middle-class expectations of appropriate femininity (p. 207).

The "situated survival strategies" described by Jones comprise modes of interaction and routinized activities that center upon securing one's personal well-being as a black adolescent girl living in the inner city. Threats to their personal safety necessitate developing strategies that physically separate girls from the streets. In contrast to girl fighters who hang out on the streets, they will stay at home, read and do school work, and generally avoid social interactions that may cause conflict (Jones 2010: 209). They will also isolate themselves from their peers, so they do not form close friendships that would require them to come to the aid of their peers in forms of physical violence. Thus, girls have "friends" and "associates" and will fight for the former but not the latter (p. 209). In this way the code of the streets impacts adolescent black girls' development by circumscribing relational connections and networks. Miller (2008) describes similar survival strategies in the black inner city of St. Louis where she noted two survival themes adopted by girls: avoiding public spaces in the neighborhood, especially at night; and relying on the company of others, especially males, for protection, including networks of family and friends in an area. As one resident, Jackie, explained:

> "I stay in the house … . I don't go outside at all when I'm at home. When I'm around my grandma's house I go outside sometimes. I know mostly everybody over there. But when I'm at home I don't go outside unless I'm going to the store, but I don't talk to nobody."
>
> (Miller 2008: 60, 61)

The views and experiences of teenage girls of violence in Scotland are presented by Michele Burman (2004: 81), "to grasp how violence is understood by them and how it is both encountered and mobilized in their daily lives." Interestingly, when asked to explain "violence" in an abstract sense, these girls offered an explanation that related violence to harmful physical actions such as fighting, punching, kicking and using weapons to injure another. However, in recounting their own experiences of being violent or suffering violence they broadened their definition to include a more diverse range of behaviors including verbal threats, self-harm, offensive name calling and bullying as well as intimidation. Most thought that these relational forms of violence were experienced as more hurtful and damaging than actual physical violence, especially when they were encountered within existing friendships (p. 85). Ongoing verbal abuse directed mainly at other girls over long periods of time was the most common conflict situation reported, and such behaviors engendered feelings of humiliation, anger and powerlessness in the target of the abuse (p. 88). Despite their definitions of violence the girls did not apply that term to describe acts of physical violence occurring between siblings in the home which, while prevalent, were never considered to qualify as acts of "violence" but rather as "not serious" and wholly "natural" events. Thus, context and relationships rendered this form of violence non-violent, and in general terms all definitions and explanations of violence were shaped by context and the relationships involved (p. 90). Thus, girls more easily characterized events that occurred outside the home, not involving family members, as violence. All the girls were prepared to use violence themselves if warranted by the situation, but generally they regarded its use as a last resort. Instances where violence was acceptable included a response to verbal attacks to prevent continued harassment, and situations where they felt compelled to "stick up" for themselves. Girls exercised agency then, taking the conceptualization of girls' violence beyond simply a response to gendered forms of victimization (p. 97).

Emphasizing the need to examine the social contexts in which violence emerges as a strategy for girls living in the central city neighborhoods of St. Louis, Miller and White (2004: 187) find that girls employ violence differently than males, shaping its use according to gender, the situation and their motives and goals. For example, in robberies the girls employ physical aggression when robbing other girls but do not use weapons and have no male assistance. In contrast, when robbing men, girls use weapons but make no physical contact with their male victims, simply pretending to be sexually interested in them to get the males to lower their guard (2004: 177). In performing robbery on the streets girls are operating in a male-dominated environment and make technical choices about modes of robbery that reflect the gender stratification of the environment in which men are perceived as strong and women as weak. As Barrie Thorne puts it (1993: 109), in terms of gender relations, "An emphasis on social context shifts analysis from fixing abstract and binary differences to examining the social relations in which multiple differences are constructed and given meaning."

For those living in the environment of the black inner cities, violence takes on an added dimension because it becomes an integral part of life. Studies of the impact of this level of violence on youth who grow up witnessing and experiencing violence reveal that it is related to increases in aggression, increases in emotional and psychological trauma, that it breeds an intense vigilance, and that there is an increased risk of being victimized (Miller 2008: 34). In addition, "repeated exposure to high levels of violence may cause children and adolescents to become uncaring toward others, and desensitized toward future violent events" (Farrell and Bruce 1997: 3). Sexual harassment and its possible consequences in one of the poorest sections of the black inner city of St. Louis were explained by one informant to Miller (2008: 36) as follows:

> "if [girls] look good, somebody might try to touch 'em or something. And they might not want them to touch them and they might say something to 'em. And the dudes in my neighborhood, they might try to beat them up 'cause the girl wouldn't let them touch em" (Dwayne).

In this inner city neighborhood many youth believe that girls could be subjected to significant personal danger if they dressed in a provocative way that draws attention to them. Victim blaming has become a way to psychologically distance themselves from violent events. Here, the public spaces are male dominated and sites for possible sexual conquest if young women are present. Mirroring the "situated survival strategies" described by Jones (2004), the rules of this neighborhood include "staying out of others people's business" and developing a "level of desensitization and callousness" to restrain any possible personal attempt to intervene when girls saw others being attacked by young males in public spaces (Miller 2008: 41, 44). In schools, where they are constantly in contact with young men and could not avoid them by staying in their homes, girls try to ward off sexual harassment by attempting to stand up for themselves but these efforts are seen by male youth as forms of disrespect and as challenges to their sexual entitlements and could provoke situations of personal danger (p. 111). The sexual double standard they experience is epitomized by male conventions which stipulate that to qualify as a "real girlfriend" girls must police their own sexual desires and also resist young men's advances (p. 156).

GIRLS' VIOLENCE AND THE "LIBERATION HYPOTHESIS"

According to this hypothesis, the supposed increase in girls' violence is explained as the outcome of the feminist agenda and feminist advocacy. In the struggle for equality with men, it is argued that feminists have now made girls resemble boys and have taken them away from their proper roles as wives, mothers and daughters. In response, feminists counter that it is patriarchy that drives girls to be violent and that girls employ violence to counter gender oppression. Both approaches assume that girls are naturally non-aggressive and non-violent. Many popular books propagate the liberation hypothesis, for example, *See Jane Hit: Why Girls Are Growing More Violent and What We Can Do About It* (2007) by James Garbarino. His overall approach is to argue that freedoms now enjoyed by girls have altered their behavior. The following exemplifies this approach to girls' violence:

> Girls in general are evidencing a new assertiveness and physicality that go far beyond criminal assault … . We would welcome the New American Girl's unfettered assertiveness and physicality … . But I believe that the increasing violence among troubled girls and the generally elevated levels of aggression in girls are unintended consequences of the general increase in normal girls getting physical and becoming more assertive. All this, the good news of liberation and the bad news of increased aggression, is the New American Girl.
>
> (Garbarino 2007: 4)

In 2005 a similar contention about girls' violence was published in *Sugar and Spice and No Longer Nice: How We Can Stop Girls' Violence* by Deborah Prothrow-Stith and Howard R. Spivak. The adverse effects of women's liberation were described as follows:

> Girls continue to break down barriers and diminish the differences between their level of achievement and that of boys in many areas, and violent behavior is no exception … . Girls have become a part of the epidemic of youth violence.
>
> (Prothrow-Stith and Spivak 2005: 1, 2)

This concern about women and girls enjoying more freedom and the dire consequences that result is not a new theme. Commentators who examined arrest data to establish whether more women and girls are being arrested have tried to link any increases to the agenda for women's rights. However, they failed to undertake a thorough evaluation of arrest data to seek explanations of what was actually being measured and so ignored changes in policing policy and practice as possible causal factors. In the 1960s and 1970s studies boldly asserted a connection between the "emancipation" of women and criminality. For example, a 1969 report submitted to the U.S. National Commission on the Causes and Prevention of Violence stated, "It is also the case that the 'emancipation' of females in our society over recent decades has decreased the differences in delinquency and criminality between boys and girls, men and woman as cultural differences between them have narrowed" (Mulvihill et al. 1969: 425).

The most celebrated example of this "liberation of women" discourse was the publication in 1975 of *Sisters in Crime: The Rise of the New Female Offender* by Freda Adler who proposed that the newly liberated women of the 1960s were becoming more criminogenic than women of previous generations. In relation to girls, Adler claimed that they had adopted male roles and were thus more involved in drinking, stealing, gang activity and fighting. She claimed that appropriating the male role and departing from the "safety of traditional female roles" at the point of the onset of adolescence created increased risk factors for criminal behaviors (Adler 1975: 95). Adler relied on interviews and FBI arrest data to make her argument but her contention that there were substantial percentage increases in girls' arrests from 1960 to 1970 ignored the fact that while boys' arrests had increased by 82 percent and girls' arrests by 306 percent during that period, the actual numbers of arrests in rates per 10,000 for 10- to 17-yearolds showed an increase for boys of 49.33 and for girls of 27.30. Critical assessments of Adler's assertions followed, including research that tried to specifically address her contention that women's liberation had resulted in more women and girls becoming involved in crime. These studies did not support Adler's arguments and consequently there exists no convincing empirical support for this "liberation hypothesis" (Sprott and Doob 2009: 17).

PROGRAMMING INADEQUACIES IN THE TREATMENT OF GIRL OFFENDERS

The domination of the juvenile justice system by male offenders means that most treatment programs have historically been designed for boys and not girls. In the 1990s in the U.S. 35 percent of delinquency programs served only males and 42.4 percent served primarily boys (Girls Incorporated 1996). Only 2.3 percent of programs served females and 5.9 percent primarily served girls (Girls Incorporated 1996). Girls have always constituted a minor proportion of youthful offenders in custody and detention, and as a result gender-specific programming has been absent and girls have been "out of sight, out of mind." In many cases, programs designed for boys have simply been expanded to include girls. Establishing gender-specific programs for girls is problematic in light of the low numbers, short custody terms and the fluctuations in demand. Nevertheless, girls in the juvenile justice system do exhibit different needs than boys in the form of an increased likelihood of mental health problems, greater experience of victimization and differences in how aggression is manifested (Antonishak et al. 2004: 171). The most promising gender-specific programs are both individualized and comprehensive. Thus, a focus on developing healthy relationships may be appropriate for a girl with issues of relational aggression while a girl who persistently runs away may need programming on family issues and victimization (p. 174).

In 1998 the U.S. Office of Juvenile Justice and Delinquency Prevention issued recommendations for gender-specific programming, specifying, for example, respectful staff, a safe supportive environment, educational services that ought to be applied generally, and for special services aimed at improving girls' self-esteem, body image, feelings of empowerment and interpersonal relationships (OJJDP 1998). The *Juvenile Justice and Delinquency Prevention Act 1992* calls for the development and adoption of policies "to prohibit gender bias in placement and treatment and establishing programs to ensure that female youth have access to the full range of health and mental health services, treatment for physical or sexual assault and abuse, self defense instruction, education in parenting education in general, and other training and vocational services." Despite legal provisions intended to specifically address the needs of delinquent girls, research reveals that some juvenile justice staff persist in rejecting gender-specific treatment approaches. For example, Gaarder and others (2004) found that four out 14 juvenile proba-tion officers in one Arizona county insisted that all juveniles had similar needs and no gender-specific approaches were warranted. Some of the staff believed that girls who did not adhere to feminine standards of behavior should be treated as if they were boys, describing these girls as follows:

> "They're not your typical girls … you know, the fingernails, the makeup, the Ms Prissy. They're just like the boys. They go out and they prove themselves like they're not feminine. You know they don't want anybody to think … well I'm helpless. I can take care of myself. So they play the role as portraying to be something that they're not."
>
> (Gaarder et al. 2004: 567)

Schaffner (2006: 160) stresses the need for programming for girls to reflect what are regarded as normative standards by contemporary youth and not to focus on topics such as getting out of prostitu-tion that involve only a tiny minority of girls. She argues that staff should be in tune with contemporary mores and be aware of gender and gender issues so that girls are not faced with "middle-aged, middle-class adults who delivered gender programming [and] bombarded girls in lock up with humiliating harangues." Similarly, Gaarder and others (2004: 555) found that probation officers in Arizona lacked any knowledge of culturally and gender-appropriate treatments, and often referred girls to treatment services that did not match their needs.

Gender-specific—also known as gender-responsive—programming draws on a feminist perspective and stresses the unique experience of being a girl in the U.S. It is one approach to the treatment of girls who have been adjudicated delinquent. Another perspective is to ask "what works" and advocates of this approach argue that the principles of effective intervention that reduce recidivism can be identified from quantitative studies that are not gender specific. This approach is associated with the work of Canadian psychologists (Hubbard and Matthews 2008: 226). In a comprehensive review of these two treatment strategies Hubbard and Matthews (2008) identify how the strategies diverge as well as the contentions put forward by the opposing advocates. For example, the "what works" approach suffers from the fact that most of the research relied on has not involved girls. In the case of the gender-responsive approach, research has tended to be qualitative and is therefore criticized on the basis of lack of generalizability. Thus, it becomes clear that as much as anything the two approaches reflect long-standing contentions about the value of qualitative versus quantitative research. At a more fundamental theoretical level the gender-specific approach is rooted in feminist arguments that girls' delinquency must be related to issues of racism, sexism, class and gender, and that societal and justice system factors play a significant role in their marginalization. The "what works" perspective is much more of a traditional theoretical approach, drawing on long-standing criminological theory such as strain as well as social learning and the cognitive-behavioral approach in psychology. It is essentially a positivist approach as compared to a feminist analysis (p. 232).

The two schools of thought diverge sharply in considerations of the most effective therapeutic approach for delinquent girls. "What works" advocates favor the cognitive-behavioral model that has been applied to boys and has come to be regarded as the most effective treatment mode in a number of countries. By contrast, a gender-specific approach asks why these psychological models should necessarily be applied to girls when the antisocial attitudes to which they are targeted are characteristic of only one gender. Of course, psychological approaches are also individualistic and take no account of social or structural issues, and therefore can be criticized for pathologizing girls' responses to their social circumstances (Hubbard and Matthews 2008: 232). Gender-specific advocates take issue with the concept of risk and how it is applied to girls (p. 234). For example, they argue that girls "may be high need" (p. 234) but not high risk given that their low crime rates are indicative that they are no danger to society. Advocates also argue that a focus on high risk usually means placing girls in detention and this works to exacerbate problems such as depression, sexual abuse and disruptions in relationships that contributed to their contact with the law in the first place (p. 234).

The gender-specific approach assumes that treatment staff must be aware of girls' individual trauma resulting from incidents of abuse, must comprehend the role that trauma plays in a girl's life, and create services that appropriately address those circumstances. This includes reinforcing survival and coping skills, and focusing on treatment goals that enhance decision making (Hubbard and Matthews 2008: 238, 239). In terms of girls' trauma, for example, the Female Detention Project found that 81 percent of girls studied reported experiencing some kind of trauma, such as sexual or physical abuse, witnessing violence or being abandoned (Chesney-Lind 2010: 64). Moreover, girls were misdiagnosed with "Oppositional Defiant Disorder" and not "Post-Traumatic Stress Disorder" with the outcome that they were not receiving appropriate treatment (p. 65).

Hubbard and Matthews (2008: 251) conclude their review of these two approaches with a balanced statement that recognizes the merits of each as follows:

> [T]he two major contributions of the gender-responsive group include their (a) explication of how the social context of being a girl in the United States facilitates girls' delinquency and (b) research and discussions on the need for gender-responsive treatment to reflect the differences in the socialization of girls and boys. The major contributions of the what works literature include (a) their empirical basis for program development and (b) their success in translating this research into practical applications for correctional and juvenile justice agencies.

Girls in the juvenile justice system struggle against cultural and gender stereotypes promoted and reinforced by juvenile justice officials. For example, research has consistently shown that girls are perceived by juvenile justice officials as being "more difficult" to manage than boys (Gaarder et al. 2004). A recent study of probation files in Arizona showed probation officers rendering value judgments such as "fabricating reports of abuse, acting promiscuously, whining too much, and attempting to manipulate the court system." Girls were viewed as "harder to work with," as being "too needy" and as having "too many issues" (Gaarder et al. 2004: 556).

Schaffner (2006: 158) reports that when she asked juvenile detention and probation staff to compare boys with girls, staff regularly regarded girls as "less good than or not as good as boys" and provided the following views:

> "Girls are more emotional than boys ... . Everything is a big ol'drama trauma with them! That's why we handle 'em a little differently" (middleaged, African American, middle-class woman, guard).

> "Girls are just harder to work with ... . The boys will follow the rules; they are quieter. The girls never listen; they just tangle with you on everything" (young, white, working-class woman, guard).

(Schaffner 2006: 158)

Why are girls regarded as so challenging? The sexualization theory of female offending sees differential treatment as the outcome of a double standard of behavior where the deviant behavior of women is regarded as a symptom of problematic sexuality requiring welfare rather than punishment. Thus, as Worrall argues, the same concern to protect exists alongside unease that a girl is dangerous and "out of control" (2001: 152).

Other issues concerning the needs of girls in custody identified by researchers include the lack of mental health services and an absence of prenatal care and health services for pregnant girls in New York City; girls experiencing sexual abuse while being detained in California; and a lack of female staff, limiting gender-specific programming and resulting in reduced outdoor recreation for girls in Florida (Chesney-Lind 2010: 65).

RECAP

As this account of the interaction between girls and the juvenile justice system has shown, enduring gender stereotypes, expanded definitions of girls' violence and the continuing criminalization of victimized girls mark the increased attention paid to girls and their delinquency. Girls' vulnerability to arrest has been enhanced by expansive redefinitions and relabeling of what constitutes "violence" and especially by the discovery of new pathologies concerning relational violence and bullying in schools. Law-enforcement policies and practices have contributed to this vulnerability because it has been more convenient for police called to domestic violence incidents to take a girl into custody than to remove a parent or both parents from the home. Thus, changes in the gendered nature of offending have adversely affected girls. From one perspective therefore, the increased focus on girls' criminality has enhanced the surveillance, monitoring and social control exercised over girls to their obvious detriment. Nevertheless, studies of the gendered forms of violence to which black girls are subjected in the inner cities (as opposed to the usual focus on girls in gangs, prostitution and drug dealing) and the debate over gender-responsive treatment for delinquent girls emerge as positives in the debate over girls' criminality. The pathways approach to girls' offending has revealed the blurred nature of the boundary between victimization and offending, and the structural factors that impact many girls' lives expose the limitations of pathologizing girls' criminality.

The fact remains that girls are far less likely to be involved in serious crime, and the majority of girls processed through the juvenile justice system commit ordinary crimes and simple assaults. Gender typing seems to be largely maintained in schools and the sexual double standard applied to girls, but not to boys, has lost none of its power. Similarly, girls continue to be punished for not conforming to expected "feminine" standards of behavior so that overall there seems to have been little change in the core elements of gender so far as girls are concerned despite claims made by the liberation hypothesis. There is a need to address not only gender differences in the type and frequency of crime but also to better understand how gender is performed in the context of offending. The history of the juvenile justice system in relation to girls has been one of sexism and paternalism, and this continues to make it a problematic site for gender-specific services.

NOTE

1. In the various editions of *Girls, Delinquency and Juvenile Justice*, Chesney-Lind and Shelden add a note to the effect that the authors learned from sources inside the juvenile justice system "that some police and probation officers are suggesting to parents the following: When a girl threatens to run away, the parent should stand in her way; if she runs into the parent or pushes the parent out of the way, then the parent can call the court and have the girl arrested on 'simple assault' or 'battery' or some other 'personal' crime that would fit into the FBI category 'other assaults'" (Chesney-Lind and Shelden 2004: 30).

REFERENCES

Adler, Freda. 1975. *Sisters in Crime: The Rise of the New Female Offender*. New York: McGraw-Hill.

Alder, C. and A. Worrall (eds). 2004. *Girl's Violence: Myths and Realities*. Albany, NY: State University of New York Press.

Antonishak, Jill, N. Dickson Reppucci and Carrie Freid Mulford. 2004. "Girls in the Justice System: Treatment and Intervention." In Marlene M. Moretti, Candice L. Odgers and Margaret A. Jackson (eds) *Girls and Aggression: Contributing Factors and Intervention Principles*. New York: Kluwer Academic/Plenum Publishers, pp. 165–180.

Batacharya, Sheila. 2004. "Racism, 'Girl Violence,' and the Murder of Reena Virk." In Christine Alder and Anne Worrall (eds) *Girls' Violence: Myths and Realities*. Albany, NY: State University of New York Press, pp. 61–80.

Belknap, Joanne. 2001. *The Invisible Woman: Gender, Crime and Justice*. Belmont, CA: Wadsworth Publishing.

Belknap, Joanne and Kristi Holsinger. 1998. "An Overview of Delinquent Girls: How Theory and Practice Have Failed and the Need for Innovative Changes." In Ruth T. Zaplin (ed.) *Female Crime and Delinquency: Critical Perspectives and Effective Interventions*. Gaithersburg, MD: Aspen Publishing.

Bishop, Donna M. and Charles E. Frazier. 1992. "Gender Bias in Juvenile Justice Processing: Implications of the JJDP Act." *Journal of Criminal Law and Criminology* 82: 1162–1186.

Brown, Marion. 2010. "Negotiations of the Living Space: Life in the Group Home for Girls Who Use Violence." In Meda Chesney-Lind and Nikki Jones (eds) *Fighting for Girls: New Perspectives on Gender and Violence*. Albany, NY: State University of New York Press, pp. 175–199.

Brown, Sheila. 2005. *Understanding Youth and Crime: Listening to Youth?* Maidenhead, Berkshire: Open University Press.

Burman, Michele. 2004. "Turbulent Talk: Girls Making Sense of Violence." In Christine Adler and Anne Worrall (eds) *Girls' Violence: Myths and Realities.* Albany, NY: State University of New York Press, pp. 81–104.

Buzawa, Eve S. and David Hirschel. 2010. "Criminalizing Assault: Do Age and Gender Matter?" In Meda Chesney-Lind and Nikki Jones (eds) *Fighting for Girls: New Perspectives on Gender and Violence.* Albany, NY: State University of New York Press, pp. 33–55.

Cain, Maureen (ed.). 1989. *Growing Up Good: Policing the Behaviour of Girls in Europe.* London: Sage.

Centers for Disease Control and Prevention (CDC). 1991–2009. *Youth Risk Behavior Survey.* Atlanta, GA: Department of Health and Human Services.

Chesney-Lind, Meda. 2002. "Criminalizing Victimization: The Unintended Consequences of Pro-Arrest Policies for Girls and Women." *Criminology and Public Policy* 1(2): 81–90.

Chesney-Lind, Meda. 2010. "Jailing 'Bad' Girls: Girls' Violence and Trends in Female Incarceration." In Meda Chesney-Lind and Nikki Jones (eds) *Fighting for Girls: New Perspectives on Gender and Violence.* Albany, NY: State University of New York Press, pp. 57–79.

Chesney-Lind, Meda and Michele Eliason. 2006. "From Invisible to Incorrigible: The Demonization of Marginalized Women and Girls." *Crime, Media and Culture* 2(1): 29–47.

Chesney-Lind, Meda and Katherine Irwin. 2008. *Beyond Bad Girls: Gender, Violence and Hype.* New York: Routledge.

Chesney-Lind, Meda and Nikki Jones (eds). 2010. *Fighting for Girls: New Perspectives on Gender and Violence.* Albany, NY: State University of New York Press.

Chesney-Lind, Meda and Vickie Paramore. 2001. "Are Girls Getting More Violent?: Exploring Juvenile Robbery Trends." *Journal of Contemporary Criminal Justice* 17(2): 142–166.

Chesney-Lind, Meda and Randall G. Shelden. 2004. *Girls, Delinquency and Juvenile Justice.* Belmont, CA: Wadsworth.

Daly, Kathleen. 1992. "Women's Pathways to Felony Court: Feminist Theories of Lawbreaking and Problems of Representation." *Southern California Review of Law and Women's Studies* 2: 11–52.

Dembo, Richard, Linda Williams and James Schmeidler. 1993. "Gender Differences in Mental Health Service Needs Among Youths Entering a Juvenile Detention Center." *Journal of Prison and Jail Health* 12(2): 73–101.

D'Emilio, John and Estelle Freedman. 1988. *Intimate Matters: A History of Sexuality in America.* New York: Harper & Row.

Devlin, Rachel. 1998. "Female Juvenile Delinquency and the Problem of Sexual Authority in America 1945–1965." In Sherrie A. Inness (ed.) *Delinquents and Debutantes: Twentieth-Century American Girls' Cultures.* New York and London: New York University Press, pp. 83–108.

Durham, M.G. 1998. "Dilemmas of Desire: Representations of Adolescent Sexuality in Two Teen Magazines." *Youth and Society* 29: 369–389.

Farrell, Albert D. and Steven E. Bruce. 1997. "Impact of Exposure to Community Violence on Violent Behavior and Emotional Distress among Urban Adolescents." *Journal of Clinical Child Psychology* 26(1): 2–14.

Federal Bureau of Investigations (FBI). 2007. *Crime in the U.S. 2006.* Washington D.C.: U.S Government Printing Office.

Feld, Barry C. 2009. "Violent Girls or Relabeled Status Offenders? An Alternative Interpretation of the Data." *Crime and Delinquency* 55: 241–265.

Gaarder, Emily and J. Belknap. 2002. "Tenuous Borders: Girls Transferred to Adult Court." *Criminology* 40(3): 481–517.

Gaarder, Emily, Nancy Rodriguez and Marjorie S. Zatz. 2004. "Criers, Liars and Manipulators: Probation Officers' Views of Girls." *Justice Quarterly* 21: 547–578.

Garbarino, James. 2007. *See Jane Hit: Why Girls Are Growing More Violent and What We Can Do About It.* Harmondsworth: Penguin.

Garland, David. 2002. *The Culture of Control: Crime and Social Order in Contemporary Society.* Chicago, IL: The University of Chicago Press.

Girls Incorporated. 1996. *Prevention and Parity: Girls in Juvenile Justice.* Washington D.C.: U.S. Department of Justice, Office of Juvenile Justice and Delinquency Prevention.

Holsinger, Kristi and Alexander Holsinger. 2005. "Differential Pathways to Violence and Self-Injurious Behavior: African American and White Girls in the Juvenile Justice System." *Journal of Research in Crime and Delinquency* 42(2): 211–242.

Hubbard, Dana J. and Betsy Matthews. 2008. "Reconciling the Differences Between the 'Gender-Responsive' and the 'What Works' Literatures to Improve Services for Girls." *Crime and Delinquency* 54: 225–258.

Jones, Nikki. 2004. "'It's not Where you Live it's How you Live': How Young Women Negotiate Conflict and Violence in the Inner City." *Annals of the American Academy of Political and Social Science* 595(1): 49–62.

Jones, Nikki. 2010. "'It's About Being a Survivor …'": African American Girls, Gender, and the Context of Inner City Violence." In Meda Chesney-Lind and Nikki Jones (eds) *Fighting for Girls: New Perspectives on Gender and Violence.* Albany, NY: State University of New York Press, pp. 203–218.

Katz, P. 1979. "The Development of Female Identity." In C. Kopp (ed.) *In Becoming Female: Perspectives on Development.* New York: Plenum Press.

Knupfer, Anne Meis. 2001. *Reform and Resistance: Gender, Delinquency, and America's First Juvenile Court.* London: Routledge.

Krisberg, Barry. 2005. *Juvenile Justice: Redeeming our Children.* Thousand Oaks, CA, London and New Delhi: Sage.

Laub, John H. and Janet L. Lauritsen. 1993. "Violent Criminal Behavior Over the Life Course: A Review of the Longitudinal and Comparative Research." *Violence and Victims* 8: 235–252.

Males, Mike. 2010. "Have Girls Gone Wild?" In Meda Chesney-Lind and Nikki Jones (eds) *Fighting for Girls: New Perspectives on Gender and Violence.* Albany, NY: State University of New York Press, pp. 13–32.

Messerschmidt, James W. 1993. *Masculinities and Crime: Critique and Reconceptualization of Theory.* Lanham, MD: Rowman and Littlefield.

Miller, Jody. 2008. *Getting Played: African American Girls Urban Inequality and Gendered Violence.* New York: New York University Press.

Miller, Jody and Norman A. White. 2004. "Situational Effects of Gender Inequality on Girls' Participation in Violence." In Christine Alder and Anne Worrall (eds) *Girls' Violence: Myths and Realities.* Albany, NY: State University of New York Press, pp. 167–190.

Mulvihill, Donald J., Melvin M. Tumin and Lynn A. Curtis. 1969. *Crimes of Violence: A Staff Report Submitted to the National Commission on the Causes and Prevention of Violence.* Washington D.C.: Government Printing Office.

Odem, Mary E. 1995. *Delinquent Daughters: Protecting and Policing Adolescent Female Sexuality in the United States 1885–1920.* Chapel Hill: The University of North Carolina Press.

Office of Juvenile Justice and Delinquency Prevention (OJJDP). 1998. *Guiding Principles for Promising Female Programming: An Inventory of Best Practices.* Washington D.C.

Platt, Anthony M. 1977. *The Child Savers: The Invention of Delinquency*. Chicago, IL: The University of Chicago Press.

Prothrow-Stith, Deborah and Howard R. Spivak. 2005. *Sugar and Spice and No Longer Nice: How We Can Stop Girls' Violence*. San Francisco, CA: Jossey-Bass.

Sabol, William J. and Heather Couture. 2008. *Prison Inmates at Midyear 2007*. Department of Justice, Bureau of Justice Statistics. Washington D.C.: Government Printing Office.

Schaffner, Laurie. 2006. *Girls in Trouble with the Law*. New Brunswick, NJ, and London: Rutgers University Press.

Schlossman, Steven and Stephanie Wallach. 1978. "The Crime of Precocious Sexuality: Female Juvenile Delinquency in the Progressive Era." *Harvard Educational Review* 48(1): 65–94.

Snyder, Howard N. and Melissa Sickmund. 2006. *Juvenile Offenders and Victims: 2006 National Report*. Office of Juvenile Justice and Delinquency Prevention, Department of Justice. Washington D.C.

Sprott, Jane B. and Anthony N. Doob. 2009. *Justice for Girls? Stability and Change in the Youth Justice Systems of the United States and Canada*. Chicago, IL: The University of Chicago Press.

Steffensmeier, Darrell, Jennifer Schwartz, Hua Zhong and Jeff Ackerman. 2005. "An Assessment of Recent Trends in Girls' Violence Using Diverse Longitudinal Sources: Is the Gender Gap Closing?" *Criminology* 43(2): 355–405.

Thorne, Barrie. 1993. *Gender Play: Girls and Boys in School*. New Brunswick, NJ: Rutgers University Press.

Vaillancourt, Tracy and Shelley Hymel. 2004. "The Social Context of Children's Aggression." In Marlene M. Moretti, Candice L. Odgers and Margaret A. Jackson (eds) *Girls and Aggression: Contributing Factors and Intervention Principles*. New York: Kluwer Academic/Plenum Publishers, pp. 57–73.

Worrall, Anne. 2001. "Governing Bad Girls: Changing Constructions of Female Juvenile Delinquency." In Jo Bridgeman and Daniel Monk (eds) *Feminist Perspectives on Child Law*. London: Routledge Cavendish, pp. 151–168.

Worrall, Anne. 2004. "Twisted Sisters, Ladettes, and the New Penology: The Social Construction of 'Violent Girls.'" In Christine Alder and Anne Worrall (eds) *Girls' Violence: Myths and Realities*. Albany, NY: State University of New York Press, pp. 41–60.

Zahn-Waxler, C. 2000. "The Development of Empathy, Guilt and the Internalization of Distress." In R. Davidson (ed.) *Anxiety, Depression and Emotion: Wisconsin Symposium on Emotion*, Volume II. New York: Oxford University Press, pp. 222–265.

CHAPTER FOUR

A Gendered View of Violence

By Denise Paquette Boots and Jennifer Wareham

The intersection of gender and violent crime has become a recent central focus of many criminological inquiries into the causes, correlates, and implications of various forms of antisocial behavior. Such studies of gendered violence can be framed within a larger conceptualization at the individual and societal level of what it *means* to be female or male. What epitomizes feminine and masculine roles and identities within respective societies? What attitudes, behaviors, and actions are acceptable today and reinforced via socialization regarding the sexes? How does society punish those persons who fail to act within the boundaries of gendered expectations? Are there gender disparities across social, legal, business, and familial spheres, and if so, why? These questions are key to understanding the intersection of gender and violence and how these pathways are formed.

Gender ideologies are central in deconstructing the aforementioned topics, as they define an individual's changing beliefs, images, and self-concepts over the life-course. Ideologies thereby influence one's assumptions regarding differences and similarities between males and females on topics such as intimacy, societal roles, expectations, and determinations of societal success or failure within the confines of gender roles. Within the context of the criminal justice system, gender stereotypes and ideologies are especially salient in determining what behaviors are deemed legally deviant, who is formally brought under corrective control, the impact of formal and informal sanctions, and the length and method by which offenders are punished and treated.

The most robust relationship in the study of crime is the underrepresentation of female offenders when compared to males. This relationship varies in both the quantity and types of crime that women commit. "Indeed, the strongest predictor of criminality is neither race nor ethnicity, nor social class, nor age, nor neighborhood conditions, nor intelligence, nor any other sociological, biological, or psychological factor. Gender unequivocally is the most discriminating factor associated with crime" (Tracy, Kempf-Leonard, and Abramoske-James, 2009, p. 172). Despite this robust and enduring relationship, the vast majority of studies examining serious violence have either ignored sex altogether or relegated gender to a peripheral variable of interest with little comparative focus in empirical inquiries. Exceptions to this rule have been few until post-1970, with even some of the most respected national longitudinal and prospective studies of violence pathways and correlates funded in the last 20 years omitting gendered perspectives and collecting data from strictly male samples (Loeber, Farrington, Stouthamer-Loeber, and van Kammen, 1998). Research on gendered violence has pointed toward a specialized subset of aggressive females who commit serious crimes involving interpersonal violence such as women who hurt or kill their children, who abuse their domestic partners, or who join gangs or engage in antisocial delinquent acts, but the origins, contexts, and motivations of these pathways are not well defined. Without question, the etiology of gendered violence trajectories and typologies of female offenders has been slow to be fully explored within the discipline of criminology.

ROOTS OF FEMINIST PERSPECTIVES ON WOMEN AND VIOLENCE

When considering the historical evolution of gendered views of criminological behaviors, several pioneers have blazed the trail. In the 1970s, critical reviews of the prominent theoretical rubrics on crime led to a number of compelling feminist writings which questioned why females were ignored, why gender was omitted as a relevant consideration in criminal pathways, and how gender stereotypes were perpetuated as fact across many mainstream theoretical frameworks. These works included Dorie Klein's (1973) seminal article regarding the propagation of sexist stereotypes in prior criminal justice theories. Klein summarized the major theorists who had influenced thinking about the predispositions and nature of women. These prior works supported the belief that "good" women were normal and kept within the boundaries of gender roles and social expectations while "bad" women were criminals who did not observe the status quo or socially-engineered restrictions on female behaviors. This traditional perspective and dichotomization of good versus bad females is commonly referred to as the virgin–whore dichotomy. Similarly, Carol Smart's (1976) classic feminist book on women and crime offered a comprehensive overview of the skewed perception of female offenders across theory and treatment. Perhaps most importantly, Smart highlighted the role of victimization in female pathways to criminal behavior. The feminist revolution was furthered by respected scholars who brought attention to the marginalization of gender within the fields of criminology and criminal justice.

With regard to early works that contribute to our understanding of women and violence, both Freda Adler (1975) and Rita James Simon (1975) advocated emancipation theory, which posits that lower rates of female crime can be explained via gender-based discrimination as well as the societal constraints of domestic roles which thereby limit criminal opportunities. Adler speculated that female violence would increase with the ongoing emancipation of women and the resulting greater equalization in social and political circles. Although emancipation theory and the "liberation hypothesis" are now generally regarded as peripheral to feminist criminology and largely unsupported due to the lack of materialization of a class of highly violent female offenders, these publications were leading-edge in igniting the debate and consideration regarding women and crime.

Additionally, a number of feminist scholars outside criminology have made relevant contributions when considering how gender roles and socialization may influence criminal behaviors. For instance, Carol Gilligan's (1982) differential gender socialization theory argues that the sexes develop fundamentally opposing worldviews during childhood, thereby producing two distinct moral perspectives or "voices." That is, men adopt an "ethic of justice" that focuses on individual rights, autonomy, condoning violence, and hierarchy and order. In contrast, women are socialized to be less violent and to adopt an ethic of responsibility and caregiving. As a result of this "ethic of care," the moral development of females over the life-course is posited to make them less prone to endorse aggression or violence and instead more likely to emphasize nurturing, protectiveness toward the weak/vulnerable, and greater social dependency and emotional attachment as caretakers (Boots and Cochran, 2011).

Despite the inroads covered and interest stirred in gendered studies of crime driven by the rise of these works and others, Daly and Chesney-Lind (1988) observed that criminology had been sluggish to fully integrate feminist perspectives into theoretical rubrics or to synthesize feminist work outside of criminology. There is a scarce amount of data collected directly from female offenders that has focused on gender-specific perspectives, motivations, experiences, and perceptions regarding crime, how and why they became involved in antisocial activities, or the social, psychological, and cultural costs of criminal participation for women across different settings and life-course stages. Despite an explosion of life-course criminology works, the field ignored the development of female criminal careers and has only recently begun to focus on the development of criminal careers for female offenders, female delinquents, and gender-sensitive programming for both treatment and prevention efforts. Relatedly, Joanne Belknap (2007) has pointed to the ongoing "invisibility" of women and young girls in both their treatment once they become part of the system and how they are studied within the larger academic community regarding the causes, correlates, and outcomes of criminogenic behaviors. The question remains as to whether similar, varying, or a combination of factors support the onset of antisocial behaviors in females and males, or whether the genesis of violence is the same across the sexes and types of crimes. Such issues persist across present-day studies of violence trajectories in youngsters and adults, with most mainstream empirical examinations relating to the gender gap attributed to emotional, familial, or social problems versus distinct gender-based differences (or similarities) in pathways to violence, even when females commit serious crimes like males (Chesney-Lind, 1997).

GENDER DIFFERENCES IN AGGRESSION IN EARLY DEVELOPMENT

A growing body of research has examined gender differences in aggression (i.e., acts or threats of verbal abuse, social harm, and physical harm) and violence (i.e., acts or threats of physical harm that is severe enough in nature to warrant a criminal offense) during childhood and adolescence. It is important to consider early developmental causes of aggression because children who are highly aggressive are at greatest risk of engaging in violence during adolescence and adulthood (see e.g., Broidy et al. 2003). The research on the stability of aggression across age is mixed. Some longitudinal studies indicate that physical aggression decreases with age (Baillargeon, Tremblay and Willins, 2005). On the other hand, some studies suggest that physical aggression, like the age–crime curve, is curvilinear, increasing during early childhood and decreasing during mid-to-late adolescence (e.g., Loeber and Stouthamer-Loeber, 1998). In general, relatively few of these studies examined gender differences in aggression trends across age. In one study of gender differences in the development of physical aggression for children ages 5 to 11, Lee, Baillargeon, Vermunt, Wu and Tremblay (2007) reported no differences in the prevalence of physical aggression across age for boys but decreasing trends across age for girls. Clearly, further research on the stability of aggression across gender is needed.

The literature on life-course criminology has also examined gender differences in subgroups of individuals who display similar behavioral patterns in aggression and violence over time. Studies of aggression and violence in subgroups of youth have revealed both similar and different patterns in offending trajectories across gender. Various trajectory studies of child and adolescent cohorts in the U.S., Canada, and New Zealand have revealed heterogeneity among boys and girls. For both sexes, the populations can be categorized into multiple (typically three to four) subgroups: non-aggressive/violent, early to late adolescent aggressive/violent, and chronic aggressive/violent youth (see Broidy et al., 2003; Lee et al., 2007). Importantly, groups of non-aggressors and chronic aggressors appear for both boys and girls; however, the proportion of girls in the non-aggressive group tends to be much larger than boys, and girls generally have lower prevalence rates than boys in similar subgroups.

With the popularity of life-course theories of aggression and violence, disagreement over gender differences in the development of aggression/violence has emerged and controversies continue as this form of sociological research explores the etiology of violence. Some of the most popular developmental theorists (e.g., Moffitt, 1993) suggest there are no etiological differences in violence with respect to gender and that gender differences are expected only in prevalence rates. Other developmental theorists such as Silverthorn and Frick (1999), however, suggest differences in the genesis of cognitive and contextual factors that are hypothesized to affect the onset of aggression for girls differently than boys.

SOCIALIZATION OF GENDER

Although the literature on aggression/violence is inconsistent, children become less aggressive and violent as they age (Tremblay, 2000). Socialization pressures and gender-typing may affect and direct differences in aggression and violence across gender, as well as other behavioral differences. The etiology of gender differentiation is a complex process that has received respectable attention in the literature from multiple paradigms. The literature on gender-typing can inform explanations about why aggression and violence decline as we age and why boys/ men tend to have higher prevalence rates of aggression and violence than girls/women. Socialization factors are gender oriented with girls, in particular, being pressured to behave less aggressively than boys. Various theories and explanations address how societal gender-typing occurs and impacts beliefs, self-concepts, behavior, and life-style (for a detailed explanation of gender-type explanations see Bussey and Bandura, 1999).

According to psychological theories, children develop an understanding of their gender identity at an early age, though there is disagreement in the literature about how early gender identity forms. This gender identity influences thought and actions to be consistent with gender stereotypes prevalent in the culture and society. From a psychological perspective, children perceive their gender as a stable or fixed condition and behave in ways that are consistent with their gender. An alternative and more controversial perspective to gender-typing is offered by biological theories, including evolutionary psychology. According to biological theories, gender differences, more accurately biological sex differences, in behavior and thinking are rooted in biological selection (i.e., evolutionary natural selection) and reproductive advantage. From this perspective, gender differences in behavior are inherent in biological sex. Neither psychological nor biological theories of gender differentiation have received much empirical validity (Bussey and Bandura, 1999).

Sociological theories of gender view gender as a social construct wherein differences are determined by social practices. Gender differences occur within and across sex depending on factors such as culture, socioeconomic status, class, race/ethnicity, and education. Gender differences in behavior are therefore viewed as a consequence of same-sex role modeling and involve learning behavior that is deemed socially appropriate for the gender. This perspective has received the strongest empirical support for understanding the causes of gender differentiation (Bussey and Bandura, 1999). In general, sociological theories of gender identity suggest that boys are pressured earlier and more rigidly to model male gender roles than girls to model female gender roles. In societies like the U.S., where aggression in males is viewed as acceptable but inappropriate in females, males are more inclined to adopt aggressive behavior, while females are less likely to adopt aggressive behavior (see Bussey and Bandura, 1999). Various social (e.g., disapproval and punishment) and personal (e.g., self-criticism) sanctions condition the likelihood and nature (i.e., direct vs. indirect types) of aggression.

CURRENT TRENDS IN REPORTS OF VIOLENT OFFENDING

Regardless of the type of data that are used, there are persistent and distinct sex differences in violent offending patterns, with females exhibiting significantly less physical aggression than males across geography, setting, chronological age, and other measures (see Moffitt, Caspi, Rutter and Silva, 2001). Contrary to media depictions of "mean," hardcore, violent girls coming into the criminal justice system in staggering numbers, various data sources indicate that females are underrepresented for most crimes (Chesney-Lind and Jones, 2010). In the latest annual official arrest data released by the Federal Bureau of Investigation (FBI) (U.S. Department of Justice, 2010), some intriguing short- and long-term trends emerge. Ten-year arrest trends from the Uniform Crime Report (UCR) data between the years 2000–2009 indicate that, overall, the total number of female arrests increased for the period by 11.4 percent; in comparison, male arrests during this decade decreased by 4.9 percent. For violent offenses, females had fewer arrests than males for murder or manslaughter, with a 10.4 percent decrease compared to a 4.7 percent decline over the decade. This trend reversed for aggravated assaults, with men having much greater reductions in arrests when compared with females, with a 13.1 percent versus 4.1 percent change over the period, respectively. For all violent offenses (including murder and manslaughter, forcible rape, and aggravated assault) across the entire decade, arrests of females increased 0.1 percent while male arrests decreased by 8.1 percent.

Self-report data show stable trends that contradicted violent arrest figures and instead indicate a decline in such female offending behaviors when compared to males. In a recent work by Steffensmeier and colleagues (2006) examining gender differences in violent crime data from the UCR and the National Crime Victimization Survey (NCVS) between 1980 and 2003, the authors report that net-widening policies, and not actual increases in acts of female violence, are to blame for inflated official arrest gender differences over this time period. Self-reported and victim-reported crime estimates are regarded as a more accurate picture of the gender–crime relationship by some researchers and show similar trends with most official statistics overall, with females underrepresented in violent crime but more gender equality found in minor and property crimes (Chesney-Lind, 2004).

TYPOLOGIES OF VIOLENT FEMALE OFFENDERS

When looking across the continuum of violent offenses, several offending typologies are relevant to the discussion of gendered offending. These include serious offenses such as: homicide and filicide, serial murder, terrorism, robbery, gangs, and domestic battery. Each of these offending types is briefly reviewed in the sections that follow.

Domestic Homicides and Filicide

Murder is a male-dominated phenomenon, much like other forms of violence. Although women in the United States comprise a small proportion of homicide offenders, with between 10 and 20 percent of such crimes attributed to women, female-perpetrated homicide rates have decreased significantly since the early 1980s and remain fairly constant (Belknap, 2007). American rates are comparable to countries such as Australia, with females constituting roughly 13 percent of homicide offenders there (Kirkwood, 2003). The relationship to the victim and motivation for homicide are quite varied for men. When women kill, however, the most common victim is a current or former intimate partner or offspring. Feminist scholars have highlighted the importance of considering the role of gender, power, and control in such homicides, as women who kill their domestic partners frequently do so to protect themselves and/or their children from further abuse or battering. Further, within this subtype of violent behavior, there are significant gender differences in rates when looking across time. In their analysis of murders committed between 1980 and 2008 by victim–offender relationship (which was known in approximately 60 percent of all homicides), Cooper and Smith (2011) estimated that the percentage of domestic homicides of male victims had decreased by 53 percent overall for that period (10.4 percent versus 4.9 percent). In contrast, across the same period, there was a 5 percent increase in females killed by their intimates, with two out of five female murder victims murdered by a former or current romantic partner. Researchers have suggested that gender equality in earnings have mediating effects on homicide, with positive social and economic empowerment and mobility reducing the probability of women committing murder (see e.g., Jensen, 2001); these findings directly contradict the emancipation hypothesis and suggest that education, economic stability, and the structure of the environment are all salient factors to consider in prevention and intervention efforts.

Another type of homicide that has received considerable empirical and scholarly attention involves gender disparities in offenders who kill their children. Such homicides include the following terms: 1) neonaticide (killing a child within the first 24 hours of birth), 2) infanticide (killing of a child under the age of one), and 3) filicide (a parent who kills any of their offspring). Frequently acknowledged as one of the most common crimes dating back to antiquity, children in the twentieth and twenty-first centuries continue to die at the hands of their biological parents, and mothers in particular, at an alarming rate. Indeed, in the United States, child deaths under the age of one are estimated at 8/100,000 versus 3/100,000 in other countries such as Canada; among maltreatment cases, roughly 32 percent of infant fatality cases are attributed to neglect, with most of these deaths associated with mothers (see Barnett, Miller-Perrin, and Perrin, 2011 for an extensive review of familial homicide and various forms of abuse and maltreatment related to child homicides). Unlike other forms of murder that are male-dominated, biological mothers disproportionately kill their children when compared to other persons (with consistent reports of over 50 percent of all child deaths at the hands of the biological mother), followed far behind by biological fathers and then step-parents.

There are serious measurement issues cross-culturally regarding the incidence of filicide since many countries do not track infant deaths, child deaths may be miscoded, a child's birth and later death may be hidden by the perpetrator, and/or government agencies may aggregate these statistics with other deaths. For the data that are available, however, researchers have estimated the incidence rates for infanticide and neonaticide between 0.5 and 6.9 per 100,000 in industrialized countries such as Hungary, the United Kingdom, the U.S., and New Zealand; infants in England and Wales were found to be at four times the risk of being murdered than any other age group, and babies born to East German women were at three times higher risk of death than those infants born to West German women (see e.g., Toro, Feher, Farkas, and Dunay, 2010; also Porter and Gavin, 2010 for a review of risk and incidence). Female infants are at greater risk of death than male offspring in some developing countries, such as China, where males are more culturally desired. The majority of neonaticides are committed by females under the age of 25 who do not suffer a form of mental illness, give birth at their own residence, are the product of an unwanted or concealed pregnancy, and whose crimes are typically characterized by drowning, suffocation, or strangulation of the newborn. In contrast, female infanticide and filicide offenders are typically older than 25 years of age, kill to retaliate against a partner, via Munchausen syndrome by proxy, or due to cumulative abuse or neglect of their children, may premeditate the homicide, are well-educated, may have a child with a handicap or who is sickly, and utilize various killing techniques including weapons and non-weapons (see e.g., Meyer and Oberman, 2001).

A subset of women who commit infanticide have been diagnosed with serious mental illness, including post-partum depression and psychosis, across American, Finnish, and Scandinavian studies (Porter and Gavin, 2010). These cases are exemplified by well-documented U.S. case studies such as Andrea Yates, who was found to have severe post-partum depression and killed her five children by drowning them systematically in a bath tub, and Dena Schlosser, who was diagnosed with bipolar disorder after she cut the limbs off her infant daughter during a psychotic episode when she heard voices command her to make a child sacrifice to God. There is controversy regarding the link between post-partum depression, psychosis, and female offenders who commit filicide, with some empirical evidence suggesting that an underlying genetic predisposition to bipolar disorder, and not pregnancy-related factors such as hormonal fluctuations, are related to acute psychotic episodes (Valdimarsdottir, Hultman, Harlow, Cnattingius, and Sparen, 2009). Occasionally a highly sensational case of matricidal filicide, such as when Susan Smith drowned her two young sons in their car seats to gain sympathy and be free to live the single life, highlights the existence of personality disorders in a small number of these female murderers. Lastly, the association between low socio-economic status, the onset of life stressors, and filicidal events has policy implications because these findings point to the need for early intervention to help at-risk families, and in particular mothers with a history of depression, psychosis, substance use, and/or personality disorders that put their children at risk.

Gender Differences in Serial Murder

As with most other forms of homicide, serial killing is a predominantly male enterprise. Contrary to public myths that males comprise virtually *all* serial killers, however, females comprise roughly 13 to 15 percent of all identified serial murderers in the U.S. since 1825 (Hickey, 2006). Critical issues surround the definition of serial killing, with those in law enforcement adopting adefinition with an emphasis on sexual motivation of the offender, and scholars debating the number of required victims (two or three) and the reliability of gender-appropriate typologies. In 1990, Aileen Wuornos, a prostitute and drug user, was infamously labeled as the first American female serial killer because she allegedly met the general profile of her male counterparts; her weapon of choice was a gun, she displayed overt aggression and anger, she had an abuse and criminal history similar to other male serial killers, and she killed seven victims over a year-long period. Perhaps most relevant to the discussion of gender roles and identity, despite a long history of severe abuse, loss, and mental illness that plagued her life, Wuornos came under intense condemnation and epitomized the "virgin–whore dichotomy" as an unjustified and evil killer. She was viewed with a mixture of horror and fascination as a socially non-feminine, unnatural anomaly or "monster" before her execution; this masculinized portrayal of her was perpetuated in the movie *Monster*. Yet there are a good number of experts who have questioned the labeling of Wuornos as a sexualized killer or the first female serial killer, both because they disagreed with the typology used and because of a lack of evidence that she killed for sexually-motivated reasons since none of her victims were violated, but rather were robbed (Gurian, 2011).

In their critique of female serial killer typologies and labeling, Farrell and colleagues (2011) present examples of female serial killers throughout history, including the first documented serial killer in history named Locusta, a woman who murdered in the first century AD in Rome via poison and the first recorded U.S. female serial killer from Delaware, Lucretia Patricia Cannon, who killed for 27 years in the late 1700s. Despite the known existence of female serial killers, few empirical studies have explored this phenomenon until quite recently. Studies that have explored the gender differences in serial killing have reported that females are more mature, likely to choose a wider variety of victims who are close in proximity and emotionally-tied to the offender (i.e., old or young family members, husbands targeted for profit), are less likely to use torture, take time to build trust with victims using ruses, kill more victims than their male counterparts, are not caught for longer periods of time, and use a wide variety of methods to kill their victims quietly (Hickey, 2006). New gender-specific serial killer typologies that acknowledge unique qualities of female offenders have been created, including: black widow, angel of death, profit killer, team killer, revenge killer, sexual predator, question of sanity, unsolved, and unexplained categories (see Hickey, 2006).

While detailed serial killing data are difficult to find or generate, recent studies have conducted both national and cross-cultural inquiries regarding female killers. For example, Gurian (2011) analyzed cross-national data compiled from academic and media sources on 134 offenders (99 partnered teams including 55 males and 44 females and 35 solo female killers) primarily from the U.S., but also including serial killers from Australia, Austria, Belgium, Canada, France, Greece, India, Mexico, Russia, Spain and the U.K. Gurian collapsed revised gendered typologies into two broad categories, pleasure-oriented vs. purpose-oriented motives, finding that solo female murderers were more likely to commit the latter when compared to teams. Partnered teams were also significantly more likely to use a variety of killing methods, chose strangers as victims, and murdered in different geographical locations, while solo female killers used a single killing method such as poison, targeted adult family members, and murdered locally. Interestingly, while most partnered serial killers received life sentences (18 percent of males versus 14 percent of females), more men in these teams received a death sentence and were executed than were their female partners (6 percent of males versus 1 percent of females), with another three males and two female offenders still on death row. Another three women who killed solo were on death row and five more had been executed for their crimes. Recent findings from an analysis of a subset of American female serial killers (Farrell, Keppel and Titterington, 2011) suggest that not only are these murderers different than male serial killers, but that the rarity and covert nature of female serial homicide has led to serious underestimations or misclassifications for deaths these offenders perpetrated. Therefore, more gendered empirical investigations need to explore serial killing.

Gender and Terrorism

In recent decades, terrorism has emerged as a global topic of interest. Terrorism refers to politically motivated violence and aggression. Stereotypically, terrorists are thought of as male perpetrators; however, women and girls have consistently been involved in acts of political violence. Often, it is believed that women's involvement in terrorism is due to coercion or brain-washing from male partners and leaders. While there may certainly be many instances where this is the case for women, as well as men, there are also cases where women's involvement in terrorism is self-motivated out of revenge, empowerment, political ideology, and a general sense of purpose.

Berko, Erez, and Globokar (2010) explored women's involvement in terrorism in Israel. They state that, as a highly patriarchal society that is very oppressive toward women, the Arab/Palestinian culture initially excluded women from participating in terrorism but now welcomes their involvement. In their interviews with imprisoned Palestinian female terrorists, Berko et al. (2010) note several motivations for the women's involvement in the Palestinian/Israeli conflict, including revenge against the Israelis, political motivation, religious motivation, and empowerment through establishment of a sense of purpose or resistance to oppression. The authors also indicated that many women became involved in terrorism because of manipulation or coercion from family and other men. Further, Eager (2008) and Gonzalez-Perez (2008) provide informative historical accounts of women's involvement in global acts of terrorism. Eager provides estimates of female memberships within specific terrorism groups, with female membership reaching almost 60 percent for some groups. Both Eager (2008) and Gonzalez-Perez (2008) describe women's roles in terrorism as diverse, with some women taking on only supportive roles and others serving as respected soldiers and killers.

A growing body of literature has begun to explore and examine gender differences in the motivations and attractions to terrorism. Unfortunately, these studies tend to focus individually on one gender and must be combined with additional research to make gender comparisons. Future research needs to further explore the etiology of terrorism and how gender affects involvement in these politically motivated acts of aggression and violence.

Gender and Robbery

In Jody Miller's (1998) instrumental work on gender, urban disadvantage, social hierarchies, and street crimes, she explored the "masculine" crime of robbery through the lens of "doing gender." Miller examined both men's and women's reasons for why offenders chose to rob others, victim selection, as well as the role of gender as it influenced the ability to execute this type of violence. The results from this study yielded valuable insights into how active offenders use their gender differently to accomplish robbery, with men in this urban environment using physical coercion, guns, and aggression to rob other males and solidify their tough street reputations. While female motivations for robbery were the same as males—economic, thrill-seeking, revenge, and quelling boredom—qualitative interviews with 14 women revealed three diverse and complex ways females enacted robbery. First, women most commonly robbed solo female victims, both by themselves and in teams with other female co-offenders, typically garnishing knives or by using threats of physical intimidation. Second, some females used their sexuality to lure male victims into compromising positions or played their victim's gendered view of females as a weaker sex to rob targets either by themselves or with female accomplices. When robbing male victims, women almost always used guns and avoided physical contact so they could maintain control. Third, some of the females reported that they participated with male co-offenders to rob male victims.

Building upon Miller's (1998) conclusions that St. Louis female robbers diverged little from male street criminals in their motivations to commit crimes but that gender played a salient role in how they accomplished these acts, Brookman and her colleagues (2007) sought to comparatively elucidate the intersection of gender and crime by interviewing 55 incarcerated street criminals in the U.K. Their findings largely concurred with previous studies on offending populations and showed similarities in U.S. and U.K. subcultures, with gender convergence found for motivations for robbery. That is, the primary focus of street robbers was an economic need to support drug habits or partying, followed by a "buzz" (p. 867) or thrill, and street justice; a small number of males stated that an assault turned into an unplanned robbery. Women were more likely, however, to self-identify as drug addicts than were male robbers, revealing their social acceptance to be viewed as dependent and neutralizing their criminal culpability. Men, on the other hand, were more likely to embrace their street crimes as evidence of their masculinity and toughness and less likely to use their drug use as an excuse. Comparatively, females in this study differed fundamentally from those in St. Louis because of their willingness to target males to accomplish robberies. Brookman and her co-authors concluded that this difference might be attributed to the gun culture of American urban environments, where the likelihood of a victim carrying a firearm is relatively common and thereby makes females less likely to target males; U.K. females still fortified themselves commonly with other weapons to ensure compliance of their male victim, however. Another substantive difference between American and U.K. robbers is the frequent targeting by female robbers of non-local middle class victims, placing more social distance between offender and victim and providing criminals with an advantage of control and intimidation. In comparison, street offenders in St. Louis were more likely to victimize others on the street or at clubs that were part of their own street culture. Such findings may be an artifact of the sampling techniques between these studies, but still point to the need to conduct further cross-cultural studies that probe the intersections of gender, power, social class, and race to determine how these factors influence and frame various violent behaviors.

Differences in Non-Lethal Intimate Partner Violence Perpetration

When it comes to intimate partner violence (IPV), results from large national data sets that failed to investigate the motives and consequences of IPV have suggested that gender symmetry exists in its perpetration (see Archer, 2000 for a meta-analytical review). These findings have proven to be quite controversial among social scientists, and have led to hundreds of studies in the U.S. and other nations such as Canada, the U.K., and New Zealand that have also indicated similar rates of domestic violence perpetration across gender. It is important to note however, that this contention of symmetry rests on different methodological approaches used to investigate the behavior and that measures may lack information on situational features that substantively contribute to gendered responses of violence in intimate relationships.

In a recent review of literature on intimate partner violence, Swan, Gambone, Caldwell, Sullivan and Snow (2008) explored gender differences in the perpetration of intimate partner violence. Swan and her associates reported no gender differences in the perpetration rates of physical and psychological abuse; however, men were more likely to commit abusive acts involving general coercion (e.g., threats, intimidation), stalking, and sexual coercion than women. Notably, Swan's review of the literature revealed women are more likely than men to be injured and require medical attention when they are the victims of domestic assault. It therefore follows that if female victims tend to require greater medical attention than male victims, this may lead to the perception that men are more likely to be the perpetrators of such violence than women. A review of the literature suggests gender differences in the motivations for committing domestic violence. Generally, men are more likely to engage in domestic abuse as a means of control over their partner, while women are more likely to engage in domestic abuse for reasons of self-defense, defense of their children, and retribution (see Swan et al., 2008); in fact, Miller's (2005) work demonstrates that most women arrested for domestic violence were either victims of battering who fought back or women who were defending their children or property (see also Osthoff, 2002). These findings are similar to those regarding lethal acts of domestic homicide and reiterate the need to critically explore the social construction of gender roles and identities in violence research. Acknowledgment of gender differences in the motivations for and types of intimate partner violence perpetration implies treatment and prevention techniques must incorporate gender differences. Moreover, there is a definitive need to look within gender categories and further explore how race, culture, and gender intersect to shape social identities as well as legal responses within the criminal justice system to various types of domestic violence, especially in cases of non-physical forms of abuse when females do not fit the "stereotypical" depiction of victims of IPV (see e.g., Goodmark, 2012 for a lengthy discussion of the evolution of the criminal justice response within the context of the intersectionality of gender, race, ethnicity, and socioeconomic status).

Gender Issues Related to Gang Involvement

Criminologists have long been interested in gangs. Studies show that gang members are responsible for a disproportionate amount of delinquency and crime, particularly more severe offenses and violence (Decker and Miller, 2006). Traditionally, studies of gang involvement have focused exclusively on the behavior and characteristics of male members. The role of girls/women were generally limited to that of male gang members' "girlfriends" and viewed as peripheral to boys'/men's roles. More recently, a few notable studies have explored more central roles of female gang membership. Much of this literature has been limited to the U.S., with few international studies such as in the U.K. (e.g., Davies, 1999).

Criminological inquiries into the gendered pathways of gang membership and outcomes have shown that female crime patterns are more complex than for their male counterparts. In their study of gender and gangs, Decker and Miller (2006) examined both offending and victimization patterns across the sexes, reporting that female encounters with rival gang members rarely result in violence, especially of a serious nature, as compared to males. Interestingly, their analysis revealed how the dynamics of gender roles and norms influence expectations of violence, females citing their femininity as a means to modify their participation in the most serious forms of violent behavior. "Thus, young women often drew on gender—and on gender stereotypes—both to negotiate and limit their involvement in gang violence, and to facilitate the success of gang members' crimes" (p. 135). Along these lines, females may be negatively impacted by intimate relationships with older boyfriends who encourage delinquency and other forms of substance use or antisocial behavior (see Richie, 1996), and the factors leading to violence for these girls appear to be different than their male peers (see Giordano, 2003).

THE ROLE OF VICTIMIZATION IN FEMALE PATHWAYS TO VIOLENCE

It has been posited that a major hurdle in the successful prediction of female criminality has been the inability to differentiate male from female offending via mainstream criminological theories. An alternate "feminist perspective of offending emphasizes consideration of female victimization and how the social organization of gender shapes female involvement in crime"(Bell, 2007, p. 367). A bounty of evidence points to the relevance when looking at female and male pathways to violence to consider physical, sexual, and verbal violations not only from an interpersonal level, but also on an institutional one. Such considerations become especially relevant as such victimization relates to girls and women and becomes the first step in their descent into offending (Chesney-Lind, 1997). Indeed, Howell (2003) hypothesizes that gendered offending pathways differ between the sexes and that childhood abuse and maltreatment is more relevant to female offending.

A large body of empirical evidence has been generated in recent years which shows that females who commit crimes are significantly more likely to have abuse histories than incarcerated men or women in the general population (Wolf Harlow, 1999), to have been a victim of intimate partner violence, and to have suffered physical, sexual, and/or emotional abuse as a youngster. While other scholarship has similarly shown the salience of victimization early in the life-course for boys with respect to gender specificoffending pathways (see e.g., Weeks and Widom, 1998), research suggests that more women than men under correctional control suffer from serious abuse histories (Wolf Harlow, 1999). Researchers have argued persuasively that serious abuse histories should have a prominent role in the empirical study of criminogenic behaviors for male and female subsamples.

For instance, in a recent article by DeGue and Widom (2009), adult women who were placed outside the home due to maltreatment were at one-third the risk of officially reported violence than females who had remained within their homes after maltreatment was reported. In contrast to female pathways, adult males with a history of delinquency *and* abuse had an increased risk of adult violent arrest, as did those who had non-foster-care placements. These gender differences further highlight the variance of short- and long-term outcomes and the need to conduct more research that can inform gender-specific, developmentally-appropriate interventions and prevention efforts.

CONSIDERATIONS FOR FUTURE RESEARCH AND PUBLIC POLICY

As more stakeholders, policymakers, and researchers enter the arena and debate the unique and similar risk factors across genders that apply toward pathways, interventions, and prevention efforts in violent offending, the greater our understanding of the complexities that surround these issues. While criminology and other related disciplines largely ignored the potential of gendered differences in trajectories of offending until the 1970s and 1980s, the emergence of interest and divergence of opinion on why girls are entering the system at increased rates, how best to treat them or prevent them from becoming criminogenic, and what gender means in the criminal justice system, are all important developments.

In their comprehensive work regarding sex differences in the Dunedin Multidisciplinary Health and Development Study cohort, Moffitt and her colleagues (2001) systematically examined gender issues surrounding antisocial behavior in the life-course of New Zealand youth. Over a decade later, the same issues the authors pointed to regarding the salience of investigating gender differences persist today when reviewing the extant literature on gender and crime. These include issues related to not testing between-sex differences in the same model, the dominance of male-only studies or employing female-only designs that exclude comparisons, a disproportionate ratio of male-to-female participants, the lack of acknowledgement in some empirical inquiries of insignificant findings that show a lack of gender differences, and an overgeneralization that sex differences are the rule when perusing through titles of academic works on the matter. As gendered pathways to offending are critically explored, there is significant potential to make positive contributions to both our understanding of the etiology of violence and to simultaneously inform programs and policies that incorporate such new knowledge to create positive outcomes for females, as well as males, who become involved in such behaviors.

REFERENCES

Adler, F. (1975). *Sisters in crime: The rise of the new female criminal.* New York: McGraw-Hill.

Archer, J. (2000). Sex differences in aggression between heterosexual partners: A meta-analytic review. *Psychological Bulletin, 126,* 651–80.

Baillargeon, R. H., Tremblay, R. E., and Willms, D. (2005). Gender differences in the prevalence of physically aggressive behaviors in the Canadian population of 2-and 3-year-old children. In D. J. Pepler, K. C. Madsen, W. Levene and K. S. Levene (eds), *The development and treatment of girlhood aggression* (pp. 55–74). Hillsdale, NJ: Lawrence Erlbaum Associates.

Barnett, O. W., Miller-Perrin, C. L., and Perrin, R. D. (2011). *Family violence across the lifespan* (3rd edn). Thousand Oaks, CA: Sage.

Belknap, J. (2007). *The invisible woman* (3rd edn). Belmont, CA: Wadsworth.

Bell, K. E. (2007). Gender and gangs: A quantitative comparison. *Crime and Delinquency, 55,* 363–87.

Berko, A., Erez, E., and Globokar, J. L. (2010). Gender, crime and terrorism: The case of Arab/Palestinian women in Israel. *British Journal of Criminology, 50,* 670–89.

Boots, D. P., and Cochran, J. K. (2011). The gender gap in support for capital punishment: A test of attribution theory. *Women and Criminal Justice, 21,* 171–97.

Broidy, L. M., Nagin, D. S., Tremblay, R. E., Bates, J. E., Brame, B., Dodge, K. A., Fergusson, D., Horwood, J. L., Loeber, R., Laird, R., Lynam, D. R., Moffitt, T. E., Pettit, G. S., and Vitaro, F. (2003). Developmental trajectories of childhood disruptive behaviors and adolescent delinquency: A six-site, cross-national study. *Developmental Psychology, 39,* 222–45.

Brookman, F., Mullins, C., Bennett, T., and Wright, R. (2007). Gender, motivation, and the accomplishment of street robbery in the United Kingdom. *British Journal of Criminology, 47,* 861–84.

Bussey, K., and Bandura, A. (1999). Social cognitive theory of gender development and differentiation. *Psychological Review, 106,* 676–713.

Chesney-Lind, M. (1997). *The female offender.* Thousand Oaks, CA: Sage.

——(2004). *Girls and violence: Is the gender gap closing?* National Electronic Network on Violence Against Women. Available at: www.vawnet.org/DomesticViolence/Research/VAWnetDocs/ARGirls Violence.php.

Chesney-Lind, M., and Jones, N. (eds) (2010). *Fighting for girls: New perspectives on gender and violence.* Albany: State University of New York Press.

Cooper, A., and Smith, E. L. (2011). *Homicide trends in the United States, 1980–2008.* Available at: http://bjs.ojp. usdoj.gov/index.cfm?ty=pbdetailandiid=2221.

Daly, K., and Chesney-Lind, M. (1988). Feminism and criminology. *Justice Quarterly, 5,* 497–535.

Davies, A. (1999). "These viragoes are no less cruel than the lads": Young women, gangs and violence in late Victorian Manchester and Salford. *British Journal of Criminology, 39,* 72–89

Decker, S. H., and Miller, J. (2006). Young women and gang violence. In L. F. Alarid and P. Cromwell (eds), *In her own words* (pp. 133–41). Los Angeles, CA: Roxbury Publishing Company.

DeGue, S., and Widom, C. S. (2009). Does out-of-home placement mediate the relationship between child maltreatment and adult criminality? *Child Maltreatment, 14*, 344–55.

Eager, P. W. (2008). *From freedom fighters to terrorists: Women and political violence.* Aldershot: Ashgate.

Farrell, A. L., Keppel, R. D., and Titterington, V. B. (2011). Lethal ladies: Revisiting what we know about female serial murderers. *Homicide Studies, 15*, 228–52.

Giardano, P. (2003). Relationships in adolescence. *Annual Review of Sociology, 29*, 251–81.

Gilligan, C. (1982). *In a different voice: Psychological theory and women's development.* Cambridge, MA: Harvard University Press.

Goodmark, L. (2012). *A troubled marriage: Domestic violence and the legal system.* New York: New York University Press.

Gonzalez-Perez, M. (2008). *Women and terrorism: Female activity in domestic and international terror groups.* New York: Routledge.

Gurian, E. A. (2011). Female serial murderers: Directions for future research in a hidden population. *International Journal of Offender Therapy and Comparative Criminology, 55*, 27–42.

Hickey, E. W. (2006). *Serial murderers and their victims* (4th edn). Belmont, CA: Thomson Wadsworth.

Howell, J. C. (2003). *Preventing and reducing juvenile delinquency: A comprehensive framework.* Thousand Oaks, CA: Sage.

Jensen, V. (2001). *Why women kill.* Boulder, CO: Lynne Rienner Publishers.

Kirkwood, D. (2003). Female perpetrated homicides in Victoria between 1984 and 1995. *Australian and New Zealand Journal of Criminology, 36*, 152–72.

Klein, D. (1973). The etiology of female crime: A review of the literature. *Crime and Social Justice: Issues in Criminology, 8*, 3–30.

Lee, K.-H., Baillargeon, R. H., Vermunt, J. K., Wu, H.-X., and Tremblay, R. E. (2007). Age differences in the prevalence of physical aggression among 5–11-year-old Canadian boys and girls. *Aggressive Behavior, 33*, 26–37.

Loeber, R., Farrington, D. P., Stouthamer-Loeber, M., and Van Kammen, W. B. (1998). *Antisocial behavior and mental health problems: Explanatory factors in childhood and adolescence.* Mahwah, NJ: Lawrence Erlbaum Associates.

Loeber, R., and Stouthamer-Loeber, M. (1998). Development of juvenile aggression and violence: Some common misconceptions and controversies. *American Psychologist, 53*, 242–59.

Meyer, C., and Oberman, M. (2001). *Mothers who kill their children: Understanding the acts of moms from Susan Smith to the "prom mom."* New York: New York University Press.

Miller, J. (1998). Up it up: Gender and the accomplishment of street robbery. *Criminology, 36*, 37–65. Miller, S. L. (2005). *Women as offenders: The paradox of women arrested for domestic violence.* New Brunswick, NJ: Rutgers University Press.

Moffitt, T. E. (1993). Adolescence-limited and life-course-persistent antisocial behavior: A developmental taxonomy. *Psychological Review, 100*, 674–701.

Moffitt, T. E., Caspi, A., Rutter, M., and Silva, P. A. (2001). *Sex differences in antisocial behavior: Conduct disorder, delinquency, and violence in the Dunedin Longitudinal Study.* New York: Cambridge University Press.

Osthoff, S. (2002). But, Gertrude, I beg to differ, a hit is not a hit is not a hit. *Violence Against Women, 8*, 1521–44.

Porter, T., and Gavin, H. (2010). Infanticide and neonaticide: A review of 40 years of research literature on incidence and causes. *Trauma, Violence and Abuse, 11*, 99–112.

Richie, B. E. (1996). *Compelled to crime: The gender entrapment of battered black women.* New York: Routledge.

Silverthorn, P., and Frick, P. J. (1999). Developmental pathways to antisocial behavior: The delayed-onset pathway in girls. *Development and Psychopathology, 11*, 101–26.

Simon, R. J. (1975). *Women and crime.* Lexington, MA: Lexington Books.

Smart. (1976). *Women, crime and criminology: A feminist critique.* London: Routledge.

Steffensmeier, D. J., Zhong, H., Ackerman, J., Schwartz, J., and Agha, S. (2006). Gender gap trends for violent crimes, 1980 to 2003: A UCR-NCVS comparison. *Feminist Criminology, 1,* 72–98.

Swan, S. C., Gambone, L. J., Caldwell, J. E., Sullivan, T. P., and Snow, D. L (2008). A review of research on women's use of violence with male intimate partners. *Violence and Victims, 23,* 301–14.

Toro, K., Feher, S., Katalin, K., and Dunay, G. (2010). Homicides against infants, children and adolescents in Budapest. *Journal of Forensic and Legal Medicine, 17,* 407–11.

Tracy, P. E., Kempf-Leonard, K., and Abramoske-James, S. (2009). Gender differences in delinquency and juvenile justice processing. *Crime and Delinquency, 55,* 171–215.

Tremblay, R. E. (2000). The development of aggressive behavior during childhood: What have we learned in the past century? *International Journal of Behavioral Development, 24,* 129–41.

U.S. Department of Justice. (2010). *Uniform crime reports.* Available at: http://www.fbi.gov/about-us/cjis/ucr/crime-in-the-u.s/2010/crime-in-the-u.s.-2010.

Valdimarsdottir, U., Hultman, C., Harlow, B., Cnattingius, S., and Sparen, P. (2009). Psychotic illness in first time mothers with no previous psychiatric hospitalizations: A population based study. *PLoS Medicine, 6.* Available at: http://www.plosmedicine.org/article/info%3Adoi%2F10.1371%2Fjournal.pmed.1000013

Weeks, R., and Widom, C. S. (1998). Self-reports of early childhood victimization among incarcerated adult male felons. *Journal of Interpersonal Violence, 13,* 346–61.

Wolf Harlow, C. (1999). *Prior abuse reported by inmates and probationers.* Washington, DC: U.S. Department of Justice, Bureau of Justice Statistics.

TOPICAL BOX 4.1

Gender and Gang Membership

By Wesley G. Jennings

While the definitional debate on what constitutes a gang and how to best operationalize gang membership has been going on for some time (Esbensen, Peterson, Taylor and Freng, 2010), empirical research in this area has been slower to acknowledge and examine the role of gender in gang membership and its related outcomes such as violent offending and violent victimization. A lot of this inattention can be attributed to Thrasher's (1927) early work where he reported female gangs as being very rare. Furthermore, he argued that in the rare instances where females were gang members, their membership was typically extended to them due to their sexual involvement with the male gang members and/or they were recruited to act as weapons carriers or lures for rival gang members (e.g., they were auxiliary gang members). More recent evidence has begun to increasingly acknowledge the significant, yet still not necessarily equal, role that females have in gangs, and this contemporary research has estimated that females now represent between 10 percent and 50 percent of gang members (Esbensen et al., 2010).

Recognizing that females are becoming much more represented in gangs in general and in empirical gang research specifically, the next set of research questions that follows are: What are the risks associated with gang membership for females? And, are these risks more similar or different compared to male gang members (who have traditionally been the focus of gang research)? With regard to violent offending, a number of scholars have reported that serious and violent delinquency is often lower among female gang members relative to male gang counterparts (Bjerregaard and Smith, 1993; Deschenes and Esbensen, 1999). This evidence would seem to indicate that the effect of gang membership on violent offending is more salient for male gang members. In contrast, there is a growing body of research suggesting that female gang members may be at a higher risk for victimization relative to male gang members, primarily stemming from their exposure to a host of unique gender-specific experiences such as an adoption of "masculine attributes" by being more heavily involved in risky and delinquent behavior, sexual exploitation by their own and/or rival gang members, and involvement in interpersonal conflicts with males in their own gangs. Furthermore, in her pioneering qualitative work on "doing gender," Miller (2002a, p. 445) argued that it is logical to assume that young women would seek to adopt "masculine attributes" or a gang identity as "one of the guys" in an effort to achieve the status and respect that is associated with gang masculinities. Comparatively, Miller (2002a) also suggested that some of these female gang members do not view themselves as "one of the guys," rather they appear to have adopted gender identities that resemble what Messerschmidt (2005) has termed "bad girl" femininity. Acknowledging the continued theoretical and conceptual debate between Miller and Messerschmidt on girls and gang identities (Miller, 2002b; Messerschmidt, 2002), it is apparent that gender and gang membership is a complex issue, but this complexity is not meant to under-emphasize the risks associated with gang membership for both males and females.

Gover, Jennings and Tewksbury (2009) provided one of the most comprehensive quantitative studies to date examining the role of gender as it relates to gang membership and violent victimization. Using data from a large sample of high school adolescents who participated in the South Carolina Youth Risk Behavior Survey (YRBS), Gover et al. found that 11 percent of the youth reported being a gang member and 36 percent of these gang members were female. This finding, in and of itself, supported the contemporary gang research demonstrating that gang membership is not an inherently male phenomenon. Furthermore, their results suggested that female gang members reported a higher prevalence of sexual assault and dating violence compared to male gang members, whereas male gang members were more likely to have been injured in a physical fight in which the injury required treatment from a doctor or nurse. Despite these differences, Gover et al.'s multivariate results revealed that after adjusting for race (e.g., African American versus Other Race), family structure, and age, the effect of gang membership on experiencing all three forms of victimization was largely invariant across gender.

Ultimately, it is clear that future research should continue to concentrate on fleshing out the degree to which gang membership affects the likelihood for reporting involvement in violent offending as well as amplifying the risk for experiencing violent victimization. The accumulating body of evidence suggests that gang membership and its associated adverse outcomes have an effect on both males and females. Acknowledging this empirical reality, it is important for future gang prevention and intervention strategies to focus on the multiple domains of risk factors that are likely relevant for joining gangs (e.g., family, peers, schools, neighborhoods) and emphasize the shared commonality of risk and involvement in adverse outcomes (e.g., violent offending and violent victimization) that accompanies gang membership for males and females.

REFERENCES

Bjerregaard, B. and Smith, C. (1993). Gender differences in gang participation, delinquency, and substance use. *Journal of Quantitative Criminology*, *4*, 329–55.

Deschenes, E. P. and Esbensen, F.-A. (1999). Violence and gangs: Gender differences in perceptions and behavior. *Journal of Quantitative Criminology*, *15*, 63–96.

Esbensen, F.-A., Peterson, D., Taylor, T. J. and Freng, A. (2010). *Youth violence: Sex and race differences in offending, victimization, and gang membership*. Philadelphia, PA: Temple University Press.

Gover, A. R., Jennings, W. G. and Tewksbury, R. (2009). Adolescent male and female gang members' experiences of violent victimization, dating violence, and sexual assault. *American Journal of Criminal Justice*, *34*, 103–15.

Messerschmidt, J. W. (2002). On gang girls, gender, and structured action theory: A reply to Miller. *Theoretical Criminology*, *6*, 461–75.

——(2005). Men, masculinities, and crime. In M. Kimmel, R. W. Connell and J. Hearn (eds), *Handbook of studies on men and masculinities* (pp. 196–212). Thousand Oaks, CA: Sage.

Miller, J. (2002a). The strengths and limits of "doing gender" for understanding street crime. *Theoretical Criminology*, *6*, 433–60.

——(2002b). Reply to Messerschmidt. *Theoretical Criminology*, *6*, 477–80.

Thrasher, F. (1927). *The gang*. Chicago, IL: University of Chicago Press.

BIOGRAPHICAL BOX 4.1

By Meda Chesney-Lind, University of Hawaii at Manoa

While in college I became interested in the power of others to define acts as crimes, even when I regarded those acts as morally correct and arguably required by international law. Of course, since biography is history, this places me in a period of time when my country was pursuing what many considered to be an immoral war, which is to say, a time, in many ways, not that different from today.

My interest in gender came about in a like fashion. Always an activist, I'd begun to hear about the women's movement from friends. At that time, there were only pamphlets on women's issues, not books, and nothing really about girls. I was reading all I could get my hands on.

Eventually, like every student I needed a topic for a thesis. So one day, I found myself in a huge room full of old juvenile court records, and I asked my friend who was coding them: "Do you ever see any girls' files?"

So, I would say that my involvement in those two movements (pacifism and women's rights) produced what some call the art of the dumb question. And, as Adrienne Rich observed, for feminist scholars this means needing to ask "but what was it like for women?" (Rich, 1976, p. 16).

I was very fortunate to have asked that question, since it has taken me in so many fascinating and important directions. It has also linked me to a network of scholars and activists that continue to be committed to not only knowing what it is like for girls and women in the criminal justice system, but also seeking to do anything we can to improve their situation. For years, I studied discrimination against girls (again, focused on the system), until one day, Mildred Pagelow, path breaking researcher on domestic violence, asked me if I knew why girls ran away from home or had ever talked with them.

Again, it is not the answers one provides that are important in life, it's the questions one asks. I owe her a huge debt for asking me that question. Interviews with women in prison and girls in detention followed, and I heard first hand what propelled girls onto the streets—sexual abuse and family violence. I believe I was the first to write about what is now being called "pathways" into girls' and women's crime as a result.

Of course, if victimization alone caused women's crime, we'd have more women arrested and in prison than men since violence against women is so ubiquitous. I've learned in the years since that other harms, particularly racism and poverty, contribute in very important and toxic ways to the contexts that produce women's involvement in crime. Certainly, I knew that when I was teaching in prison, I was often one of the very few white people in the room.

When mass imprisonment began to sweep huge numbers of women into prison, I began writing about the "causes" and consequences of the misguided war on drugs that was quickly morphing into a war on women. I also worked to refute arguments that "an inmate is an inmate is an inmate," instead noting that girls' and women's lives and their crimes were inextricably mixed, so that solutions to their gender troubles are essential if they are to heal and live a life free from involvement with the justice system.

More recently, I've been kept busy by the onslaught of racist and sexist media constructions of hyper violent "bad" girls, who are constructed both in words and images as just as menacing as their male counterparts. The corporate media loves bad news about girls and women, and of course, the female offender has become a go-to staple in this kind of "journalism," so much of my work is really fighting backlash journalism.

My current work (and the work I'm reading) focuses on efforts to prevent the mass incarceration seen in the adult system from spilling over into the juvenile system. To do this, I have focused on the terrible consequences of imprisoning girls and women. Sadly, there is plenty of material to document the harms that come with imprisonment.

REFERENCE

Rich, A. (1976). *Of women born*. New York: W.W. Norton.

CHAPTER FIVE

The Influence of Patriarchy and Traditional Gender Role Attitudes on Violence Against Women

By Melinda R. York

I t is important to examine the social context of the research being done for this study before delving into the more specific areas of gender attitudes, the social capital concept, and violence against women. The concept of *patriarchy* sets the overall framework for this research, especially since much of the literature on traditional gender attitudes specifically addresses or incorporates patriarchy into the development of ideas and framing of research regarding this topic. Once the concept of patriarchy is explained in sufficient detail, the literature linking traditional gender attitudes and violence against women is presented.

PATRIARCHY

Some very strong arguments have been made in the research literature that the social, legal, economic, religious and political climate of the United States clearly values male dominance in most social settings and supports male-centered hierarchy in most social institutions (Freeman, 1995). These systems and institutions intermingle in multiple ways, causing gender-based inequality in a systemic (deep-seated and pervasive) way. This is not to say that people are consciously taught male privilege, but such gender-based privilege becomes something that is expected with little question by most people. Goldrick-Jones (2002) defines the term patriarchy as "any practices and systems that oppress, control or dominate women," (p. 5) and Eisenstein (1980) observes that patriarchy is best defined as "a sexual system of power in which the male possesses superior power and economic privilege" (p. 16). Feminist scholars have sought to expose, document, critique, and bring an end to this type of domination, focusing specifically in the area of violence against women in their work (Anderson & Collins, 2004; Belknap, 2001).

Patriarchal societies are not only male-dominated, but they are male-identified, male-centered, and tend to cause the oppression of women by devaluing the work they do or treating them as though they are "invisible" (not worthy of due notice and reward) (Johnson, 1997; Johnson, 2000; Anderson & Collins, 2004; Barak, Flavin, & Leighton, 2001; Merlo & Pollock, 1995; Messerschmidt, 1997; Muraskin, 2007; Sheldon, 2001; Schwartz & DeKeseredy, 1997). As the term is used here, oppression is meant to convey a social phenomenon by which men dominate over and receive benefits from the ongoing exploitation and/or subordination of women (Johnson, 1997). This oppression can be achieved either overtly or inadvertently. For instance, a woman may be passed over for a promotion simply because she is a woman, or the same outcome of being passed over may be the result of a male superior preferring to train and mentor someone more like himself. Not all women will suffer the same degree of oppression in a patriarchal society because they may be the beneficiaries of a privileged race and/or social class. In Johnson's (1997) widely read book entitled *Gender Knot*, the knot reference in the title is representative of the concept of patriarchy. Johnson explains this connection by arguing that patriarchy is not reinforced by a mere collection of malevolent individuals, but rather it is deeply rooted and inherent within the institutions making up the social system.

The literature on—explains that masculine and feminine social constructs are particular patterned behavioral aspects of social roles which are deeply embedded in a patriarchy. In such a society girls are socialized to be submissive, docile, and place a high value on emotions and relationships. Boys, in contrast, are socialized to value thinking and performance while being aggressive (versus timid), dominating (versus submissive), competitive (versus cooperative), and avoiding virtually all things feminine. Those boys that exhibit feminine traits receive negative consequences in the form of disapproval and/or punishment, consequences which may force them into the reaction of *hyper-masculinity* (Kilmartin, 2000). The trait of hyper-masculinity is associated with the denial of emotions, homophobia, an intensified rejection of all things feminine, and the desire for exercising power over others (Haywood & Mac an Ghaill, 2003).

PATRIARCHY'S ROLE IN VIOLENCE AGAINST WOMEN

It is important to recognize the key role that patriarchy plays in creating a climate conducive to the perpetration of violence against women. In a societal structure permeated with patriarchy, violence directed against the least powerful people in society is not only permissible, but it is to a considerable degree encouraged and normalized as a way of preserving "traditions" and protecting an established culture (Kandel-Englander, 1992). Dutton (1994) is correct in noting, however, that the occurrence of domestic violence cannot be explained by any "single-bullet" theory such as that of patriarchy because the maintenance of patriarchy is not the sole motivation for the use of violence against women in a society. LaViolette and Barnette (2000) correctly note that not all men in the U.S. employ violence against women, and there are certainly some women who employ violence against men. For these reasons it cannot be claimed that patriarchy is the cause of violence against women; however, patriarchy is used to set the context of this study because it is frequently cited in the research literature as the fundamental reason for male aggressiveness and inclination to resort to physical force and a significant predictor of various forms of violence perpetrated against women (Anderson & Collins, 2004; Belknap, 2001; Johnson, 1997; Johnson, 2000; Kilmartin, 2000; Barak, Flavin, & Leighton, 2001; Merlo & Pollock, 1995; Messerschmidt, 1997; Muraskin, 2007; Sheldon, 2001).

Sex role socialization in American society largely dictates that men are expected to be the breadwinners in a typical household and women's work is typically to be viewed as supplemental to that of the breadwinner. In recent decades information technology has transformed service sector work leading to a pronounced increase in women's employment, although such work tends to be done for low wages, involves insecure work, and is often carried out under poor working conditions. Manual work is considered masculine, but it tends to pay low wages (Haywood & Mac an Ghaill, 2003). Crime becomes a way for men to "do gender" when they do not have the resources to accomplish masculinity, either because they are in poorly paid jobs or have no job at all. Some of these economically marginalized males will engage in intimate partner violence, resort to violence in high stress situations, perpetrate rape, engage in pimping, exhibit sexual harassment, or commit robbery in order to accomplish the goals reflecting their masculine role (Messerschmidt, 1993).

In addition to the ubiquitous influence of the patriarchal society of the U.S., there is also *familial patriarchy* which refers to the power held by men in domestic or household settings. According to Schwartz & DeKeseredy (1997), familial patriarchy includes dating relationships as well as cohabitating couples and traditional family units featuring a husband, wife and one or more children. They also explain the term *courtship patriarchy* in which men use their power in dating relationships to decide when and where sex will take place. This can also be *quid pro quo* in that men provide services or money by taking the female to dinner or fixing their car for them and expect sex to be given in return. When women do not meet these expectations, some men feel a sense of entitlement and become physically aggressive with the females in question. Kanin (1967) provides evidence that men often develop a "vocabulary of adjustment" that justifies sexual aggressiveness with females by labeling them a 'tease' or characterizing them as being 'loose' in character. For the purposes of this research, patriarchy will be used in a comprehensive sense as it relates to the structural system of the U.S. and encompassing its ubiquitous effect on interpersonal relationships.

TRADITIONAL GENDER ATTITUDES

Beyond the contextual and structural factors influencing violence toward women, the social and cultural acceptance of traditional gender roles plays an important role in the prediction of violence toward women. Gender roles are "normative behaviors and attitudes which are expected from individuals, based on their biological sex, and which are often learned through the socialization process" (Ben-David & Schneider, 2005, p. 386). The research done in this area strongly suggests that hostile attitudes toward women are strongly correlated with traditional gender or sex role attitudes in regard to the distinctive roles prescribed for men and women in the family, in the workplace, and in the area of commonplace social behaviors (Bookwala, Frieze, Smith, & Ryan, 1992; Hilton, Harris, & Rice, 2003; Marciniak, 1998; Walker, Rowe, & Quinsey, 1993). The position of women in a society rests upon the social arrangement of the sexes, and this arrangement is held in place by socializing members of society in regard to norms, expectations and behaviors (Martin, 1995).

Socialization of Traditional Gender Roles

At birth, people are placed into a sex category of male or female and then socialized to act in accordance with the socially prescribed attributes of this label. Parents generally give their children gender-specific toys and games, tend to decorate their room according to gender, and tend to dress them according to gender scripts as well (Lips, 1995). Furthermore, there is empirical evidence that parental behavior is adjusted either subconsciously or consciously depending on the gender of the child, and such behavior adjustment typically reinforces society's gender role expectations of the child (Block, 1984; Frankel & Rollins, 1983). There are few if any inherent traits present at birth that cause women to be passive, to be dependent, to be relationship-oriented, and to be physically and emotionally weak. In fact, females are generally trained to exhibit and internalize these traits through socialization. When young women demonstrate these feminine traits they are nearly always socially rewarded, and they are nearly always penalized when they act outside of these role designations. In the same way, males are taught to be strong, dominant, independent, aggressive, initiators of sexual interactions, and taught as well to reject feminine traits (Martin, 1995).

Social interactions from childhood on will feature the insistence of "doing gender," a term which means responding to a wide variety of different situations and inter-personal interactions with the expected gender role behavior (West & Zimmerman, 1989). Men and women are held to their gender expectations and are continuously evaluated according to them. Both school peers and teachers are an integral part of socialization as well. They tend to ostracize those students acting outside the bounds of their gender roles, and issue acceptance to those who comply with these expectations. School peers can be especially cruel to those students who do not adhere to gender expectations. Most youth want very badly to "fit in" and to "be liked" by peers, so they are inclined to conform strictly to the expected gender norms.

Once young children reach adolescence, however, gender role socialization more narrowly addresses gendered understandings of vocation, sexuality, and family (Lips, 1995). Men are expected to be the initiators of sexual activity, and it is socially acceptable for males to engage in a variety of sexual activities and to talk about sex openly. Women, in stark contrast, are taught to be protectors of their virginity and to deny sexual advances. Women are socialized to want a "family" consisting of a husband and one or more children. They are encouraged to be the primary caretaker of the family, emotionally and through domestic activities, even if their employment status outside of the home imposes upon those responsibilities. Men maintain the primary role of 'breadwinner' by providing for the monetary needs of the family. In this way, women's work is considered secondary to the work performed by the man and the male maintains a position of power over all family members (Steil, 1995).

The system of maintaining gender role adherence starts early on in life and carries on throughout adulthood. For instance, women who initiate sexual interactions are called "whores," and those who are aggressive in business are called "bitches" (Brescoll & Moss-Racusin, 2007). Similarly, men displaying feminine qualities are taunted with words characterized by female names, female body parts, or other words descriptive of femininity, vulnerability and weakness (Lutze, 2003), or they are accused of homosexuality. These types of social reprimands not only give men social power in general, at school, and at the workplace, but they also confer sexual power as well by allowing men as a social group to control the intimate relationships that become established between men and women (Martin, 1995).

Moreover, there are noteworthy differentiations in patterns of socialization within American society. For instance, research in this area clearly shows that working class families are more restrictive of women's behavior and more likely to enforce strong gender stereotypes than are middle class families

(McBroom, 1981; Rubin, 1976). Also, due to the diverse racial and ethnic composition of the United States, there are substantial differences in socialization patterns across American racial and ethnic sub-populations. Hispanics tend to emphasize feminine subservience and the importance of the domestic role during the socialization process (Garcia, 1991). In contrast, while African Americans too practice substantive gender differentiation in their youth socialization process, gender role differentiation is not nearly as strict as tends to occur in the socialization practices of either Caucasians or Hispanics (Dugger, 1991).

Traditional Gender Attitudes and Violence against Women

People who adhere to traditional gender role expectations are more likely to blame female victims of violence more than male perpetrators. This is especially true in cases of date rape (Willis,1992) and domestic violence (Esqueda & Harrison, 2005). Perpetrators of violence toward women, with certain perceptions of women based on the aforementioned gender role stereotypes, may be supported in their actions to varying degrees, a fact which serves to reinforce those attitudes and behaviors. Traditionalist police officers may not make arrests in domestic violence situations where the victim does not adhere to traditional gender roles and perpetrators may receive shorter jail or prison sentences due to the traditionalist ideas of a judge or jurors (Willis, Hallinan, & Melby, 1996). It seems to follow that in areas with strong traditionalist ideals, there will be more violence against women because of the level of social acceptance present in those communities. The violence against women crimes of physical/domestic violence and sexual assault featured in the NIBRS will be studied as they relate to the presence of traditional gender role attitudes within a group of American counties.

Homicide

The Bureau of Justice Statistics reported that 33% of women who were homicide victims in recent years were an intimate partner of a male suspect. Between the years of 1976 and 1995, 34% of female homicide victims were intimate partners while only 6% of male homicide victims were likewise an intimate partner (Puzone, Saltzman, Kresnow, Thompson & Mercy, 2000). In 2000, intimate partners killed 1,247 women (Rennison, 2003; Cole, 2004). It is not surprising that women are more often than men the victim of homicide since they hold less power, command less money, and have lower status in society. However, it is important to note that, in general, in the United States and in other countries men's risks of homicide have always been much greater than that of females (Gartner, Baker & Pampel, 1990).

Fortunately, there has been a decline in intimate partner homicide over the last two decades, and this favorable trend can be attributed to several likely factors. Dugan, Nagin and Rosenfeld (1999) collected data from 29 U.S. cities and found that the decline was likely a result of shifts in marriage, divorce and other declining domesticity factors, women's improved economic status, and the great increase in domestic violence services present across the country. Nagin and Rosenfeld speculate that this observation lends partial support to Russell's (1975) 'backlash' theory. This theory holds that men will respond violently to a loss in status or power in their relationships with women. It appears this happens at first, but this reaction declines as men either become accustomed or reserved to the new shifts in power toward gender equity. Whaley and Messner (2002) also found mixed support for the 'backlash' theory in their study of homicide in 191 large U.S. cities. The extent of gender equality present was significantly and positively associated with female (and other male) murders committed by males *only in Southern cities* when controlling for structural predictors.

In most cases female homicides are not an isolated event. The homicide usually follows upon many instances of physical, sexual and/or verbal abuse (Edwards, 1987). Female homicide victims come from all races, classes, ages, and geographical areas. Several studies have examined the risk factors that lead to the murder of an intimate partner. However, no predictive model has been developed that completely accounts for this phenomenon. Most studies focus on gender inequality, but they do not include measures of traditional gender attitudes—even though the theoretical literature strongly supports this link.

Titterington (2006) studied 217 central U.S. cities over the period 1989–1991 to examine the link between gender inequality and female homicide victimization. Gender inequality was operationalized as divorce rates, socioeconomic inequality, legislative, political and extra-legal inequality. Using structural equation modeling, Titterington found a strong positive connection between divorce and homicide rates and between socioeconomic inequality and female homicide levels. Furthermore, when laws are less favorable to women there are also higher numbers of female homicides. Avakame (1998) also found economic deprivation, social disorganization, the proportion of people in metropolitan areas, the presence of a culture that accepts violence, a location in the South, and gender inequality as contributing conditions for the occurrence of domestic homicide.

Much of the gender inequality and homicide research available for review focuses on economic and status measures rather than gender role attitudes. DeWees and Parker (2003) examined American cities with populations over 100,000 and found that socioeconomic status and political inequality contributed to homicide victimization for both males and females. Specifically, gender inequality in education was most predictive of female homicide victimizations. More recently, Vieraitis, Kovandzic, & Britto (2008) used 2000 census data and crime data to determine whether gender inequality was related to female homicide victimization. Gender inequality was measured by level of formal education, occupation, employment, and income. They found a significant correlation between a woman's status and homicide victimization, but this variable was only conclusive for intimate partners.

The aforementioned studies confirm that gender inequality is present and represents an important aspect of American society, as predicted by the patriarchal analytical framework used in this research. They also show that it affects the incidence of female homicide victimization. However, the literature review presented here indicates as well that there are no studies looking directly at gender attitudes and how they relate to the incidence of the homicide of women in the United States.

Domestic Violence and Physical Assaults

In the United States, it has been estimated that 22% of women have been the victims of domestic violence at some point in their lifetime (Johnson & Hotton, 2003). Some people criticize the victims of intimate partner violence for not leaving the abusive relationships in which they are involved. However wise this advice might be in the abstract, LaViolette and Barnett (2000) identified several valid reasons for why women often do not leave violent relationships. First, women are socialized to believe that their role in the family is to please their partner and to be a "good wife," which can mean being "supportive," "forgiving," and "self-sacrificing." Battered women may view their partner's violence as a failure in their relationship, and many women blame themselves for that failure. Also, many loving parents use physical discipline on their children when they misbehave, so women sometimes grow up thinking that love and physical force are generally synonymous. Many women are deeply committed to making their relationship work. The idea of being committed to one's partner is generally reinforced by society (i.e., family, friends, song lyrics, literature, religion and media).

Second, the cycle of violence often leads battered women to think that their partners will change, or that they are truly repentant for their acts. The abuse generally starts with minor incidences of violence, which lead in time to a major violent incidence. However, it is the honeymoon phase and fear that keeps a battered woman in the relationship because, in this part of the cycle the batterer will usually cry, apologize, buy gifts, promise to change, or tell the victim he is going to or is seeking help from some type of counselor (LaViolette & Barnett, 2000; Websdale, 1999). Many battered women become disillusioned through "learned hopefulness" in that they truly believe their partner will change. Either because of counseling or believing their partners' promises to change, these women often stay with their abuser because of the belief that the violence will stop in due course if they persist in being patient and forgiving.

Third, the approach-avoidance conflict situation is sometimes in evidence. On the one hand, many of the victim's emotional and economic needs are being met and she/he wants to approach the love that is hopeful, but on the other hand she/he wants to avoid the violent episodes and abuse. Other reasons for staying with abusive partners include: legal bonds, does not want to hurt their partner, fear of being alone, fear of retaliation and/or fear of not finding anyone better, believing that she can change her partner, believing she/he can make the relationship better, does not want to be a quitter, needs to protect the children or parents, and/or religious convictions (Barnett & LaViolette, 2000; Websdale, 1999). Finally, when these women leave the relationship or move out, in many cases they are actually putting themselves at a higher risk of becoming a victim of intimate partner homicide (Campbell Webster, Koziol-McLain, & Block, 2003; Wilson and Daly, 1992; Glass, Koziol-McLain, Campbell, & Block, 2004).

Despite the reasons for victims' staying, there are many people, mostly men, who blame the victims for their own victimization. Garimella, Plichta, Houseman and Garzon (2000) surveyed 76 physicians working in a large general hospital about their attitudes toward victims of domestic violence. Although 97% of physicians said it was part of their job to help domestic violence victims, 30% held victim-blaming attitudes. Overall, 55% of the physicians believed that the women's "personalities" caused the beatings, and 34% believed the women must like something about the relationship or they would leave. Women, younger physicians, those working in obstetrics-gynecology, and those with fewer years of experience in the field were less likely to engage in victim-blaming.

Ulbrich and Huber (1979) sought to determine the effects on children's gender role attitudes when parental violence was observed. They employed a telephone survey to obtain a random sample from the U.S. consisting of 1,092 women and 910 men. They asked questions about the observation of violence in the home as a child, attitudes about women's employment and motherly roles, and attitudes regarding the use of violence against women. Domestic violence in the home as a child did not show a significant relationship with traditional gender role attitudes. Interestingly, a father hitting the mother in the home was significantly correlated with victim-blaming by males in cases of rape. Overall, the researchers found that of all the child witnesses of domestic violence, men were more approving of violence against women while women were more disapproving, findings which were similar to those of Garimella, Plichta, Houseman, and Garzon (2000) and Locke and Richman (1999).

Nabors and Jasinski (2009) examined intimate partner violence perpetration among college students and found a positive relationship between physical violence and attitudes supporting gender role stereotypes. However, they argue their results do not indicate that the gender role attitudes led to the abuse, but were a way of justifying it afterwards. They also found gender to be important in that males' attitudinal acceptance of relationship violence predicted physical assaults, but female's acceptance of male violence did not predict the assaults. Despite these findings and the expression of support for the patriarchal theory in the literature, a strong correlation between traditional gender role attitudes and domestic or physical violence against women in the U.S. has not been substantiated in the extant research literature.

Sexual Assault

Sexual victimization is likely to occur in societies with a patriarchal orientation because of the institutionalized inequality between men and women that is present in values, attitudes and behaviors (Johnson, 1997; Kilmartin, 2000; Russell, 1975; Schwartz & DeKeseredy, 1997). The research literature indicates that most rapes are not purely sexual in nature, but rather they are more often crimes of power as opposed to crimes of desire (Brownmiller, 1975). The structural factors associated with patriarchy provide the reasons why men tend to choose women as recipients of their unwanted sexual behaviors and how society tends to uncritically accept these forms of violence against women (Franklin, 2008). Women are especially at a disadvantage when it comes to sexual assaults because of their diminished status in society, the aspect of socialization into traditional gender roles that require women to accept men's violence against them, and the natural physical strength of males relative to females.

Societies which emphasize male dominance, provide for the strict separation of the sexes, take a permissive stance on interpersonal violence involving physical force applied against women, and deprecation of women's social roles generally witness high levels of sexual victimization. The research clearly shows a strong connection between adherence to traditional gender roles and engaging in sexual assault at the individual level (Johnson, Kuck, & Schander, 1997; Kopper, 1996; Lonsway & Fitzgerald, 1994; Shotland & Goodstein, 1983). Underlying reasons for the occurrence of this relationship include the existence of the broader cultural context of patriarchy (Johnson, 1997; Kilmartin, 2000) and the socialization of individuals into variegated gender roles featuring dominant and subordinant statuses (Bridges, 1991; Burt, 1980; Check & Malamuth, 1983; Koss, Goodman, Browne, Fitzgerald, Keita, & Russo, 1994; Simonson & Subich, 1999). In this regard, Burt (1980) found that in her study of rape in the U.S. the acceptance of "rape myths" was predictive of adherence to sex role stereotypes and the holding of permissive attitudes toward interpersonal violence. Rape myths refer to the justification or minimization of the raping of women with a plethora of rationalizations. For example, when considering an alleged rape some people will express the commonly held views that 'women often say no to sex when they mean yes' or 'she led him on' or 'the way she dresses invites that kind of response from men'.

In a more recent study of similar design involving 212 sixteen-year-olds, traditional sex role attitudes were found to predict strongly decreased perceptions of seriousness in sexual or physical victimization scenarios (Hilton, Harris, Rice, 2003). Self-reported perpetrators also rated the scenarios as less serious than non-perpetrators. Generally, males had more traditional sex role attitudes than females, and men rated the scenarios as less serious than did the females as well. In another study carried out along these lines, Check & Malamuth (1983) found that men with strict traditional gender role attitudes experienced stronger sexual arousal when presented with rape scenarios than men without such attitudes. Much of the empirical research would seem to agree that sexually aggressive males are more likely to embrace traditional gender roles than their non-sexually aggressive counterparts (Lackie & de Man, 1997; Loh, Gidycz, Lobo, & Luthra, 2005; Muehlenhard & Linton, 1987; Sigelman, Berry, & Wiles,

1984; Truman, Tokar, & Fischer, 1996). These findings, in turn, are consistent with the literature on hypermasculinity (Check & Malamuth, 1985; Koss et al., 1985; Sanday, 1981).

Men with traditional gender role attitudes report higher rates of past sexual aggression than those holding egalitarian or sex-neutral attitudes, and some studies suggest they are also more likely to engage in sexual offenses in the future as well (Check & Malamuth, 1983; Malamuth, Sockloskie, Koss, & Tanaka, 1991; Mosher & Anderson, 1986). Empirical research also tends to indicate that men holding traditional gender role attitudes are predisposed to engage in victim-blaming, especially in cases of acquaintance or date rape, and to subscribe to rape myths (Anderson & Lyons, 2005; Bell, Kuriloff, & Lottes, 1994: Bridges, 1991; Kopper, 1996; Simonson & Subich, 1999; Whatley, 2005). There appears to be strong support for the link between traditional gender role acceptance and sexual aggression, both in theory and in the empirical research done on individuals.

CONCLUSION

Men who cling to traditional conceptions of gender roles and masculinity learn norms and mores through socialization within a patriarchal culture implying that the exercising of power and control over women constitute the normal state of affairs. Strict adherence to traditional gender roles leads to the belief that violence against women is acceptable, in part because women are of inferior social status to men. Physical assaults, some of which may lead to homicides, and sexual aggression are clearly the most violent and extreme expressions of violence against women. Those males possessing rigid gender role expectations, hypermasculinity traits, social support for violence against women, and/or fixation upon power and control issues are most likely to commit these severe acts. In order to resolve the inconsistencies in methodology, sample size and composition, and location of studies, the current research is especially important to validate the theory and assess its generalizability. Moreover, it is important to note that most of these studies involve the study of individuals, and the study to be undertaken here entails cross-sectional comparisons on the county-level.

CHAPTER SIX

Women's Human Right to Health

By Julie A. Mertus and Nancy Flowers

States Parties shall take all appropriate measures to eliminate discrimination against women in the field of health care in order to ensure, on a basis of equality of men and women, access to health care services, including those related to family planning.
—*Convention on the Elimination of All Forms of Discrimination Against Women, Article 12*

States Parties recognize the right of the child to the enjoyment of the highest attainable standard of health and to facilities for the treatment of illness and rehabilitation of health. States Parties shall strive to ensure that no child is deprived of his or her right of access to such health care services.
—*Article 24(1), Convention on the Rights of the Child*

OBJECTIVES

The exercises and background information contained in this chapter will enable participants to work towards the following objectives:

- Define the right to health.
- Explain the importance of women's health for women's equality.
- Understand the interrelationship between the right to health and other human rights.
- Identify ways in which women's right to health has been promoted or denied.
- Explain women's double work burden arising from their multiple roles and its effect on their health.

- Identify ways to balance respect for culture and tradition with respect for women's health.
- Describe the provisions regarding health in the Convention on the Elimination of All Forms of Discrimination Against Women (CEDAW).
- Remember core concepts.

GETTING STARTED: THINKING ABOUT WOMEN'S HEALTH

Women's *de facto* second-class status in society gives rise to both direct and indirect threats to their health. Since women are far more likely than men to be poor,[1] they often receive less nourishment and are more vulnerable to disease. Many women who suffer from poor health lack information, skills, purchasing power, and access to health care services. Too often, women are not part of the formal decision-making processes concerning the formulation of health care laws and policies. Violence against women, substandard working conditions, and a poor living environment also undermine women's health. As noted by the International Labour Organisation (ILO):

> The health problems reported in the literature on the informal sector are generally the same as in the formal sector, with a common presence of poor housekeeping, poor lighting, long work hours, poor work place design, unawareness of chemicals risks and increased use of drugs as home medication. Job-related risk factors are compounded by overcrowding, poor nutrition and other public health problems, inadequate sanitation, lack of adequate storage and the more general effects of poverty.[2]

The World Bank estimates that health care costs plunge 100 million people into poverty every year, with 60 percent of care spent on medicine:

> Women bear the brunt of the high cost of health care. If someone falls ill in the family, women take on the added burden of becoming the carer, and women are often the last to seek health care for themselves if any cost is involved, because they prioritise the rest of their family over themselves.[3]

Women may experience some or all of these problems regarding their health-related rights:

- Exposure to HIV
- Pregnancy-associated health issues
- Lack of clean drinking water
- Insufficient vaccination programs for girls
- Failure to treat anemia in women and girls
- Lack of general gynecologic care
- Lack of birth control and sex education
- Unsafe abortions
- Unsanitary and otherwise inadequate birthing facilities
- Treatment with unsafe drugs
- Inadequate attention to diseases mainly affecting women, such as breast cancer

- Medical research predominantly based on male subjects, yielding inadequate evidence for making decisions about women's health
- Lack of mental health care and therapy
- Lack of therapy for women victims/survivors of rape, incest, and other forms of violence
- Insufficient number of women trained as counsellors, physicians, and health care professionals
- Cultural barriers to women's health, such as the prohibition against allowing women to be attended by male health care providers and researchers
- Lack of education for women about child care, hygiene, nutrition, and other family health matters
- Barriers to general health care services for people with disabilities, especially disabled women
- Lack of appropriate, responsive health care for women living in rural areas; migrant, refugee, and displaced women; older women; lesbians; women of ethnic and racial minorities; and women in prison.

In short, poor health can prevent a woman from realizing other human rights. Women and girls who are ill often cannot participate fully in society; for example, they may not be able to attend school, work outside the home, or organize and participate in groups.

❋ Learning Activity 1: Defining Women's Health ❋

Objective   To write a broad definition of women's health
Time   60 minutes
Materials   Chart paper and markers or blackboard and chalk

1. Brainstorm
Draw the outline of a woman on chart paper or a blackboard. As a group, brainstorm the qualities that characterize a healthy woman and list these inside the outline. Consider the emotional and psychological aspects of health in addition to the physical ones.

Brainstorm the factors that are necessary for women to achieve these qualities of good health and list them in the margins outside the outline. For example, if the group included *energetic* as a quality of a healthy woman, *adequate food* or *rest and leisure* might be listed as necessary factors.

2. Analyze
Circle the items on the list of factors necessary for health that most women in your community do not have. Discuss what happens when women lack these factors:
- What are the effects on the woman herself?
- What are the effects on her children? On other members of her family?
- What are the effects on the community, especially if many women lack good health?

3. Discuss
The image of the woman in Step 1 represents all women in the community. Make a list of three or four subgroups of women (e.g., disabled, refugee, older, widowed, or unmarried women) who might have special health care concerns different from most women.

Divide into small groups and pick one of these subgroups to discuss. In the context of the factors necessary for health listed outside the outline during Step 1, address the following questions:

- Are there additional factors necessary for health among this subgroup?
- Are there additional factors necessary for health that this group generally lacks?
- What are the obstacles to this group's enjoyment of good health?

Compare the findings of the small groups and discuss:

- What are some of the main obstacles to these subgroups' enjoyment of good health?
- Do these obstacles prevent them from exercising their human rights?
- Is good health a human right?

DEFINING THE RIGHT TO HEALTH

Building on the broad definition of *health* adopted by the World Health Organization (WHO) in its Constitution and other principles, the Beijing Platform for Action reaffirms that *health* as it specifically relates to women is

> a state of complete physical, mental and social well-being and not merely the absence of disease or infirmity. Women's health involves their emotional, social and physical well-being and is determined by the social, political and economic context of their lives, as well as by biology. However, health and well-being elude the majority of women.[4]

International human rights law does not guarantee the right of people to be healthy. Rather, it recognizes the right of all to have access to health care to ensure that people may attain the highest standard of health of which they themselves are capable. States are required to guarantee the right to access health services, a right that is further elaborated in some international documents. Article 12 of the Convention on the Elimination of All Forms of Discrimination (CEDAW), for example, requires states to eliminate discrimination against women in their access to health care services, throughout the life cycle, particularly in the areas of family planning, pregnancy, confinement, and postnatal well-being.

As the above Platform for Action definition of *health* makes clear, access to health care is broadly defined. Indeed, states are required to take certain measures with the aim of safeguarding public health.[5] For women to be healthy, their basic needs must be fulfilled. These include assured income, safe working and living conditions, adequate and clean food and water, education, and available, affordable, and appropriate health care. In addition, women need equal status in society, equitable division of labor (including production, child care, and housework), and freedom from violence. Accordingly, rights relating to health care imply only access to hospitals, clinics, medicines, and health professionals. While this access is important, it is insufficient for comprehensive "health."

Often poor health can be traced to oppression and human rights violations. As noted in the Beijing Platform for Action:

> The prevalence among women of poverty and economic dependence, their experience of violence, negative attitudes towards women and girls, racial and other forms of discrimination, the limited power many women have over their sexual and reproductive lives, and lack of influence in decision-making are social realities which have an adverse impact on their health (paragraph 92).

One important aspect of health is *reproductive and sexual health*, which the Platform for Action defines as a "state of complete physical, mental and social well-being … in all matters relating to the reproductive system" (paragraph 94). This section focuses on the *totality* of women's health needs. (See also Chapter 4, "The Human Rights of Young Women and Girls.")

❋ Learning Activity 2: Health Needs at the Community Level ❋

Objective   To identify the health needs of women at the community level
Time   60 minutes
Materials   Small pieces of paper, pens, adhesive tape or tacks, chart paper or surface on which to attach pieces of paper

1. List/Prioritize/Compare
Divide participants into small groups and ask them to do the following:

- Write or draw the health needs of women and girls in your community. Use a separate piece of paper for each need.
- Arrange the needs in a triangle, according to their importance. Put the most pressing needs at the top.
- Circle those needs in the triangle that are poorly met or not at all. Star those needs that are particular to women and girls.
- Post your chart and compare with others.

2. Discuss
In the full group, discuss the following points:

- What were the principal differences among the triangles?
- In what respect(s) is each item in the triangle important to the health of women and girls?
- What happens if any of these health needs are denied? Give examples.
- Why are those needs that are circled not met?
- Is there any relationship between the needs you have starred and those you have circled? Discuss.
- What steps are being taken in your community to improve women's health? What further might be done?

HEALTH FOR ALL

Many women live with long-term health problems. Countless women and girl children suffer from nutritional deficiencies and anemia that make them prone to illnesses such as tuberculosis, malaria, diarrhea, and pneumonia. Many are subjected to constant stress and injuries resulting from work responsibilities and social restrictions as well as abuse and violence. In industrialized countries, health-related problems are often worst among women of color and women from minority groups.

Within any country, great disparities exist in health needs among different regions and different socioeconomic, ethnic, and age groups. Although many countries have made significant advances in primary health care, the worldwide HIV/AIDS epidemic has eroded much of this progress, and women's general and maternal health care and treatment for complications from pregnancy and childbirth remain inadequate. Of the 515,000 women who die from childbirth-related illnesses each year, almost 99 percent come from developing countries.[6] Between 2005 and 2007, 1 million women died for lack of medical care during pregnancy or while giving birth—a figure equivalent to the total number of German and Canadian women who gave birth in 2006. During the same two-year period, 21 million children under the age of 5 died from inadequate care—the same number as the total of children under 5 born in Ger-many, France, Canada, Japan, Italy, and the United Kingdom combined.[7]

No matter what the country, not just poor women but women from rural areas, refugee, displaced, and migrant women, and women heads of households—who are also likely to be of lower economic status—usually face great obstacles in exercising their health rights. Women with disabilities, too, often have restricted access to general health care as a result of discriminatory attitudes, physically inaccessible health facilities, or ignorance about the health needs of disabled women.

Women's multiple work responsibilities often endanger their health. In many societies women bear a double burden, expected to work outside the home for pay as well as to be responsible for work inside the home and to take care of their husband and children's needs—and often those of other relatives as well. Even when women do not work outside the home, their work may be difficult and never ending. In many homes around the world, women are the first to rise in the morning and the last to go to bed at night. Some women may become conditioned to think of their own health needs last. In some societies, women can see a doctor only when escorted by a husband or father. As a result, women are likely to delay or do without treatment. In addition, in some families boys are more likely to receive proper medical care than girls.[8] When the family resources are limited, money for proper nutrition and medicines may go first to boys, leaving the girls with little or none.[9]

A sick woman faces particular problems, especially if her disease bears some social stigma, as with tuberculosis, HIV/AIDs, or other diseases commonly transmitted sexually. Women with such diseases may be ostracized by their family, get fired from their job, or suffer domestic violence. Fearing such repercussions, many women do not seek treatment and attempt to hide their illness. For example, women may avoid being screened for HIV/AIDS out of fear of the husband's or family's reaction and, as a result, fail to get medication or treatment. Even women with a less stigmatizing illness such as heart disease, diabetes, or malaria often face greater obstacles to full recovery because of chronic overwork, poor care, and undiminished family responsibilities.[10]

Facts About Women's Health

- The World Bank has warned that violence against women is as serious a cause of death and incapacity among women of reproductive age as cancer, and a greater cause of ill health than traffic accidents and malaria combined.[11]
- The life expectancy of women has either remained the same or risen since 1995 in every region of the world except sub-Saharan Africa.[12]
- Pregnant women are more susceptible than the general population to malaria and its consequences. Malaria-related maternal mortality can be very high, particularly during epidemics and in areas of low transmission and therefore low immunity.[13]
- Women are more likely than men to become disabled during their lives, due in part to gender bias in the allocation of scarce resources and in access to services. When ill, girls and women are less likely to receive medical attention than boys and men, particularly in developing countries where medical care may be a considerable distance from home. They are also less likely to receive preventive care, such as immunizations. Due to social, cultural, and religious factors, disabled women are less likely than men to make use of existing social services, including residential services, and it is estimated that disabled women worldwide receive only 20 percent of rehabilitation care.[14]
- Globally, 45 percent of adults living with HIV/AIDS are women. By region, this percentage varies considerably, from 57 percent in sub-Saharan Africa to 28 percent in East Asia and the Pacific. In 2004, 17.6 million women were living with HIV/AIDS worldwide.[15]
- Women between the ages of 35 and 60 account for 60 percent of all cases of cervical cancer. There appears to be an increased risk of this cancer in women who are farm workers, cooks, cleaners, and maids as well as in those who work, or have partners who work, in environments that involve contact with certain chemical substances (i.e., those in the mining, textile, metal, or chemical industries).[16]
- Women living in poor social and environmental circumstances with associated low education, low income, and difficult family and marital relationships are much more likely than other women to suffer from mental disorders.[17]

RESPECTING CULTURE AND TRADITION

A number of international human rights instruments require that states take effective action to abolish traditional practices prejudicial to the health of women and girls. In 1990, for example, members of the Committee on the Elimination of All Forms of Discrimination Against Women, the body responsible for monitoring the implementation of CEDAW, expressed its concern at the continuation of traditional practices harmful to the health of women.[18] And in 1999 the fifty-fourth UN General Assembly adopted a resolution condemning traditional or customary practices that affect the health of women and girls. Yet despite these developments, many societies continue adhering to customs, often rationalized in the name of religion or culture, that endanger women's health. One such custom prevents a woman from travelling to see a doctor; another accepts violence against women by male family members.

In some societies, early marriage and pregnancy have a grave effect on the health of women and girls. A preference for sons often results in preferential treatment for male children that, in turn, results in neglect or discriminatory treatment of girls, compromising their health and well-being. According to UNICEF, more than 100 million women are "missing" from global population figures, a majority of them from South and East Asia, victims of infanticide, malnutrition, neglect, abandonment, and, more recently, sex-based abortion relating to the misuse of technologies for prenatal sex determination.[19] Another study estimates that 60–100 million fewer women are alive today than would exist in a world without gender discrimination and without social norms that favor sons.[20]

Because of their lower status, women and girls often eat only after all male family members have eaten and suffer higher rates of malnutrition as a result. In addition, although women are often expected to have numerous children, many are forbidden or unable to access professional medical help and die during childbirth. Traditional birth practices pose further health risks, including, for example, dietary restrictions for pregnant women, harmful practices during labor and childbirth, and inappropriate treatment of conditions such as obstructed labor. According to the United Nations, at least 1,600 women die from complications of pregnancy and childbirth every day. These complications are the leading cause of death and disability for women aged 15 to 49 in developing countries.[21] For more on the impact of culture and tradition on health and human rights, see Chapter 4, "The Human Rights of Young Women and Girls."

The Case of Female Genital Cutting Continued[22]

The World Health Organization (WHO) estimates that, around the world, 100–132 million girls and women have been subjected to female genital cutting (FGC) or female genital mutilation (FGM). Each year, an estimated 2 million girls are believed to be at risk for the practice. The majority of survivors live in twenty-eight African countries; others live in the Middle East and in Asian countries and, to an increasing extent, among immigrant populations in Europe, Canada, Australia, New Zealand, and the United States of America.

Female genital cutting is a cultural practice harmful to women that violates women's human rights to life, bodily integrity, health, and sexuality. As noted by the WHO, "FGM is linked to gender inequalities entrenched in the political, social, cultural and economic structures of societies in which it is practiced. It is a reflection of the discrimination against women in both public and private life." The health consequences of the practice can be severe, leading to lifelong mental and physical disability and even death and implicating the right to life, the right to freedom from violence, the right to bodily integrity, and reproductive rights. Because it is practiced mostly on young girls, female genital cutting violates a range of human rights of the girl child, including informed consent.[23]

The WHO defines *female genital cutting* as "all procedures which involve partial or total removal of the external female genitalia or other injury to the female genital organs whether for cultural or any other non-therapeutic reasons."

The United Nations Population Fund has identified four types of female genital cutting practices:

Type 1: Excision of the prepuce, with or without excision of part or all of the clitoris.
Type 2: Excision of the clitoris with partial or total excision of the labia minora.[24]
Type 3: Excision of part or all of the external genitalia and stitching/narrowing of the vaginal opening (infibulation). Sometimes referred to as pharaonic circumcision.

Type 4: Others. For example, pricking, piercing or incising, stretching, burning of the clitoris, scraping of tissue surrounding the vaginal orifice, cutting of the vagina, introduction of corrosive substances or herbs into the vagina to cause bleeding or to tighten the opening.[25]

Abolition of these harmful cultural practices is a complex and challenging issue, as FGM has important cultural and symbolic significance for some women and communities. The practice, much like plastic surgery to increase breast size, is understood to enhance the femininity of women, and to make them more attractive to men. It is also seen as a ritual in the process toward womanhood. Although groups have been working against the practice of female genital cutting in African countries for many years, the increased visibility of this problem has resulted primarily from the growth of women's movements around the world as well as from attention from the international human rights community to issues related to gender.

❋ Learning Activity 3: Impact of a Woman's Health on Her Life Cycle ❋

Objective   To identify the impact of health on the life cycle of a woman
Time   45 minutes
Materials   None

1. Create a Story

Divide participants into small groups. Explain that each group will construct a life story of a typical women from their community from the standpoint of health, covering her life cycle from birth to old age. Each group should decide in advance the social, ethnic, and economic setting for this woman and assign her a name, life, and health experience typical for that setting. Encourage a wide choice of such settings.

Begin the story with "A baby girl was born into the community ..." and let the story pass from one participant to another, with each telling about a different period in this woman's life. Include factors that affect women's health in this community, both positively and negatively, such as traditional health practices, access to health care, education, leisure, family planning, child bearing, and cultural influences reflected in the media.

Alternative: These stories might be illustrated by drawings, dancing, role-play, or other creative methods.

2. Present

Each small group summarizes its life story for the whole group.

3. Discuss

Conclude with discussion of questions like these:

- What factors were common to all stories?
- Which illnesses and practices most affect women of low economic status? Women of high economic status?

- Aside from reproductive factors, how would the stories be different if the baby had been a boy?
- What factors contribute to a lifetime of good health? To bad health?
- How do poor childhood health care and nutrition affect a person's life cycle?
- Is it possible to justify any custom that has a negative effect on women's health?
- How can women's bodily integrity be protected at the same time that culture and religion are respected?

THE ROLE OF AUTHORITIES IN WOMEN'S HEALTH

Most public health systems aim to make health care available for the whole population. This goal is reinforced by evolving human rights documents that obligate the states that have ratified them not only to promote and guarantee health care but also to ensure that health care facilities are equally accessible to everyone.

The United Nations Charter (1947), the founding document of the United Nations, calls on the UN to promote solutions for international health problems (Article 55b), and the Universal Declaration of Human Rights (UDHR, 1948) states that everyone has the "right to a standard of living adequate for the health and well-being of his [sic] family, including food, clothing, housing and medical care and necessary social services" (Article 25). In short, all UN Member States have an obligation to create the conditions for the health and well-being of all people in those states. These general documents were followed in later decades by covenants and conventions that placed legally binding obligations on the governments that ratified them, referred to as "States Parties to the treaty."

Some of these legal responsibilities require a government to refrain from interfering with or harming people's health; others obligate a government to actively promote health. Whether acting directly through official government programs or indirectly through institutions such as hospitals and doctors, governments cannot discriminate between the health care available to women and girls and that available to men and boys.

States that are parties to the International Covenant on Economic, Social, and Cultural Rights (ICESCR, 1976) are obligated to take the steps necessary to "recognize the right of everyone to the enjoyment of the highest attainable standard of physical and mental health" (Article 12). The Convention on the Elimination of All Forms of Discrimination Against Women (CEDAW, 1979) guarantees women the right to equal access to health care (Article 12), as well as to information and advice on family planning (Article 10). And in addition to guaranteeing the right of the child to the "highest attainable standard of health" (Article 24), the Convention on the Rights of the Child (CRC, 1989) gives the child the right to sources of information including "those aimed at the promotion of his or her … physical and mental health," thus implicitly including information about sexuality and reproductive health.

In its 1999 General Recommendation on women's right to health, the Committee on the Elimination of All Forms of Discrimination Against Women recommended that states should "implement a comprehensive national strategy to promote women's health throughout their lifespan" and that "States Parties should allocate adequate budgetary, human and administrative resources to ensure that women's health receives a share of the overall health budget comparable with that for men's health, taking into account their different health needs." The Committee also issued the following more specific recommendations:

31. States parties should also, in particular:

(a) Place a gender perspective at the centre of all policies and programs affecting women's s health and should involve women in the planning, implementation and monitoring of such policies and programs and in the provision of health services to women;

(b) Ensure the removal of all barriers to women's access to health services, education and information, including in the area of sexual and reproductive health, and, in particular, allocate resources for programs directed at adolescents for the prevention and treatment of sexually transmitted diseases, including HIV/AIDS;

(c) Prioritize the prevention of unwanted pregnancy through family planning and sex education and reduce maternal mortality rates through safe motherhood services and prenatal assistance. When possible, legislation criminalizing abortion could be amended to remove punitive provisions imposed on women who undergo abortion;

(d) Monitor the provision of health services to women by public, non-governmental and private organizations, to ensure equal access and quality of care;

(e) Require all health services to be consistent with the human rights of women, including the rights to autonomy, privacy, confidentiality, informed consent and choice;

(f) Ensure that the training curricula of health workers include comprehensive, mandatory, gender-sensitive courses on women's health and human rights, in particular gender-based violence.[26]

Governments differ greatly in their ability to provide health care, but they are obliged, to the extent that they are able, to ensure that their citizens attain a standard of living adequate to their health and well-being. Too often, however, even the wealthiest nations fail to meet this standard in a fair and nondiscriminatory manner.

HEALTH CARE AND EQUALITY BETWEEN MEN AND WOMEN

Governments have the obligation to avoid discriminating between men and women in the provision of health care. However, providing health care on the basis of equality between men and women means more than simply providing identical facilities. The Committee on the Elimination of All Forms of Discrimination Against Women, in its General Recommendation regarding women's human right to health (1999), emphasized that "States Parties should report on their understanding of how policies and measures on *health care* address the health rights of women from the perspective of women's needs and interests and how it addresses distinctive features and factors which differ for women in comparison to men."[27] This means recognizing and addressing the differing health needs of men and women. A prenatal health service does not discriminate against men because they do not need such a service. Similarly, screening for prostrate cancer does not discriminate against women as long as other programs exist that address women's cancer concerns such as breast cancer.

Adequate health services for women must address their particular health care needs. For example, women may suffer from forms of cancer and other illness that are rare or unknown in men. Women may also be particularly susceptible to the effects of chronic fatigue, malnutrition, and anemia as well as to the health consequences related to these conditions. Governments and communities have to take steps to make health care more accessible to women, such as ensuring that hospitals and clinics:

- maintain working hours that correspond to times during which women are available
- are conveniently located (as women are less likely than men to be able to travel distances)
- are affordable
- offer quality care and consistently available medications
- employ culturally appropriate staff (including, if possible, local health professionals who speak the same languages and female staff for gynecological exams)
- design services in consultation with women to fit their needs (including the particular needs of rural, refugee, migrant, displaced, older, single, widowed, and disabled women)
- offer a welcoming atmosphere, not one that is cold or frightening.

REMEMBERING CORE CONCEPTS

❊ Learning Activity 4: Speaking Out for Women's Health ❊

Objectives   To examine women's right to health care in the community and consider how to take action to improve such care

Time   60+ minutes

Materials   Chart paper and markers

1. Brainstorm

Ask participants to list the health problems of women in their community and, after dividing into small groups, to choose a problem on which they wish to concentrate.

2. Discuss/Plan

Ask each small group to prepare a five-minute presentation to a "panel of community leaders" on their chosen problem. Each presentation should:

- describe the health problem as well as identify the group of women it impacts and, if possible, the cause(s) of the problem
- relate the problem to women's human rights
- clarify how the problem affects women's lives
- show how addressing the problem can improve their lives
- propose specific actions that should be taken to address the problem
- show how members of the community can get involved in addressing the problem.

For a group-oriented class: Ask each group to choose a spokesperson to make the presentation and a "community leader" to serve on the panel. While the groups plan their presentations, the panel of leaders meets to decide on their roles, representing a variety of differing but typical attitudes within the community leadership.

3. Present/Role-Play

The spokesperson from each group makes a presentation and members of the panel listen and respond, asking questions and offering comments, objections, or suggestions in keeping with their chosen roles.

4. Discuss

After the presentations and role-play, discuss the following questions:

- How did the spokespersons feel when presenting the problem?
- How did the "community leaders" respond to the presentation? What attitudes in the community were they representing?
- How did the audience, composed of the rest of the group, respond to the presentations?
- Did any spokesperson discuss the problem as a human rights violation? Did putting the problem in a human rights context strengthen the argument? Why or why not?
- Are these ideas for improving women's human right to health feasible in your community? Why or why not?

5. Conclude

Challenge the participants by asking them to evaluate their knowledge of the problem and the inclusiveness of their perspective:

- How did you obtain your information about the health issues facing women in your community? Was it accurate and complete? If not, what additional information do you need and how can you obtain it?
- Did you personally consult women about the problem and how it affects them? About actions that could improve the problem?
- Why is it important in real-life human rights advocacy to include the active participation of those directly involved and affected?
- How can you apply the example of this exercise to planning and implementing advocacy for women in your community?

NOTES

1. UN Platform for Action Committee Manitoba, Women and the Economy, "What Are the Causes of Women's Economic Inequality?" (2002), from the BRIDGE Briefing Paper on the feminization of poverty, available online at http://www.unpac.ca/economy/ whatcauses.html.
2. International Labour Organisation, "Health Impact of Occupational Risks in the Informal Sector in Zimbabwe," Chapter 2, February 2000.
3. Oxfam International, "The World Is Still Waiting," *Oxfam Briefing Paper 103*, May 2007, available online at http:// www.oxfam.org.uk/what_we_do/issues/debt_aid/bp103_g8.htm.
4. *The World's Women 1995: Trends and Statistics* (New York: United Nations, 1995).
5. Asbjørn Eide, "Economic and Social Rights," in *Human Rights: Concepts and Standards*, edited by Janusz Symonides (UNESCO, 2000).
6. UNICEF Maternal Health, December 4, 2005, available online at http://www .unicef.org/health/index_maternal-health.html.

7. Oxfam International, "The World Is Still Waiting," *Oxfam Briefing Paper 103*, May 2007, available online at http://www.oxfam.org.uk/what_we_do/issues/debt_aid/ bp103_g8.htm.

8. United Nations, Expert Group Meeting on the Elimination of All Forms of Discrimination and Violence against the Girl Child, *Violence and Discrimination—Voices of Young People: Girls About Girls*, Florence, September 25–28, 2006, available online at http://www.unicef.org/voy/media/UNICEFEGM_GirlaboutGirlsFINAL.doc.

9. Ibid.

10. *UNAIDS, "AIDS Epidemic Update, December 2004," from Why Is There Stigma Related to HIV and AIDS?* (Avert.org), available online at http://www.avert.org/aidsstigma.htm.

11. Cited in Shelley Anderson, "'More Training!' Towards Gender-Sensitive Nonviolence Training," International Fellowship for Reconciliation Women Peacemakers Program, The Netherlands, available online at http://www.ifor.org/WPP/TOT%20report %202002.pdf.

12. United Nations, *The World's Women 2000: Trends and Statistics* (New York: United Nations).

13. Philippe J. Guerin et al., "Malaria: Current Status of Control, Diagnosis, Treatment, and a Proposed Agenda for Research and Development," *The Lancet Infectious Diseases*, vol. 2 (September 2002), available online at http://www.accessmed-msf.org/upload/ReportsandPublications/25920021619148/malaria.pdf.

14. Human Rights Watch, "Women and Girls with Disabilities," available online at http://www.hrw.org/women/disabled.html.

15. USAID Health Overview, Washington, DC, available online at http://www.usaid.gov/our_work/global_health.

16. United Nations Sustainable Networking Development Program (SNDP), New York, United Nations, available online at http://www.sdnpbd.org.

17. World Health Organization, "Women and Mental Health," available online at http://www.who.int/mediacentre/factsheets/fs248/en/.

18. CEDAW, General Recommendation No. 24 (20th session, 1999), Article 12: Women and Health, available online at http://www.un.org/womenwatch/daw/cedaw/recommendations/recomm. htm#recom24.

19. UNICEF, "Equality, Development, and Peace," available online at http://womenshistory.about.com/library/etext/speech/bl_sp_beijing_un_1.htm.

20. UNICEF, "Early Childhood: Investment in Early Childhood Can Break the Cycle of Poverty," available online at http://www.unicef.org/earlychildhood/index_investment .html.

21. United Nations Chronicle, "Safe Motherhood: A Matter of Human Rights and Social Justice" (Rita Luthra, 2005), available online at http://www.un.org/Pubs/chronicle/ 2005/issue2/0205p14.html.

22. Unless otherwise noted, references in this section are to "Female Genital Mutilation Information Pack, FGM: Prevalence and Distribution" (1996), available online at http://www.who.int/docstore/frh-whd/FGM/infopack/English/fgm_infopack.htm #THE%20PRACTICE.

23. UNICEF, "Changing a Harmful Social Convention: Female Genital Mutilation/Cutting" (Alexia Lewnes, 2005), available online at http://www.unicef-icdc.org/publications/pdf/fgm-gb-2005.pdf.

24. Ibid. See also Fran Hosken, *The Hosken Report: Genital and Sexual Mutilation of Females*, 4th rev. ed. (Lexington, MA: Women's International Network News, 1993); National Demographic and Health Surveys, Macro International, Inc., 11785 Beltsville Drive, Calverton, Maryland; and Nahid Toubia, *Female Genital Mutilation: A Call for Global Action* (New York: Women, Ink., 1993).

25. UNFPA, "Harmful Practices: Frequently Asked Questions on Female Genital Mutilation/Cutting," available online at http://www.unfpa.org/gender/practices2.htm#2.

26. CEDAW, General Recommendation No. 24 (1999).

27. Ibid.; see also http://www.unicef-icdc.org/publications/pdf/fgm-gb-2005.pdf.

CHAPTER SEVEN

Women's Human Rights to Reproduction and Sexuality

By Julie A. Mertus and Nancy Flowers

[R]eproductive rights embrace certain human rights that are already recognized in national laws, international human rights documents and other consensus documents. These rights rest on the recognition of the basic right of all couples and individuals to decide freely and responsibly the number, spacing and timing of their children and to have the information and means to do so, and the right to attain the highest standard of sexual and reproductive health.
— *Programme of Action, United Nations International Conference on Population and Development, Paragraph 7.3*

We, the Governments participating in the Fourth World Conference on Women, are determined to ... [e]nsure equal access to and equal treatment of women and men in education and health care and enhance women's sexual and reproductive health as well as education.
— *Beijing Platform for Action, Paragraph 1.30*

OBJECTIVES

The learning activities and background information contained in this chapter will enable participants to work toward the following objectives:

- Recognize the importance of reproductive and sexual rights for women and their interconnection with other human rights.

- Identify obstacles to women's reproductive and sexual rights.
- Define the role of government, community leaders, the media, and women themselves in protecting and advocating for women's reproductive and sexual rights.
- Critically analyze the relation between population policies and reproductive and sexual rights.
- Debate the issue of reproductive and sexual health education from the perspective of women's human rights.
- Remember core concepts.

GETTING STARTED: THINKING ABOUT REPRODUCTIVE AND SEXUAL RIGHTS

About half the world's female population is of reproductive age (15–49). Over the next twenty years, this group will increase by 30 percent. Half of the world's population is under the age of 25, and within fifteen years—less than one generation—all 3 billion will have reached reproductive age.[1] The lives and health of women of reproductive age are greatly influenced by their potential reproductive roles. Although rates of mortality and illness related to reproductive health have declined throughout the world, this progress is being eroded by the HIV/AIDS epidemic, especially in Africa and parts of Asia. As noted in the Beijing Platform for Action (paragraph 95):

> Reproductive health eludes many of the world's people because of such factors as: inadequate levels of knowledge about human sexuality and inappropriate or poor-quality reproductive health information and services; the prevalence of high-risk sexual behavior; discriminatory social practices; negative attitudes toward women and girls; and the limited power many women and girls have over their sexual and reproductive lives. Adolescents are particularly vulnerable because of their lack of information and access to relevant services in most countries. Older women and men have distinct reproductive and sexual health issues that are often inadequately addressed.

Facing the Facts on Women's Reproductive Health

- Pregnancy and childbirth and their consequences are still the leading causes of death, disease, and disability among women of reproductive age in developing countries.[2]
- Maternal mortality is highest by far in Africa, where the lifetime risk of maternal death is 1 in 16 women, compared with 1 in 2,800 in wealthy countries.[3]
- Worldwide, 61.1 percent of births are attended by a professional who, at least in principle, has the appropriate skills. In sub-Saharan Africa, however, only 40 percent of births are accompanied by a skilled attendant.[4]
- Over 300 million women in the developing world suffer from short-term or long-term illness brought about by pregnancy and childbirth; 529,000 die each year.[5]

REPRODUCTIVE DECISION MAKING

✳ Learning Activity 1: Discussion Circle on Reproductive Rights ✳

Objectives   To get started discussing reproductive rights and to relate them to personal experience

Time   45 minutes

Materials   None

1. Discuss

Arrange the group in two concentric circles, with each participant on the inside circle facing a participant on the outside circle. Explain that as you read out a question from the list below, each pair should speak to each other about the question for four minutes. For the next question, those on the outer circle rotate one place to the right to face a new partner. Repeat this process for every question.

Note to Facilitator: Some of these questions would be inappropriate in certain cultural settings; develop a set of five or six questions appropriate to a particular group and its culture. Other questions may need to be rephrased from the personal to the general (e.g., not "How did your mother protect herself from unwanted pregnancy?" but "How did women of your mother's generation protect themselves?"). Still others may need to be omitted altogether; clarify that everyone is free to decline to discuss a question.

- What is the first thing that comes to mind when you think of reproductive and sexual rights? The next thing?
- What major decisions in your life have been related to reproduction and sexuality (e.g., choosing a partner, taking a job, finishing education or training)?
- Has anyone tried to make decisions about reproduction and sexuality for you?
- What are the main controversies in your community about reproduction and sexual rights?
- What are the main incentives in your community for large families? For small families? Which arguments are most influential to you?
- How many children did your mother have? How did she protect herself from unwanted pregnancy?
- What kinds of decisions have you made about having or not having children? Did you make these yourself? Did your partner pressure you in any way? Your partner's family? Your family? Your community?
- What is the main family planning method used in your community, if any? What method, if any, do you use? Did you or most women in your community always choose family planning methods freely, or did someone do it for you? How did you and/or women in your community learn about them?
- What is the general attitude in your community toward abortion?

2. Discuss

After participants have discussed a number of questions for about half an hour, ask them to form one large group and discuss what they experienced in discussing the questions with others.

- How did you feel about discussing these topics with others?
- What did you learn about others' attitudes and information? About your own?
- Did this exercise help you to focus on issues related to reproductive health in your community? What do you think are the main concerns of women in your community?

Women and girls face many decisions about their reproduction and sexuality, including the following:

- Whether to obtain information regarding sex
- Whether to engage in sexual activity and with whom
- Which contraceptive methods to use, if any
- Whether to require a male sexual partner, including a spouse, to use a condom
- Whether to have children
- Whether to seek medical attention during pregnancy
- With whom to have children
- When to have children
- How many children to have
- Spacing of children
- With whom to bring up children
- Whether to abort an unwanted pregnancy.

Women's choices are often imposed or limited by direct or indirect social, economic, and cultural factors. For example, in some countries where women are allowed little participation in reproductive decisions, or where governments impose strict population policies and there is a strong preference for sons, women may feel forced to decide between abortion of the female fetus, infanticide of the female newborn baby, or neglect of a female child until she dies. In many countries an unmarried pregnant girl is told to have the baby quietly and then to give the child away to a married couple. Her only other option may be to raise the child alone in poverty with few prospects for the future.

It is often assumed that women and girls with disabilities cannot or should not exercise reproductive choices, and as a result they are denied access to information and services needed to make such choices, pressured into making particular choices, or made subjects of substituted decision-making (whereby someone else, such as a doctor or relative, makes the decision for them).

❋ Learning Activity 2: Decisions About Reproduction and Sexuality ❋

Objective	To identify decision makers over reproduction and sexuality
Time	60 minutes
Materials	Chart paper and markers or blackboard and chalk, slips of paper, string or tape, copies of the above section headed "Reproductive Decision Making"

1. List/Discuss
Hand out copies of "Reproductive Decision-Making" or post this list on a prepared chart or blackboard. Ask participants:

- Is the list comprehensive?
- If not, what would you add to the list?

2. Analyze
Ask participants which of these decisions women in their community make and mark them with a *W*. Mark with an *M* decisions made by men. Write both *M* and *W* only when the decision making is shared equally. Discuss these questions:

- Do all members of the group agree?
- Did your mother make the decisions marked with *W*? Your grandmother? You?
- If there has been a change over time, discuss what explains this change.

3. Create/Gallery Walk
Draw a long horizontal line on a blackboard or chart paper or hang a string across the room. Explain that this represents women's lifeline. Mark ten equal units along the line to represent each decade of life.

Divide participants into small groups and ask them to write or draw on slips of paper decisions about reproduction and sexuality that women are likely to make or have made for them at different periods of their lives. Then attach these slips to the line in the appropriate decade, forming a "reproductive lifeline." When all of the slips are attached, have everyone examine them.

4. Discuss
Ask these questions about the reproductive lifeline:

- At what stages in life do most decisions about reproduction and sexuality occur? Least?
- Are there any decisions on the reproductive lifeline that women in your community may not or cannot make? Remove those from the line. What percentage remains? What percentage was removed? What conclusions can you draw from these percentages?
- How would your own reproductive lifeline change if you had more or less access to economic resources? To education?
- How would your own reproductive lifeline change if you were from a different racial, ethnic, or social group in your community?
- What happens when women cannot make decisions about their reproduction and sexuality? How are women's human rights affected when they cannot make these decisions?
- What other factors would alter women's reproductive lifeline?

DEFINING REPRODUCTIVE AND SEXUAL RIGHTS AS HUMAN RIGHTS

Many reproductive rights advocates have long linked their cause to human rights, and support for reproductive rights as human rights can be found in many international instruments. Yet reproductive and sexual rights were not firmly at the forefront of human rights advocacy until the issue was raised at a series of international conferences in the 1990s.

A major advance in the international recognition of reproductive and sexual rights as human rights took place in Cairo, Egypt, in 1994 at the UN International Conference on Population and Development (ICPD). There, the 180 countries in attendance agreed that population growth can be stabilized and development efforts enhanced by the advancement of women. The documents that were agreed upon at the ICPD thus recognized reproductive rights as part of the international human rights agenda and as crucial measures for promoting development. Specifically, the ICPD Program of Action, the main document resulting from the 1994 conference, recognized the need for women and men to be informed about and have access to safe, effective, and affordable means of contraceptives and other health care services.

The 171 state representatives at the UN World Conference on Women in Beijing in 1995 reaffirmed that reproductive rights are human rights. The main action plan drafted at the meeting, the Beijing Platform for Action, provides the following definitions of reproductive rights:

- Reproductive health "is a state of complete physical, mental and social well-being and not merely the absence of disease or infirmity, in all matters relating to the reproductive system and to its functions and processes. Reproductive health therefore implies that people are able to have a satisfying and safe sex life and that they have the capability to reproduce and the freedom to decide if, when and how often to do so" (paragraph 94).
- Reproductive health care "is defined as the constellation of methods, techniques and services that contribute to reproductive health and well-being by preventing and solving reproductive health problems. It also includes sexual health, the purpose of which is the enhancement of life and personal relations, and not merely counseling and care related to reproduction and sexually transmitted diseases" (paragraph 94).
- Reproductive rights "embrace certain human rights that are already recognized in national laws, international human rights documents and other consensus documents. These rights rest on the recognition of the basic right of all couples and individuals to decide freely and responsibly the number, spacing and timing of their children and to have the information and means to do so, and the right to attain the highest standard of sexual and reproductive health" (paragraph 95).

With the momentum of the Cairo and Beijing meetings behind them, reproductive and sexual rights advocates increasingly framed their struggles in human rights terms. This strategy met the most success in Africa, where advocates succeeded in persuading the African Union—the regional body charged with promoting unity and solidarity among its fifty-three member nations—to include strong statements on reproductive and sexual rights in a new treaty on women's rights. The treaty, known as the "Protocol on the Rights of Women in Africa,"[6] which, in turn, supplemented the African Charter on Human and Peoples' Rights, went into effect in November 2005. Among many global "firsts," this was the first human rights treaty to include a specific provision on a woman's right to abortion when pregnancy resulted from sexual assault, rape, or incest; when continuation of the pregnancy endangered the life or health of the pregnant woman; and in cases of grave fetal defects incompatible with life. Among other measures, the treaty also called for the prohibition of harmful practices such as female genital cutting.[7] (For more information on women's health, see Chapter 5, "Women's Human Right to Health.")

Reproductive and sexual rights under international human rights law are considered to be a composite of several separate human rights, including:[8]

- the right to life, liberty, and security
- the right to health, reproductive health, and family planning
- the right to decide the number and spacing of children
- the right to consent to marriage and to equality in marriage
- the right to privacy
- the right to be free from discrimination
- the right to be free from practices that harm women and girls
- the right to not be subjected to torture or other cruel, inhuman, or degrading treatment or punishment.

Governments' obligations to respect these rights can be found in many international treaties, as well as in several consensus documents arising from international human rights conferences. As with other human rights, government has both an affirmative duty to promote reproductive and sexual rights and a negative duty not to interfere with these rights. For example, in order for women to have full reproductive rights, governments should provide a wide range of information and health services to all women to enable them to make informed decisions about their health.

One highly significant development has been the support for reproductive rights incorporated into the Human Rights Committee's "General Comment 28," on equality. This document represents the thinking of one of the most important international human rights bodies. Among other provisions related to reproductive health, "General Comment 28" notes that states may fail to respect women's privacy "where there is a requirement for the husband's authorization to make a decision in regard to sterilization ... or where States impose a legal duty upon doctors and other health personnel to report cases of women who have undergone abortion ... . Women's privacy may also be interfered with by private actors, such as employers who request a pregnancy test before hiring a woman."

Since the Cairo Conference on Population and Development, a number of countries have introduced laws to combat discrimination against pregnant women and also to ensure greater access to health care.[9] According to a survey of the UN Population Fund, nearly fifty countries have introduced such legislation since 1994.[10]

❊ Learning Activity 3: Taking Action for Reproductive Rights ❊

Objective   To define what women need for their reproductive health and strategies to achieve it
Time   60 minutes
Materials   Chart paper and markers or blackboard and chalk

1. Brainstorm
Ask participants to list all the factors a woman needs in order to achieve full reproductive health. List these and, when finished, read the full list aloud. Ask participants which factors women in their community have access to and circle these.

Discuss the items not circled:

- What is the reason that each of these factors is not available?
- What happens to a woman when such needs are not met?

2. Prioritize
Consider the items not circled in Step 1 (i.e., the unmet needs). Read this list aloud and ask participants to rank each item on a scale of 1 to 5, giving the highest score to the most urgent needs.

3. Discuss
Compare your list with the list below.

For full reproductive health, all people need:

- information, education, and communication on reproductive health and reproductive freedom, sexually transmitted diseases (STDs), human sexuality, responsible parenthood, gender power relations, sexual abuse and incest, sexual differences, and the reproductive health effects of toxic substances
- safe, appropriate, available means of family planning, including a broad range of methods
- promotion of responsible sexual behavior, including increased condom use
- access to adequate medical care, including but not limited to gynecological care and maternal pre-, peri-, and post-natal care
- in countries where abortion is legal, access to safe and legal abortion and pre- and post-abortion care
- prevention and treatment of STDs, including but not limited to HIV/AIDS
- prevention of and appropriate treatment for infertility
- recognition and support of many kinds of family structures
- elimination of threats to women's reproduction, such as environmental and workplace hazards
- the inclusion of women's perspectives and women's organizations in the planning, implementation, research, and development of new reproductive methods and forms of family planning and prevention of sexually transmitted diseases, and in programs and policies for the provision of reproductive health care and sex education
- access to adequate employment, housing, health care, and education.

Keeping in mind the priorities from Step 2, ask these questions:

- What could women do to lobby the government for better information and services?
- What could women's groups and other nongovernmental organizations (NGOs) do to meet these needs for full reproductive health?
- Can you begin a public education project or discuss family planning?
- Can you set up counseling, family planning, or other needed services?
- Could you conduct campaigns and demonstrations against unsafe contraceptive and coercive reproductive technology? Would this be safe in your country?
- Can you undertake research to document medical polices and prac-tices that abuse the rights of women with respect to reproduction and sexuality?
- Which of these approaches are most likely to be feasible and successful in your community?

The World Health Organization Facts on Abortion

- Thirteen percent of maternal deaths worldwide are the result of unsafe abortions.[11]
- Thirty-eight percent of pregnancies each year are unplanned, and 22 percent result in abortions.[12]
- Of the 19 million unsafe abortions performed throughout the world each year, 18.5 million take place in developing countries.[13]
- Women aged 15–24 experience 59 percent of all unsafe abortions in Africa.[14]
- Complications from unsafe abortion procedures lead to the deaths of 68,000 women each year, primarily in developing countries.[15]
- The risk of death from unsafe abortion procedures in developing countries is estimated to be 1 in 270.[16]

ABORTION

Many women's attempts to assert their claims to reproductive and sexual rights have centered on access to safe abortion. An unsafe abortion is "a procedure for terminating an unwanted pregnancy either by persons lacking the necessary skills or in an environment lacking the minimal medical standards, or both."[17] Where women are denied access to abortion, the death rate from illegal and self-induced abortions may increase. Lacking resources to pay for higher-quality care, women who are poor, those who live in isolated areas, and vulnerable women such as refugees and adolescents are most likely to rely on unsafe abortions without skilled providers. Unsafe abortions can cause complications including infections, infertility, and even death.[18]

According to a 2000 World Health Organization study, 19 million unsafe abortions take place each year. Almost all abortion-related deaths occur in developing countries, where unsafe abortions are most prevalent.[19] Health care providers have found several ways to reduce the number of deaths from abortion, including improving the quality of abortion services, where legal; better post-abortion care; legalization of the procedure; increased use and quality of contraception; and increased information and education about reproductive health.[20]

✳ Learning Activity 4: Conflicting Messages About Reproduction ✳

Objective	To illustrate the pressure and conflicting messages women receive about reproduction
Time	30 minutes
Materials	None

1. Role-Play

Ask one volunteer to be the representative "woman." She can circulate and listen in on any of the groups while they plan their arguments. Divide the rest of the participants into six groups, which will prepare the arguments for each of the following roles:

- A government health official encouraging a large number of children
- A government health official advocating restricting the number of children
- A traditional authority opposing any form of family planning
- A feminist health worker encouraging family planning
- A government official offering food and medical support in return for sterilization
- A family elder encouraging the birth of many children as security for old age, a necessity for economic survival, and/or as a major component of a woman's social status.

Ask the representative "woman" to sit in the center while a spokesperson from each group tries to persuade her about how to use her fertility. She may ask questions at the end of each argument, but should not express any opinion.

2. Discuss

Discuss the role-play, considering some of these questions:

- How did it feel to be the "woman"? Do many women get such conflicting messages?
- What are some of the coercions or incitements offered the woman?
- What advice or support would the group like to give this woman?
- What might motivate the government actors?
- Imagine that these arguments were made to persuade a man to have a vasectomy; would they be persuasive? Why are so few population control programs directed toward men?
- Which argument is most likely to persuade a woman in your society? Why?
- Do women really get to make choices about their reproduction? Why or why not? What factors interfere with choice? Do women have the right to choose?

REPRODUCTION, SEXUALITY, AND SOCIAL CONVENTIONS

The 1995 World Conference on Women in Beijing recognized a woman's right to decision making in a broad range of areas, including choice of partner and the option of not marrying. In many societies, however, this right may be limited by a variety of factors, including prejudice against women who break traditional social codes. These conventions usually include certain ideals of what a woman is supposed to be (e.g., mother, caretaker of the house, dutiful wife).

This narrow vision of women is limiting for all women, inhibiting their ability to express and enjoy their sexuality, to choose their partners, to make decisions about whether and when to have children, to protect themselves from disease and violence, and to participate equally in all aspects of economic and social life. Because of such norms, women are often unaware that they can view experiences (especially those affecting their bodies)—and exercise choice in sexual and reproductive matters—in ways other than those into which they have been socialized.

Although limiting to all women, such conventional social expectations have a particularly harsh impact on women who are not married to men. These women face violence, harassment, and discrimination in all spheres of life, including family and work.

REPRODUCTIVE RIGHTS VERSUS POPULATION CONTROL

Global population growth is a cause for legitimate concern. Although fertility rates are falling in many regions, global population increased by 2 billion during the last quarter of the twentieth century, reaching 6 billion in 2000. Despite declining fertility rates, population is expected to increase by another 2 billion during the first quarter of the twenty-first century. Nearly all of this growth will occur in developing countries and will be concentrated among the poorest populations and in urban areas.[21] Fertility rates have a direct impact on the lives of women. Reductions in birth rates most often lead to the improvement of the overall status of women, and family planning can save the lives of mothers and their babies by reducing the burden of too many pregnancies. Moreover, high fertility rates in poorer countries are usually an indicator of high infant and child mortality; families feel they must have many children to guarantee at least one child's survival. High fertility rates also may be an indicator that families feel they must have many children to take care of the sick and elderly. Finally, high rates reflect poor education; for example, women lack access to information on how to safely regulate their own pregnancies and men do not learn about their reproductive roles and responsibilities.

Promoting reproductive and sexual rights implicitly includes promoting the means for regulation of fertility. However, this is not the same as advocating population control. The assumption behind promotion of reproductive and sexual rights is that individuals have the capacity to make decisions about their lives and that denying them this capacity can erode both their human dignity and their health, whereas advocates of population control assume that women cannot make such decisions and that government and/or international organizations must make them for women. When governments resort to coercive methods of population control, whether encouraging or discouraging reproduction, women need to respond by claiming their sexual and reproductive rights. They can demand programs that improve their well-being as well as enhance their ability to make decisions about choice in how to change fertility patterns, including guarantees of informed consent and proper counseling for all family planning methods, including their side effects.

Another difference between reproductive rights and population control concerns the focus of government programs. The population control policies of some governments have prejudicially targeted specific groups, especially minorities and the poor; they have also viewed women in the limited roles of pro-creators of children, devoted spouses, and mothers within the context of marriage, thus ignoring the sexual and reproductive health needs of other women such as childless, divorced, widowed, or abandoned women. Such policies thus violate the principle underlying reproductive and sexual rights, which are intended to apply to *all* women equally, regardless of their status or identity.

By contrast, policies based on reproductive and sexual rights prohibit coercive government laws, population politics, and adverse social customs. At the same time, reproductive and sexual rights policies promote affirmative efforts by governments and the international community to adopt social, economic, and cultural conditions that will protect women's self-determination, health, and livelihood.

Case Study: Reproductive Rights and Racism[22]

"Slovak healthcare providers throughout eastern Slovakia are complicit in the illegal and unethical practice of sterilizing Romani women. [There are] clear and consistent patterns of healthcare providers who disregarded the need for obtaining informed consent to sterilization and who failed to provide accurate and comprehensive reproductive health information to Romani patients, resulting in the violation of their human rights.

[In-depth interviews were conducted] with more than 140 women who were coercively or forcibly sterilized or have strong indications that they were forcibly sterilized. Approximately 110 of these women [were] sterilized or [have] strong indications that they were sterilized at the fall of communism … . In many of these cases, doctors and nurses furnished misleading or threatening information to Romani women in order to coerce them into providing last-minute authorizations for sterilizations that were performed when women were undergoing a cesarean delivery … . In other cases, Romani women were given no information about sterilization procedures nor were they informed that they would be sterilized *prior* to undergoing the procedure … . In a few cases, women under the age of 18 were forcibly sterilized without the authorization required by law from their legal guardians. Many other women were never even told that they had been sterilized … . It sometimes took these women years, if ever, to confirm that they had been sterilized."

THE POLITICS OF POPULATION CONTROL

❋ Learning Activity 5: Blaming the Poor[23] ❋

Objective   To examine common attitudes toward the poor and overpopulation
Time   30 minutes
Materials   None

1. Take a Position/Discuss

Draw or indicate a line at the front of the room. Explain that the left side represents strong disagreement, the center represents neutrality, and the right side represents strong agreement; when you read a statement, participants should take a position along the line according to whether they disagree or agree. After participants have taken their positions on a statement, ask those at opposite ends to discuss their differences. At the conclusion of the discussion, ask whether any participants wish to change their position and invite them to explain why.

Some sample statements follow:

- Overpopulation is the cause of poverty.
- Poor people have too many children. As a result, they need too much food and too many resources.
- The poor have too many children because they are illiterate.
- The world's problems arise because poor people are too many, and they multiply at an alarming and uncontrolled rate.
- Poor people stay poor because they mindlessly have children that they cannot afford.

2. Discuss

Ask these questions about attitudes toward the poor and overpopulation:

- What other factors contribute to overpopulation?
- Why would authorities want to blame the poor? Why would ordinary people?
- What kinds of policies are authorities who blame the poor likely to support?
- Who or what do you think is responsible for overpopulation?

THE NEEDS OF YOUNG PEOPLE

One of the main points of debate at the 1994 International Conference on Population and Development in Cairo concerned adolescents. Some governments simply refused to acknowledge that adolescents engage in sexual relationships and have their own reproductive and sexual health care needs. The conference recognized that male behavior and attitudes must change if the reproductive needs of all people are to be met.

Among the principal barriers to the promotion of good adolescent health is a lack of effective sex education, particularly a scarcity of information about family planning and sexually transmitted diseases for girls and boys. One consequence is that many young people are not treated for sexually transmitted diseases, some of which can lead to infertility or even death.

Another consequence is that HIV/AIDS has become a disease of young people, with young adults aged 15–24 accounting for half of the 5 million new cases of HIV infection worldwide each year. Yet young people often lack the information, skills, and services needed to protect themselves from HIV infection. Providing these is crucial to turning back the epidemic. An estimated 6,000 youth a day become infected with HIV/AIDS (1 every fourteen seconds), the majority of them young women. At the end of 2001, an estimated 11.8 million young people aged 15–24 were living with HIV/AIDS— one-third of the global total of people living with HIV/AIDS. Only a small percentage of these young people know they are HIV-positive.[24]

Adolescent girls have limited power to refuse sex or negotiate condom use, and in many countries married adolescent girls are at greater risk for HIV/AIDS than unmarried girls their age. Many girls do not understand the health dangers of early pregnancy, which can lead to permanent organ damage, infertility, and even maternal mortality, as well as low birthweight and survival rates for their babies. And, as noted, many girls are vulnerable because they are not in a position to refuse sexual advances, particularly those of older men.

Lack of information on sexual health can have a particularly devastating impact on gay, lesbian, bisexual, and transgendered adolescents. Suicide rates and severe depression are highest among this population, frequently because the boy or girl feels all alone with no way out.

Even when available, sex education is too often limited to information on the physiology of reproduction. Family planning is seldom mentioned, and little mention is made of boys' responsibility for preventing pregnancy. HIV is seldom addressed or is treated as a disease of some outside group of people, despite the fact that women's rates of HIV infection are rising in all parts of the world. The primary concern of most young people is not pregnancy but love, courting, and sexuality. Health care experts have found that to be effective, sex education programs need to address young peoples' real concerns and anxieties and promote a positive and healthy sexual life—one that emphasizes self-determination, equal communication between partners, and shared responsibility for birth control.

Designed principally for the adult population and usually ignoring adolescent sexual activity, health services often fail to meet the needs of young people. In particular, many young people avoid seeking sexual and reproductive health care because they fear exposure owing to lack of confidentiality on the part of health professionals. (See also Chapter 4, "The Human Rights of Young Women and Girls.")

Information on Adolescence and Reproductive Health[25]

- Adolescents are between the ages of 10 and 19 and make up 20 percent of the world's population.
- Adolescents bear about 10 percent of the children in the world. About 14 million adolescent girls give birth each year.
- In developing countries 1–4 million adolescent girls have illegal, and usually dangerous, abortions each year.
- In 1998, 30 million people were diagnosed with HIV/AIDS; at least one-third of these were between 10 and 24 years old. When this statistic was obtained, young people were contracting AIDS at a rate of 2.6 million per year, or 5 every minutes.

✳ Learning Activity 6: Sex Education for Whom? ✳

Objective	To examine the need for information about sexuality and reproduction, and to evaluate the quality of information available to girls
Time	60 minutes
Materials	Slips of paper, three baskets or bags

1. Remember
Give participants three slips of paper each. Ask them to write on the first a question or misunderstanding they had about sexuality or reproduction as a child; on the second, a similar question from

adolescence; and on the third, a question from the present. Explain that all questions are anonymous. Gather the finished slips into the three different baskets or bags.

Invite a participant to draw a slip from the "childhood" basket and read it aloud. Based on this example, request input from other participants about how they learned such information as children. List these sources of information. Read at least three slips from each basket or bag.

Ask these questions regarding the sources of information about sex:

- What was the source?
- Was the information accurate and complete?
- What values, if any, did the information source emphasize?
- Was the information related to women's human rights? Could it be? Should it be?

2. Discuss
Ask these questions about sex education:

- How do young people in your community learn about reproduction and sexuality?
- Do they receive any information from schools, health care centers, and/or other social institutions?
- Is the information from these sources accurate and complete?
- What values do these sources of information emphasize?
- Does the information they receive mention women's human rights? Should it?
- How would you revise the information and materials about sexuality that are currently available?
- If no educational materials exist in your community on reproductive and sexual rights, would you want to create some?
- How would you evaluate the information on sexuality and reproduction available in your youth? Available today?
- Where improved information is needed, who is or could be acting for change? Who opposes change?
- If you had the resources to publish anything for girls on reproduction and sexuality, what would you do?
- Where would you distribute this publication? How?
- Would you also offer courses to teach information in your publication?
- Would parents be permitted to forbid their children from receiving materials?

Actions to Promote Reproductive and Sexual Rights

- *Ireland, Poland, and Portugal.* Women on Waves, a Dutch organization whose mission is to "prevent unwanted pregnancy and unsafe abortions throughout the world," provides safe reproductive health services to women on a ship that sails to countries where abortion is illegal. On ocean waters, such services as nonsurgical abortions, contraception, and counseling are fully legal. Thus far, the organization has operated off the coasts of Ireland and Poland. In 2004, it was blocked from entering Portuguese waters,26 but on April 10, 2007, the Portuguese president ratified a law permitting abortion until the tenth week of pregnancy.[27]

- *Mexico.* In 2007, one year after Colombia legalized abortion, abortion was declared legal in Mexico City—the capital of the world's second-largest Roman Catholic country.[28]
- *Nepal.* Legal experts met for the first time in August 2004 "to look for remedies to human rights violations in women's reproductive health."[29] High-profile officials discussed such wide-ranging issues as gender inequality, child marriage, and sexual violence.[30]
- *Japan.* For more than thirty years, oral contraceptives were illegal in Japan. However, thanks in part to the persistent media advocacy of Midori Ashida and her organization, the Women's Center for Sexuality and Health in Tokyo, oral contraception was legalized in June 1999.[31]
- *United States.* When the Bush administration withheld money from the United Nations Population Fund (UNFPA) for the third year in a row, Jane Roberts and Lois Abraham decided to get involved. They founded an organization, 34 Million Friends for the UNFPA, which is dedicated to raising the amount of money for the UNFPA that the Bush administration blocked—$34 million—by asking 34 million Americans to donate $1.00 each.[32]

Women in the United States and worldwide have participated in similar fundraisers and other political actions to demonstrate against other U.S. policies such as the policy that "restricts foreign non-governmental organizations (NGOs) that receive U.S. family planning funds from using their own, non-U.S. funds to provide legal abortion services, lobby their own governments for abortion reform laws, or even provide accurate medical counseling or referrals regarding abortion."[33] This policy inspired the March for Women's Lives in Washington, DC, on April 25, 2004, which opposed the policy.[34] The march drew throngs of protesters numbering from 800,000[35] (according to police sources) to more than 1 million marchers from at least sixty different countries.[36]

REMEMBERING CORE CONCEPTS

✳ Learning Activity 7 ✳
Speaking Out for Women's Reproductive and Sexual Rights

Objective	To examine women's right to reproduction and sexuality in the community and consider how to take action to improve it
Time	60+ minutes
Materials	Chart paper and markers

1. Brainstorm

Ask participants to list reproduction- and sexuality-related problems faced by women in their community. Then, after dividing them into small groups, ask them to choose a problem on which they wish to concentrate.

2. Discuss/Plan

Ask each group to prepare a five-minute presentation to a "panel of community leaders" on their problem. Each presentation should:

- describe the problem, identifying the group(s) of women it impacts and, if possible, the cause(s) of the problem
- relate the problem to women's human rights
- clarify how the problem affects women's lives
- show how addressing the problem can improve their lives
- propose specific actions that should be taken to address the problem
- show how members of the community can get involved in addressing the problem.

Ask each group to choose a spokesperson to make the presentation and a "community leader" to serve on the panel. While the groups plan their presentations, the panel of leaders meets to decide on their roles, representing a variety of differing but typical attitudes within the community leadership.

3. Present/Role-Play

The spokesperson from each group makes a presentation, and members of the panel listen and respond, asking questions and offering comments, objections, or suggestions in keeping with their chosen roles.

4. Discuss

After the presentations and role-play, discuss these questions:

- How did the spokespersons feel when presenting the problem?
- How did the "community leaders" respond to the presentation? What attitudes in the community were they representing?
- How did the audience, composed of the rest of the group, respond to the presentations?
- Did any spokesperson discuss the problem as a human rights violation? Did putting the problem in a human rights context strengthen the argument? Why or why not?
- Are these ideas for improving women's human rights to healthy reproduction and sexuality feasible in your community? Why or why not?

5. Conclude

Challenge the participants by asking them to evaluate their knowledge of the problem and the inclusiveness of their perspective:

- How did you obtain your information about the reproduction- and sexuality-related issues facing women in your community? Was it accurate and complete? If not, what additional information do you need and how can you obtain it?
- Did you personally consult women about the problem and how it affects them? About actions that could improve the problem?

> • Why is it important in real-life human rights advocacy to include the active participation of those directly involved and affected?
> • How can you apply the example of this exercise to planning and implementing advocacy for women in your community?

NOTES

1. Population Action International, "Young People's Reproductive Health Needs Neglected," April 26, 2002, Washington, DC, available online at http://www.population action.org/news/press/news_042302_Youth.htm.

2. World Health Organization, "Facts and Figures from the World Health Report 2005," in *The World Health Report World Health Day 2005: Make Every Mother and Child Count*, available online at http://www.who.int/whr/2005/media_centre/facts_en.pdf.

3. Ibid.

4. Ibid.

5. Protocol to the African Charter on Human and Peoples' Rights on the Rights of Women in Africa, 2nd Ordinary Session, Assembly of the Union, adopted July 11, 2003.

6. Ibid.

7. "Protocol on the Rights of Women in Africa," *Equality Now*, available online at http://www.equalitynow.org/english/campaigns/african-protocol/african-protocol_en.html.

8. Center for Reproductive Law and Policy, *Reproductive Rights are Human Rights* (June 2003), available online at http://www.crlp.org.

9. United Nations Population Fund, *State of World Population 2004: Reproductive Health and Family Planning* (2004), p. 38, available online at http://www.unfpa.org.

10. Center for Reproductive Rights, *Surviving Pregnancy and Childbirth: An International Human Right* (December 2003), p. 11, available online at http://www.reproductiverights.org/pdf/pub_bp_survivingpregnancy.pdf. See also "Key Actions for the Further Implementation of the Programme of Action of Special Session," New York, June 30–July 2, 1999, paragraph 62(b), UN Doc. A/S-21/5/Add.1 (1999), available online at http://www.unfpa.org/icpd.

11. Center for Reproductive Rights, *Surviving Pregnancy and Childbirth: An International Human Right* (December 2003), p. 10, available online at http://www.reproductiverights.org.

12. Alan Guttmacher Institute, *Sharing Responsibility: Women, Society, and Abortion Worldwide* (1999), p. 42, available online at http://agi-usa.org/pubs/sharing.pdf.

13. Elisabeth Ahman and Iqbal Shah, *Unsafe Abortion: Global and Regional Estimates of the Incidence of Unsafe Abortion and Associated Mortality in 2000*, 4th ed. (Abstract) (World Health Organization, 2001), p. 9, available online at http://www.who.int/reproductive-health/.

14. Ibid.

15. Ibid.

16. Ibid.

17. World Health Organization, "Safe Abortion: Technical and Policy Guidance for Health Systems" (2003), available online at http://www.who.int/reproductive-health/publications/safe_abortion/safe_abortion.pdf.

18. Ibid.

19. Elisabeth Ahman and Iqbal Shah, *Global and Regional Estimates of the Incidence of Unsafe Abortion and Associated Mortality in 2000*, 4th ed. (Geneva: World Health Organization, 2004).

20. World Health Organization, "Safe Abortion"; Ahman and Shah, *Unsafe Abortion*.

21. United Nations Population Fund, "Population and Demographic Dynamics: World Population Still Growing," available online at http://www.unfpa.org/pds/.

22. "Body and Soul: Forced Sterilization and Other Assaults on Roma Reproductive Freedom in Slovakia," Center for Reproductive Rights (2003), pp. 14–45, available on-line at http://www.reproductiverights.org.

23. Adapted from *Na Shariram Nadhi: My Body Is Mine*, edited by Dr. Mira Sadgopal (Bombay: Sabala and Kranti, 1995), p. 47.

24. United Nations Population Fund, "State of the World Population 2003," available online at http://www.unfpa.org/swp/2003/english/ch3/index.htm.

25. Center for Reproductive Rights, "Ensuring the Reproductive Rights of Adolescents," available online at http://www.reproductiverights.org/.

26. Feminist Majority Foundation, "Women on Waves Leaves for Portugal," August 23, 2004, available online at http://www.feminist.org/.

27. Women on Waves Press Release, "'Yes' to Abortion!" April 10, 2007, Amsterdam, available online at http://www.womenonwaves.org/article-1020.1745-en.html.

28. Ibid.

29. Center for Reproductive Rights, "Nepalese Legal Experts Seek to Remedy Reproductive Health Violation," August 3, 2004, available online at http://www.crlp.org.

30. Ibid.

31. Midori Ashida, founder, Women's Coalition for Sexuality and Health, Tokyo, at Annual Japan Studies Association of Canada Conference October 4–6, 2002, Calgary, Alberta. p. 1, Haskayne School of Business, University of Calgary Press Release, available online at http://www.haskayne.ucalgary.ca/news/media/2002/jsac2002pressre-lease.pdf#search='women's%20activism%20Japan%20oral%20contraceptives.

32. "34 Million Friends of the UNFPA," available online at http://www.unfpa.org/support/friends/34million.htm. (See also "34 Million Friends of UNFPA homepage: www.34millionfriends.org.)

33. Center for Reproductive Rights, "The Bush Global Gag Rule: Endangering Women's Health, Free Speech, and Democracy" (July 2003), available online at http://www.reproductiverights.org/.

34. Planned Parenthood Federation of America, "More Than a Million March in Washington for Reproductive Rights," April 25, 2004, available online at http://www.plannedparenthood.org/.

35. Associated Press, "Abortion-Rights Supporters Rally in Washington: Marchers Take Aim at President Bush's policies," April, 25, 2004.

36. Ibid.

CHAPTER EIGHT

Rape and Child Molestation

By Rudy Flora and Michael L. Keohane

OVERVIEW

The word *rape* comes from the Latin word *rapere* which means to "steal, seize, or carry away" (Flowers, 2006, p. 22). Rape may be defined as a form of aggression against another; it is an act of violence expressed by forced sex, without passion or caring. Such sexual behavior is used on the victim to display anger, control, domination, hostility, and power. Victims are often coerced, forced, or manipulated in some manner to engage in sexual activity.

The federal definition of rape changed in January 2012—the first time in 80 years—and is more comprehensive and includes both men and women. Rape is now defined as "the penetration, no matter how slight, of the vagina or anus with any body part or object, or oral penetration by a sex organ of another person, without the consent of the victim" (Holder, 2012, para. 1). Although laws differ from state to state, the legal definition of rape, in broad terms, implies that some form of sexual intercourse occurred against the will of the victim. The specific defining element of rape is lack of consent.

On occasion such assaults can be experimental, opportunistic, preferential, sadistic, or situational in occurrence. Victims who are unable to render informed consent as the result of being mentally incompetent or who are minors are also considered victims of rape.

Crime Classification Manual (CCM)

The *Crime Classification Manual: A Standard System for Investigating and Classifying Violent Crimes*, written by Douglas, Burgess, Burgess, and Ressler, was published in 1992 and updated in 2006. The manual was created to assist criminal justice and law enforcement officers in the assessment, arrest, and prosecution of violent offenders. Rape and sexual assault are included.

Douglas *et al.* (2006) noted that assault includes offenses in which victims are forced, coerced, or manipulated into engaging in sexual activity. Violence may or may not occur.

This manual may serve as a helpful guide not only for criminal justice professionals, but also for others in human services and mental health. (An index coding is used and each point is summarized in Appendix I.)

RAPE STATISTICS

Every year the FBI puts out the Uniform Crime Reports that statistically track rape and sexual assault in the United States. By the end of 2010 there were 84,767 forcible rapes, attempted forcible rapes, or assaults with intent to rape that were reported—a 5% decline from 2009. However, this number is still very high, especially considering the underreporting of rape by both women and men. The statistic is also misleading because sexual assaults committed on males are not included in the statistic for forcible rape—they are included under aggravated assaults or sex offenses. However, this may change since the new definition of rape. The 2010 forcible rape rate was around 54 per 100,000 female residents, comprising 93% of total rapes, while the attempts or assault to commit rape made up the last 7% (FBI, 2011).

Rape is such an emotionally charged word that most people would prefer not to discuss it; however, it merits in-depth discussion. The rate of rape crimes has declined since 2000—but past, current, and future victims of this heinous crime will find little solace in this statistic since it is approximated that a woman is raped in the United States every two to three minutes (RAINN, 2009). In addition, only one in five women who are raped will go on to report her rape experience to the criminal justice system (Black *et al.*, 2011; Tjaden & Thoennes, 2006). In a study conducted for the *National Violence Against Women Survey*, women were asked why they didn't report their rapes. The top three answers were "fear of their rapist, embarrassment, and not considering their rape a crime or police matter" (Tjaden & Thoennes, 2006, p. 2).

It is important to note that statistical data sometimes fail to capture the full extent of a sexual crime, its impact upon the victim, and the surrounding community. The sheer volume of reported sexual offenses and the estimated number of victims are alarming and not easily discounted. The sexual assault and rape statistics that we have today will continue to grow in the coming years; especially now that the definition for rape is more comprehensive.

Public awareness of sexual violence against women and children has dramatically increased. Sexual crimes are now being treated in a serious manner which is promoting new research, knowledge development, and clinical expertise. Still, the majority of sex crimes go unreported.

In 2010, the *National Intimate Partner and Sexual Violence Survey* completed a national phone questionnaire that asked 16,507 respondents (7,421 males and 9,086 females) about their experiences involving different types of violence, including rape. The study found that in the United States:

- Over 18% of women (one in five) and 1.4% of men (one in 71) reported that they had been raped at some point in their lives. In real numbers this translates to close to 22 million women and almost 1.6 million men.
- More than 91% of female rape victims knew their rapist (intimate partner rape, 51.1%; acquaintance rape, 40.8%) and over 52% of the males in the study reported being raped by an acquaintance.
- Almost 80% of the women interviewed reported that their rape happened before their twenty-fifth birthday. Close to half (42.2%) experienced forced completed rape before their eighteenth birthday (11 to 17 years old—29.9%; ten years and under—12.3%).
- Around 35% of the women who had a completed forced penetration before the age of 18 were also raped as an adult, compared to 14.2% of adults who did not report a rape before their eighteenth birthday.
- Almost 28% of the males in the study reported that they were raped before or by their tenth birthday.
- In the 12 months prior to taking the survey it is estimated 1.3 million women were raped.
- About one in 20 women (5.6%) and men (5.3%) reported that they were victims of sexual violence (outside of rape) in the 12 months prior to the survey (Black *et al.*, 2011).

Salholz, Clift, Springen, and Johnson (1990) have reported that the United States has a rape rate nearly four times higher than Germany's, 13 times higher than the United Kingdom's, and more than 20 times higher than Japan's.

International Rape Statistics

South Africa consistently reports more rape crimes than any other country in the world. It is estimated that a female is raped every 26 seconds in South Africa, giving credence to the theory that more South African women and girls are raped than know how to read (Basu & Mabuse, 2012). During 2010/2011 there were a little over 66,000 cases of reported rape; however, those numbers are likely to be much higher due to underreporting (Basu & Mabuse, 2012).

Jewkes, Sikweyiya, Morrell, and Dunkle of the Medical Research Council in South Africa (as cited in Smith, 2009) interviewed 1,738 South African men regarding their experiences with rape. To increase the likelihood of truthful answers, the men reported their answers anonymously into an APDA (audio-enhanced personal digital assistant). Of the men interviewed, one in four admitted to rape, one in ten reported that they were forced to have sex with another man, and three out of four who had raped admitted that their first rape was during their teenage years. Out of the 487 men who admitted to rape, 7% reported that they had participated in retaliatory gang raping or "jack rolling." Just as disturbing, one in 20 men interviewed reported that they had raped a woman or girl within the last year of the research conducted (Jewkes *et al.*, as cited in Smith, 2009).

While underreporting distorts rape statistics from one end of the criminal justice process, attrition distorts rape statistics at the other end of the criminal justice process.

Attrition, the process by which rape cases fail to proceed through the justice system, has been highlighted as a critical issue in several English-speaking countries with common-law systems, and there is emerging research in some European countries (for example, Austria,

Germany and parts of Scandinavia). In virtually all countries where major studies have been published, the number of reported rape offences has grown over the last two decades, yet the number of prosecutions has failed to increase proportionately, resulting in a falling conviction rate. (Lovett & Kelly, 2009, p. 5)

In 2006, the European Commission's Daphne II organization ranked Sweden the highest in rape crime attrition with 46.5 convicted rapes per 100,000 residents, approximately 5,000 rape crimes per year. Although 73% of the rape suspects were identified, only 43% were charged and 10% were convicted. Sweden's conviction rate is the fourth lowest in Europe while its rape rate is twice as high as England and Wales. However, it should be noted that Sweden has a wide definition of rape and that the reporting rate for rape has increased 426% between 1977 and 2006 (Lovett & Kelly, 2009).

During the Bosnian War (1992 to 1995) rape and sexual violence was widespread and used by all parties involved in the conflict, although Amnesty International reports that most of the victims were Bosnian Muslims. Estimates of rape and sexual abuse during this time period has varied from 20,000 to 50,000 women and girls, some as young as 12 years old. Amnesty International does not give an exact number, but instead reports that several thousand were raped (House, 2009). To avoid their cultural stigma only 7% to 10% of the women in former Yugoslavia actually reported rape and sexually violent crimes. After the war, many of the rape survivors were traumatized, shamed, humiliated, and without psychological and social supports, making it more difficult for them to report the crime to family members or the police. Amnesty International reports that the majority of those involved in the rape and sexual violence of many Bosnian Muslims have never been brought to justice (House, 2009).

It appears that regardless of global context rape most often occurs in the "context of familiarity, and intersects with domestic violence, sexual harassment, stalking, forced marriage, trafficking, and other forms of violence against women. It is a form of gender-based violence and needs to be understood through this lens" (Lovett & Kelly, 2009, p. 112).

THE EFFECTS OF PORNOGRAPHY

Sexual offenders tend to depersonalize their victim(s). The more deviant the fantasy, the more the victim(s) becomes simply a means to a sexually gratifying end. Most often, pornography plays a role in this objectification. Oddone-Paolucci, Genius, and Violato (as cited in Foubert, Brosi, & Bannon, 2011) found that increased exposure to pornography was connected to more aggressive behavior, not taking rape seriously, and greater acceptance of rape myths. The Oddone-Paolucci *et al.* study also found that the men viewing pornography had a decreased understanding or concern regarding victims subjected to sexual assault (as cited in Foubert *et al.*, 2011).

As individuals view pornography they become more desensitized to the images that they are viewing. A pornographic picture on a page or a website is devoid of feelings, personality, or reality. While studying the correlation between sexual assault behaviors and pornography, Malamuth, Addison, and Koss (as cited in Foubert *et al.*, 2011) found that men who repeatedly viewed pornography were more likely to also embrace the attitudes and behaviors associated with rape.

Foubert *et al.* (2011) completed a study involving 489 college-aged fraternity men and how viewing pornography affected their response and behavior towards rape. The results indicated that the men who viewed more extreme pornography (rape and sadomasochistic) were more likely to also embrace the behaviors associated with rape, commit sexual assaults, and accept rape myths and were less willing to help if they viewed a sexual assault situation occurring before them. The study further indicated that "[m]en who watch rape pornography and sadomasochistic pornography were significantly more likely to indicate willingness to rape women if they could be assured of not being caught or punished" (p. 225).

RAPE MYTH SNARE

Field (as cited in Page, 2008) surveyed individuals in the public about their perception and attitude toward rape. Male respondents felt that it was the woman's responsibility to avoid the rape. Men in the study also supported the rape myth that the more provocative the clothing, the more that the victim could be expected to be raped.

Unfortunately, rape victims can also become caught in the rape myth snare. They may believe that they are responsible for their rape because of what they wore, said, or did or didn't do. Victims will rightfully voice anger toward the offender, but most often will self-blame for the offense. Various research studies have indicated that up to 90% of rape victims have symptoms consistent with PTSD shortly after the sexual assault; several months after the rape almost 50% continued to exhibit symptoms related to trauma (Moor & Farchi, 2011).

Many people in society have been conditioned to think they know what rape looks like when it happens. Rape myths are made more complicated due to the misinformation surrounding sexual violence. It is important to challenge rape myths individually and in public dialogue. Sexual violence is very real and happens more often than reported. Harris (2011), in speaking about rape myths, has stated:

> The word *rape* is a vital, strategic tool that disrupts the acceptance, denial, dismissal, and excusal of many forms of nonconsensual sex. Yet this label is only one part of a political intervention that must transform the ideas that make the word's sharp lines necessary. (p. 60)

Rape can and does happen to both genders; however, it is predominantly violence against women by men. The *National Violence Against Women Survey* indicated that almost 86% of all rape victims were women (Tjaden & Thoennes, 2006). Rape is still a traumatic event regardless of gender and should be taken seriously. However, there are still people in the community that will accept rape myths to some degree.

In addition, accepting rape myths has been shown to decrease the empathy level toward rape victims and reduce the social support that they receive from people in the community (Smith & Frieze, as cited in Moor & Farchi, 2011).

Changing rape myths begins with changing the culture that tolerates the devaluing of women. The first step in educating the community about the nature of rape is to debunk the rape myths that percolate within pockets of each community. A difficult part of this equation resides in what communities allow to come into their homes through media sources (television, computer, print material, newspapers, trade journals, and music). The more that women are defiled, debased, and disrespected through these landscapes, the more difficult it is to destroy the misinformation and myths about the "how" and "why" rape occurs.

Indeed, rape may be seen as a dynamic action of the offender who cannot express him- or herself in a more socially appropriate manner. Sexual assault may be considered displaced aggression by the offender. Anger, aggression, conflict, and fear are often associated with rape. Anxiety and problems with intimacy may be found. Sometimes, forced fellatio or anal penetration may occur during a sexual assault incident.

Rape, as a dynamic action, is a representation of sexual behavior that is influenced by status, hostility, control, and dominance. Victims are the medium through which such inappropriate behaviors are expressed. The trauma and long-term psychological damage to a victim are not issues for offenders.

Polaschek and Ward (2002), in regards to rapists' deviant thoughts, have stated, "Clinical experience and theoretical work suggest that a tendency to attribute to women certain beliefs, capacities, and desires increases the likelihood that some individuals will commit sexually aggressive acts" (p. 386). It is not uncommon for rapists to have distorted views fueled by deviant fantasies regarding women wanting and desiring to have sex with them.

PARAPHILIAC COERCIVE DISORDER

The American Psychiatric Association (2000) does not currently classify rape as a mental disorder. The *DSM-IV-TR* does list two types of sexual abuse that may be considered a focus for clinical attention. These are identified as "sexual abuse of child" and "sexual abuse of adult." Several task forces have been assembled over the years; they have been unable to resolve the issue as to whether rape is a clinical disturbance or a criminal offense or both, or what special conditions should be factors.

As a result, rape remains a controversial issue in criminal justice, human service, and mental health circles. Some researchers believe that some rapists have diagnostic features similar to other paraphilias. It is the inability to make a valid diagnosis with some reliability that continues to restrict the mental health community from actually defining rape as a clinical disorder.

The American Psychiatric Association (1999) reports that a category tentatively titled "paraphiliac coercive disorder" has been examined. Individuals with this disorder would need to experience intense, repetitive urges to commit an act of rape during a six-month time frame and would either have acted on these urges or have experienced a form of distress related to the problem. Also, it was noted that some specialists now believe there is enough scientific evidence for the creation of a rape disorder; others have reservations. However, there is wide agreement that the number of individuals qualifying for such a clinical disturbance is small.

Groth (1990) has noted that all non-consenting sexual encounters are assaultive as an interaction. Therefore, the defining characteristics of rape are the forced assault of another, the victim's perceived fear of harm, and the concern for their physical safety. Sexual assault is a psychological dysfunction that may be either temporary and transient or chronic and repetitive.

Groth (1990) has also said mental health professionals have been slow to respond to rape as a possible sexual disorder which inadvertently places the public and future potential victims at risk. Only paraphiliac acts are currently considered sexually deviant and are recognized as a clinical disturbance. The more passive and unconventional disorders such as fetishism and transvestism have been researched more thoroughly and found to meet the criteria for a clinical disturbance. As a result, a large proportion of sexually inappropriate behaviors, including rape, are left to the criminal justice system for resolution.

It has been noted that the criminal justice system may be impacted if a clinical diagnosis of rape is offered. The fact that some rapists would attempt to use a clinical disorder to avoid being held accountable for their actions is a noteworthy consideration in regards to creating a new paraphilia category. Yet, more aggressive sexual disorders such as pedophilia already exist and punishment appears to be occurring when merited. In fact, many future victims may be spared harm if a diagnosis was created. Already many rape typologies have been created in an effort to assist those professionals in criminal justice, human services, and mental health in their work with sex offenders. Therefore, it now appears to be feasible that a clinical diagnosis be offered, which may be identified as sexual assault disorder.

RAPE TYPOLOGIES AND TAXONOMIES

Rape typologies have come under scrutiny for stereotyping and categorizing all rapists. Before lambasting the typologies as outdated and not currently useful, it should be noted that the typologies allowed for a starting place. Also, it allowed the clinical community to begin gathering empirical data. Over the years, the process has been refined and more empirical data have resulted in a better understanding of rapists. Also, research completed by McCabe and Wauchope (2005) indicated that there is some validity in the characteristics associated with the four types of rapes as outlined in rape typology (anger, power exploitative, power reassurance, and sadistic).

Reid, Wilson, and Boer (2011) have indicated that to understand how to effectively adapt treatment for rapists, it is important to understand rape subtypes. Reid *et al.* (2011) went on to say, "Such an approach recognizes the diversity within the rapist population and allows attention to be given to the multiple motivations underlying rape behavior" (p. 295). Reid *et al.* (2011) concluded their remarks by indicating that the main focus of research surrounding rape is to "gain a greater understanding of this crime and the offenders who perpetrate it, so that future rapes can be prevented and future victims protected" (p. 296).

Several typologies and taxonomies have developed in regard to the sex offender who rapes or sexually assaults an adult. Below is one such typology that highlights the different types of rapists.

Hazelwood Rape Model

Hazelwood (2009) expanded upon the Groth, Burgess, and Holmstrom (1977) rape typology model as follows.

Power-reassurance—This type of offender possesses many of the common features of a sexually disordered person. There are feelings of inadequacy concerning sexual performance. This offender is ritualistic and will fantasize about being in a consensual relationship with the potential victim. Sexual dysfunction may be a problem. Issues regarding masculinity and sexual orientation are sometimes present. These offenders usually do not intend to harm their victims. Force is limited and is used only to gain submission. Most assaults occur during the early morning hours when he would not be suspected. Attacks are premeditated and there can be more than one victim selected at a time in the event that the first attempt fails. Victims are selected in advance and are of similar age to the offender. An apology may be offered regarding the assault. Strangers are the most likely targets of such an attack. Clothing is often removed to incorporate a fantasy of willingness. This type of offender may keep a record of his offenses. In the law enforcement community, this type of offender has been referred to as the "gentleman rapist" (Hazelwood, 2009, p. 104).

Power-assertive—Such offenders will use rape as an expression of their need to control and dominate a woman. This offender has a sense of entitlement and women are seen as sexual objects to be had. A moderate level of force is used during the attack. There is no concern for the emotional state of the victim. Female victims tend to be of a similar age to the offender. The location of the rape is selected for isolation. Clothing may be torn or ripped as a part of the fantasy affirming the offender's perceived virility. Sexual acts may be repeated. To impair reporting, victims are sometimes left nude without transportation. This type of offender can be moderately impulsive and is often linked to date, spousal, and acquaintance rapes.

Anger-retaliatory—These offenders use rape as an expression of their anger toward women. The anger is displaced and these offenders target women for real or imagined wrongs done to them earlier in life. The anger is openly displayed during the attack. Assaults may be impulsive and unplanned. Excessive force is used to overwhelm the victim quickly and to gain control of the situation. Victims may be the same age or older. Victim availability is a factor. Physical beatings may be a part of the assault. Clothing may be torn or ripped off the victim. Profanity is sometimes used. The offender will experience a sense of calmness following the assault.

Anger-excitation—Features of sadism are found in these rapists. Such persons obtain sexual pleasure by harming others. Arousal is dependent upon the physical and emotional suffering of the victim. Attacks are premeditated. Victims are usually strangers. This type of offender prefers women and girls, but has no compunction about sexually assaulting men and boys. He has been described as a "polymorphous offender—one who is aroused in a variety of ways and experiments sexually" (Hazelwood, 2009, p. 107). The fear experienced by the victim is sexually exciting to the offender. Bondage and demeaning sexual acts are characteristic in such assaults. Victims are often physically harmed in some manner or tortured. The offender may record a part of the sexual assault. No victim empathy or remorse is expressed. This type of rapist is rare, but when found is the most violent of rape offender. Baker (as cited in Johnson, 2006) has indicated that sexually sadistic rapists account for less than 10% of the rapist population.

Opportunistic—This type of offender commits rape while in the process of committing another crime, such as breaking and entering a home. Such an offender may discover a woman alone and then choose to sexually assault her. The motivation is sexual.

Gang rape—This type of offense occurs where two or more individuals are involved in the sexual assault of a victim. Usually such offenses have a leader; in cases where there are three or more offenders, one of the rapists may appear somewhat protective of the victim. The motivation of such an attack revolves around the potential victim's perceived weakness, vulnerability, or because the group feels that the victim deserves to be sexually assaulted.

Hazelwood (2009) recommended that professionals use caution when using these groups for assessment purposes.

RAPE AS A CRIMINAL DISTURBANCE

Rape as a criminal disturbance occurs on a regular basis within the United States, and is a universal phenomenon in all countries. Groth (1990) has stated that rape is a legal definition and not a diagnostic term. Rape is a disturbance that severely impacts the victim in both a psychological and physical way. Such a crime is significantly different from other crimes of violence, such as physical assault.

Sexual assaults by strangers are reported most often to law enforcement, giving a skewed view of actual rape cases. Studies conducted by the British Crime Survey indicated that date, acquaintance, and marital rape are more common (45%) than stranger rape (8%) (Craig & Giotakos, 2011).

As a criminal act, Nadelson, Notman, and Carmen (1986) have cited rape with the following characteristics:

> Rape has been defined as the act of taking anything by force. Most rapes include force or violence applied to the victim in order to accomplish the act, but acquiescence can be obtained by verbal threat or other circumstances indicating lack of consent. (p. 339)

RAPE AND IMPLICIT THEORY

Research completed by Polaschek and Gannon (2004) suggests how implicit theories may direct a rapist's contact with his or her victim. Implicit theories are developed in early childhood and "people derive everyday understanding of their own beliefs, desires, needs and behaviors, and those of people with whom they interact by developing and using casual theories in a quasi-scientific fashion" (p. 300).

Polaschek and Ward (2002) have offered five specific implicit theories to help further clarify some of the underlining reasons as to why rapists engage in distorted thinking regarding their victim. However, they have also offered the following caveat:

> The theoretical proposal we make here is not intended to be a comprehensive explanation for rape. Instead, we hope it provides some speculations about the cognitive aspects of rape, as they are captured in existing rape scales. Further, implicit theories are only one way in which information can be stored and organized. (p. 399)

They conclude that their implicit theory is not designed to be a comprehensive approach that would explain rape or the rapist mind set. Although the implicit theories explained are not designed to be a one-size-fits-all approach, the theories do provide clinical implications that can be useful in treatment. The implicit theory model also provides a solid foundational piece and provides a "fertile theoretical framework for an area of clinical work that has often appeared to be atheoretical" (Polaschek & Ward, 2002, p. 399).

Women are unknowable—This theory proposes that due to the natural difference between the ways that men and women think, it is impossible to really understand how a woman's mind works. In essence, the theory indicates that women are deceptive and that they are unpredictable. The theory further suggests that it is fruitless to try and understand women and so there is no reason to attempt it. As a result of the way that women think they will always seek to mislead men. Example: *"Many times a woman will pretend she doesn't want to have intercourse because she doesn't want to seem loose, but she's really hoping that a man will force her"* (p. 395).

Women as sex objects—This theory is self-explanatory. The main reason that women exist is to be sexual objects for men. Women should always be ready and willing to have sexual relations any time that the man is ready. This theory also suggests that the way that a woman behaves also means that she wants to have sexual relations. If she is nice it's really because she wants to have sex; the way that she dresses says that she wants to have sex. Men with this view will always be able to find a reason that women wants to have sex with him. Another aspect of this theory purports that a woman's "no" and her body language may actually be in conflict. Under this distorted view, women are sexual objects and therefore can't be injured unless from too much physical force. Women are essentially the gatekeepers to men's sexual gratification. Example: *"Rape of a woman by a man she knows can be defined as a 'woman who changed her mind afterwards'"* (p. 396).

Male sex drive is uncontrollable—The sexual energy that men derive from being male can be overwhelming and being denied access to a sexual outlet (women) can be dangerous. Women who deny this access bring it upon themselves when men lose control. Men ascribing to this implicit theory view women as being solely responsible for preventing rape. Example: *"In most cases when a woman is raped, she was asking for it"* (p. 397).

Entitlement—Women should always be on standby to meet the needs of men. This theory postulates that once a woman has allowed a man to do something nice for her then she has agreed for him to have sex with her regardless if she wants to or not. Men are superior to women and women are sexually clueless, and therefore men are in control of women's sexuality. Men are entitled to shape a woman's sexual and non-sexual behavior. Rape is not seen as wrong, but as punishment for bad behavior. Example: *"Being a whore, or acting too good for a man, justifies rape"* (p. 398).

Dangerous world—Sex offenders and non-offenders can have this foundational view that the world is not a kind but a hostile, indifferent place that is full of pitfalls. Another belief is that people are out to deceive and harm. When this theory is applied to rape, it assumes that if the rapist didn't perform the crime, the victim might have raped the offender instead. This theory often works in conjunction with the entitlement theory in order to justify the rapist's aggressiveness and harm to other people. Example: *"She would have done the same to me, if I hadn't gotten to her first"* (p. 398).

CHILD MOLESTATION TYPOLOGIES AND TAXONOMIES

Typologies (analyses or classifications of groups with similar features) and taxonomies (scientific classifications) are used to define characteristics of sexual offending in a manner useful to those in the criminal justice, human service, and mental health professions, as well as those in academia and in research settings. Other reference groups for child victim assault are not listed as a particular typology or taxonomy category, but are used to identify specific sexual misconduct. There are many excellent assessment categories. To provide some reference for the reader, several of these profiles have been included for review.

Groth's Patterns of Pedophilic Behavior

Groth (1990) has reported that child molestation is a form of sexual activity in which the offender will hug, kiss, fondle, masturbate, suck, and touch the child victim in some inappropriate manner. Penetration does not occur. Developmentally such individuals are, in many cases, at the same sexual maturation level as the child victim. Pedophilia is a disorder that can be found in both child molesters and rapists.

One of the first classifications of child molesters was developed by Groth (1978). Two groups were identified, the fixated offender and the regressed offender.

Fixated Offender

This offender is sexually attracted to children exclusively. The onset usually begins in adolescence and involves a compulsive type of mood. The offending is premeditated. Males are usually the primary target for such victimization; however, female victims are also targeted. The emphasis for this type of offender is on sexually stimulating the child and eliciting an erotic response. Such individuals are developmentally immature.

Regressed Offender

This offender has a sexual orientation that is primarily toward adults, with a sexual attraction to children during a temporary lapse. This type of offender has pedophilic interests that have emerged during adulthood. A precipitating stress is usually a contributing factor to the offense. Sexual incidents may be episodic, with the first offense as an impulsive reaction without premeditation. This offender sexually acts out to replace a conflicting adult peer—the child is used as a temporary substitution. The emphasis is on sexual interaction, with the child being elevated to adult status. Alcohol is often used during such incidents.

Lanning's Situational and Preferential Child Molester Typology

Lanning (2010), in an updated analysis combining past research, outlined a typology of child exploitation used primarily by law enforcement officers. This can also be helpful to other disciplines (Hazelwood, Dietz, & Warren, 1995; Knight & Prentky, 1990; Abel *et al.*, 1988; De Young, 1988; Lanning & Hazelwood, 1988; Abel *et al.*, 1987; American Psychiatric Association, 1987; Hartman, Burgess, & Lanning, 1984; Dietz, 1983; Groth, Hobson, & Gary, 1982; Groth, 1978).

Lanning (2010) has reported that two separate categories of child sex offenders exist: situational and preferential. It should also be noted that as part of Lanning's (2010) typology all sex offenders (not just child molesters) are placed along what he calls a "motivational continuum (Situational to Preferential) instead of into one or two discrete categories" (p. 32). Although primarily motivated by deviant needs and desires, the offender can also have motivations that are not sexual in nature. The offender can exhibit motives and behavior patterns that are identified with both situational and preferential, but along the continuum will display a stronger association with one of the two categories (Lanning, 2010).

Situational Child Molester

Such offenders may experience one or more sexual encounters with a child or develop an extended relationship. Usually, only a limited number of victims are reported. Other victims may include the elderly, sick, or disabled. These offenders may be experiencing a particular psychosocial event that promotes their sexual aggression. The situational type of offender doesn't have a preference for children, but will molest them for a variety of reasons. The more often that the situational child molester molests a child the further he moves along the continuum (Lanning, 2010).

There are three subgroups in this category: regressed offenders, morally indiscriminate offenders, and inadequate offenders.

Regressed offender—This type of offender has poor coping skills, low self-esteem, and will often turn to children due to his inadequacy and inability to have an appropriate relationship with an adult partner. The regressed offender will display sexual misconduct when under such stress as marital or job conflict. Others will offend after a drinking or drug-use episode. Victim availability is important. Incest is often found. Such offenders may or may not use child pornography, but if they do it is generally homemade videos of the child that is being harmed.

Morally indiscriminate offender—These offenders abuse as a lifestyle pattern. Sexual abuse is an enactment of their global view of life. Often a personality disorder is found, especially anti-social personality disorder. This offender's criteria for victimization include vulnerability and opportunity. Due to the high degree of impulsivity and blatant disregard for other people, the morally indiscriminate offender is at a high risk of molesting teenagers. It is common for such offenders to lie, cheat, and manipulate others. Few will demonstrate victim empathy or remorse for their actions. Spouse abuse is sometimes found. They can be involved in nonsexual criminal activity, molest without motivation, use force, and may lure victims with gifts. Violent and nonviolent methods to obtain a victim are used. Most often the victims are strangers or acquaintances, but incestuous relationships are also reported. Pornography and adult magazines can be found. Offenses are impulsive and reckless.

Inadequate offender—Offenders may include those with a mental illness, a mental retardation, an eccentric personality disorder, or some form of dementia. Other features include depression, self-isolating behaviors, impaired social skills, and poor personal hygiene. Victims may be either acquaintances or strangers. Such offenders tend to have multiple victims. Victim availability is important. Parks, playgrounds, and schools are areas used by such offenders to find and later assault children.

Sexual involvement with children for these types of offenders appears to be out of curiosity or insecurity. Children are seen as sexual objects for the offender to satisfy whatever sexual curiosities or interests they may have; however the elderly may also be at risk. Most often the inadequate offender will target the very young or the very old due to perceived vulnerability. If these offenders possess pornography it is generally of adults. Due to their poor interpersonal skills, inadequate offender types are clumsy at grooming/seducing their child victims. Such individuals can appear childlike, harmless, or gentle in interaction. Some will live at home with elderly parents and are viewed by the community as social outcasts. Most are involved only in child molestation, but some have been involved in the death of a child.

Lanning (2010) has reported that almost any child molester is capable of violence or even murder; however, the FBI has found that those situational molesters most likely to be involved in the death of a child are either morally indiscriminate or inadequate offenders.

Preferential Child Molester

The preferential child molester possesses many features found in pedophiles. Such persons report sexual fantasies, urges, and erotic imagery involving child victims. Many have a large number of victims. The majority of child victims harmed by this offender group is boys. Lanning (2010) discusses that there are four subgroups: seduction offenders, introverted offenders, sadistic offenders, and diverse offenders.

Seduction offender—This offender seduces children both emotionally and physically. Such offenders will engage in the grooming of victims. They will court a child in a romantic manner. Attention, affection, and gifts are used to lower the child's guard. The offender's ability to seduce children lies in his or her ability to identify with them. The offender will talk with the potential victim and, more importantly, listen to them since victims are often from single-parent or dysfunctional home environments.

Seduction offenders select children who are emotionally or physically neglected. Such offenders may engage in a number of concurrent relationships. Threats of harm or physical violence to the victim may be used to protect the identity of the offender.

Introverted offender—Such offenders experience problems maintaining a relationship with an adult partner. Some may display courtship and intimacy deficits or general social skills problems. Victims will include prepubescent children or strangers. The introverted offender will frequent places that children are commonly known to visit. Exhibitionist behaviors and obscene telephone calls may be used by these offenders. Other paraphiliac behaviors may be found. Some offenders will develop a superficial relationship with a woman who has children in order to abuse them. Some will use child prostitutes; some will use the Internet to communicate with children across the world. Erotic imagery, fantasy of children, and masturbation with child pornography is usually found. It is not unheard of for this type of offender to marry and have children for the purpose of molesting them, beginning in their infancy.

Sadistic offender—Sadistic paraphiliac disturbances and personality disorders are found in such offenders. Such perpetrators will use force to obtain access to a potential victim. Others will use lures such as gifts. Sexual arousal is based on the physical and psychological pain of a victim. These individuals lack victim empathy or remorse for their actions. Victims are viewed as objects for their sexual gratification and need. Behavioral traits include depersonalization. The sadistic child offender is the most likely of this subgroup to kill a child. This sex offender is considered to be rare.

Diverse offender—This type of offender was formerly classified as the *sexually indiscriminate offender* and placed under the situational child molester category. Diverse offenders are sexual experimenters. Many will possess a paraphiliac disturbance or characteristics of a sexual addiction. These individuals are constantly in search of a new sexual experience and can be involved in affairs or spouse swapping.

This type of offender may use the Internet to chat with a woman who has children. The offender will then encourage the mother to engage in sexual activity with her children and ask that he be able to watch it online or send him the photos (Lanning, 2010).

Others will have contact with prostitutes. Outside of prostitution they tend to be law-abiding. Many are of a higher socioeconomic background. Most will collect pornography. Child sexual abuse occurs during the search for new experiences. Multiple victims can sometimes be found (Lanning, 2010).

SUMMARY

Underreporting is the biggest concern when looking at reported rape statistics. Although rape is primarily violence against women, the number of men who have reported rape should not be overlooked. The new definition of rape introduced by the federal government in January 2012 will more than likely net additional numbers over the next few years for both genders, which should give a new statistical look at how pervasively rape affects the nation.

Studies seem to indicate that men who view more extreme pornography are at a greater risk of accepting the behaviors associated with raping, committing sexual assaults, and agreeing with rape myths, and are less willing to intervene if they view any form of sexual assault happening before them. However, it should also be noted that not all men who view pornography will graduate to behaviors associated with rape. Although no definitive research will ever be able to answer the correlation between the two behaviors, it does stand to reason that people who view pornography on a regular basis may embrace more rape myths, although they may never engage in behaviors associated with sexual assault.

Another issue associated with rape is whether the behavior is a criminal behavior, clinical disturbance, or both. The American Psychiatric Association has defined a category of paraphiliac coercive disorder in order to address this hotly contested issue. Task forces have been put together many times, but to no avail. Rape as criminal behavior, clinical disturbance, or both continues to be a controversial topic that currently does not have a solution.

Lastly, the mental health or criminal justice system should not put all of their proverbial eggs in one basket with any typology. There will always be people who don't fit into a specific category, but it doesn't mean that the typologies should be dismissed completely. The typologies can be useful as an aid, but should never be used exclusively to diagnosis or convict a person.

CHAPTER NINE

An Old Enemy in a New Outfit: How Date Rape Became Gray Rape and Why It Matters

By Lisa Jervis

I t's very, very tempting to call gray rape a myth. As much as I want to (would that make it go away?), I can't. Because it's not a myth. No, no, my friends, gray rape—a term popularized by retro slut-shamer extraordinaire Laura Sessions Stepp, in September 2007's *Cosmopolitan* article "A New Kind of Date Rape," as "sex that falls somewhere between consent and denial" due to "casual hookups, missed signals, and alcohol"—is more like what one of the math teachers in my high school used to call an old friend in a new hat. More accurately, in this case it's an old enemy in a new short skirt. But hey, he was talking about a calculus variable and I'm talking about a disgusting, destructive, victim-blaming cultural construct that encourages women to hate ourselves, doubt ourselves, blame ourselves, take responsibility for other people's criminal behavior, fear our own desires, and distrust our own instincts.[1]

I'd love to dismiss this as the reactionary claptrap it is, but in the wake of Stepp's article and her casual-sex-will-damage-you-emotionally book *Unhooked: How Young Women Pursue Sex, Delay Love, and Fail at Both,* the concept has attracted the attention of criminal justice scholars, prosecutors, and sexual assault experts; news outlets from *The New York Times* to *Slate* to PBS's *To the Contrary;* college journalists; and countless bloggers, feminist and otherwise. And don't forget the other books that couch their disdain for sexual women in faux-concerned terms and urge us all to stifle our nasty urges in order to better society and/or preserve our chances of finding the love of a good man: Wendy Shalit's recent *Girls Gone Mild* (and its predecessor, the 1999 call to high collars *A Return to Modesty*), Dawn Eden's 2006 *The Thrill of the Chaste,* and Miriam Grossman's *Unprotected* in 2007. When mixed with the still-far-too-influential sentiments articulated by rape apologists like Camille "Woman's flirtatious arts of self-concealment mean man's approach must take the form of rape" Paglia and Katie "If 25 percent of my women friends were really being raped, wouldn't I know it?" Roiphe, it's a potent cocktail indeed.

Cosmo's sensationalistic headline declaration notwithstanding, everything about so-called gray rape seems awfully familiar: The experience is confusing, makes victims feel guilty and ashamed, and leaves them thinking they could and should have done something differently to prevent the attack. One of *Cosmo's* sources, Alicia, says she "ha[d] this dirty feeling of not knowing what to do or who to tell or whether it was my fault .... Maybe I wasn't forceful enough in saying I didn't want it." Women also don't want to name their experience as rape because of the stigma of victimhood and the fear of not being believed: "While it felt like rape to her," writes Stepp of Alicia, "she was not sure if that's what anyone else would call it .... Even today, she is reluctant to call it rape because she thinks of herself as a strong and sexually independent woman, not a victim."

Having some déjà vu? That's because any therapist, sexual assault counselor, rape survivor, or close friend or family member of a rape survivor knows that feelings of guilt, shame, self-blame, and denial are common almost to the point of inevitability, no matter what the circumstances of the crime. People raped by strangers are going to torture themselves with thoughts of why they didn't know better and take a "safer" route home; people raped by dates, so-called friends, or the hot guy at the other end of the bar are going to torture themselves with thoughts of how they might have brought it on themselves by flirting, kissing, having that one last cocktail, fill in the blank with any detail a mind can seize upon in the wake of trauma. Rape survivors tend to echo one another in their comments, things like "I thought it was my fault. I felt humiliated and ashamed," and "I was too ashamed and confused to tell anyone what had happened. I tried to forget about it."[2]

Survivors of any attack that doesn't fit the most extreme stranger-in-the-bushes-with-a-knife paradigm are very often reluctant to name their experience as rape. When the culture teaches you that lack of consent is measured only in active, physical resistance, when *your* actions are questioned if your date refuses to respect "no," you're going to have a hard time calling rape by its real name. This is one of the reasons why feminists had to (and continue to) battle so hard for date rape to be taken seriously in the first place, and the reason why the title of the first major book examining the phenomenon, published in 1988, is *I Never Called It Rape*. It's a vicious cycle: Stigma and fear fuel guilt, shame, and denial, which our culture uses to shore up stigmas and fear. You can see the cycle at work in Alicia's experience above, in her desire to preserve her self-image as strong and sexually independent, as if someone else's actions were the key to those qualities in herself. You can see it in the way she worries that others might not agree that she was raped—and how she depends on their opinions to shape her own knowledge. You can see it in what Jezebel blogger Moe writes about her own assault, twisting herself like a verbal and emotional gymnast to cast her experience—with a "smarmy hair-product using type from [her] ex-boyfriend's frat" who, after being told repeatedly that she didn't want to have sex, waited until she slipped into a beery sleep before "sticking it in"—not as rape but as "one drunken regrettable night" and noting with something like approval that "*Cosmo* has come up with a new name for this kind of nonviolent collegiate date-rape sort of happening."

This is how the language of "gray rape" accelerates the victim-blaming cycle. The very concept the phrase relies on—that a supposed gray area of communication or intoxication means that you cannot trust your own memories, instincts, or experiences—is designed to exploit the stigma and fear that fuel the guilt, shame, and denial. But make no mistake—it is not a new concept, it's simply a new tactic. Gray rape and date rape are the same thing: a sexual assault in which the victim knows the attacker and may have consented to some kind of sexual activity with hir. Survivors of such attacks have always been reluctant to name their experience "rape." Despite gray rape proponents' eagerness to use this phenomenon to shift responsibility from rapists to victims, the fact remains that the reluctance in question is a symptom of the very social disease—sexism, misogyny, men's entitlement to women's bodies, and the idea that sexual interaction involves women's guarding the gates to the land of the sexy goodies as men try to cajole, manipulate, and force their way in—that enables rape in the first place.

And that social disease is evolving as fast as we can keep up. Weakness is no longer the prized quality of womanhood it once was, and despite the long, hard efforts of survivors and advocates to make clear that being a victim of rape says nothing about you and everything about your attacker (as Melissa McEwan of the blog Shakespeare's Sister puts it, "To be a survivor of rape does not have to mean shame and brokenness and guilt … it is brave, not weak, to say, plainly: 'I was raped'"), too many people still equate victimhood with frailty. Plus, though sexual expression for women has become destigmatized in some ways, culturally praised and accepted sexual expression (think *Girls Gone Wild*, pole-dancing classes, porn chic, and the Pussycat Dolls) tends to be more about display for a (presumably male) audience than about any kind of subjective pleasure. Women are now encouraged to look sexy for other people, but not to be sexual for ourselves. These messages about sexuality as culturally overdetermined sexiness have intensified over the last decade or so, keeping pace with supposed cultural acceptance of women's sexual activity in general—but they make it harder than ever for women to center our own authentic sexuality. When you're steeped in messages about looking hot at the expense of (or as a substitute for) feeling aroused or having sexual desire, it becomes all the easier for you to question your own judgment about what happened to you and believe the cultural forces telling you that your assault was just miscommunication and bad sex.

In the end, it's not all that surprising that someone would come up with an idea like "gray rape." Date rape and the cultural phenomena connected to it are something feminist anti-violence activists have been fighting to respond to and eradicate since there have been feminist anti-violence activists; anti-feminists, rape apologists, and proponents of a return to the days when women were roundly punished for doing anything but pinching a penny between their ankles have been trying to discredit our side all along the way. Over the two decades since the idea of date rape entered the public imagination, we've been pretty successful in getting cultural and institutional recognition that it's, um, wrong. Not that we've solved the problem or anything (if we had, this essay—and much of this book—wouldn't need to be written). But we've changed some cultural attitudes and taught many young people of all genders that consenting to some sexual activity with a person, or having consented to sex with a person in the past, doesn't mean you've consented to anything and everything with that person, or that you automatically consent to fuck that person again, and that a quiet "no," even if it's not accompanied by a knee to the groin or any other physical struggle, is still a valid "no." In other words, we've been at least moderately successful in demonstrating that date rape is, in fact, rape.

But backlash is a devious little douchebag, and there are still people who think that women are ruining everything with our slutty, sexually aggressive, entitled-to-our-own-pleasure (gasp!) attitude; these folks are always in need of ammunition, both legal and conceptual. The fact that feminism's battles are unfinished means that it's all too easy to enlist flat-out lies—that consent to kissing means consent to more, or that one person's drunkenness excuses another person's criminal acts—in service of beating back new sexual mores, ones with the potential to free women from being punished just for wanting the full human experience of sexuality and sexual exploration. So they've gone and rebranded their old friend, dressing her in a new outfit in the hope of keeping women feeling good 'n' guilty about our sexuality and our desires, scared to stand up for ourselves and demand accountability for violence against us, scared to insist on acceptance of our sexuality on equal terms with men's. *Cosmo* shows its ass quite clearly here, making obvious an investment in threats of violence to keep women in line: "So how do you avoid being a victim without giving up the right to be sexually independent and assertive? Many psychologists feel that the first step is to acknowledge the dangers inherent in the free-and-easy hookup approach to dating and sex. 'We all have vulnerabilities, and we all can be taken advantage of,' says [psychotherapist Robi] Ludwig. 'Though you're successful at school, sports, whatever, *you must see yourself—as a woman—as vulnerable"* (emphasis added). In the context of the article, this is not an encouragement of commonsense caution; it's an attempt to enlist women in the project of our own subjugation. The message is clear: Your sexual desire is dangerous. You can stifle it or you can be a slut who lives in fear and gets what she deserves. These are the only two choices in the world of gray rape.

The cherry on top of this backlash sundae is that to the Laura Sessions Stepp/Wendy Shalit modesty-or-bust crowd, feminism is to blame for gray rape because feminism has promoted women's sexual freedom and power—and if women weren't feeling all empowered and happy about their sexuality, they wouldn't go hitting on guys, making out with them, or having consensual hookups. But here's the thing: Flirting and hookups do not cause rape. Rapists and the culture that creates them—with its mixed messages and double standards—cause rape. Feminism is working to dismantle that culture, but we've been only partly successful so far. Blaming feminism for the damage remaining when we've made insufficient change is just like exploiting a rape survivor's totally normal feelings of confusion and shame, far from a new strategy. Feminism has been blamed by right-wing commentators for everything from drinking among teen girls (because we've encouraged them to do anything boys can) to women's postdivorce poverty (because we've convinced women they can get along just fine without a man), when really those things have just as much to do with sexism as with anything else (in these cases, the need to relieve gendered social pressure toward perfectionism and a little thing called the wage gap, respectively). I'll happily admit that feminism has helped pave the way for more sexual autonomy (not, it's well worth noting, just for women but for people of both genders). The progress we've made toward integrating the virgin/whore split—that now women can want sex and still be good people (as long as their desire is bounded by love and commitment)—was driven by feminism. But the fucked-up attitude our culture has about consent, illustrated by the fact that too many people still think that "no" can be part of a coy seduction strategy, has nothing to do with feminism, except that it's still our goal to change it. The attitude itself is clearly the fault of our old friend misogyny, and we must continue to be vigilant about keeping the blame for sexual assault squarely where it belongs.

If you want to read more about Is Consent Complicated?, try:

- Beyond Yes or No: Consent as Sexual Process by **Rachel Kramer Bussel**
- Reclaiming Touch: Rape Culture, Explicit Verbal Consent, and Body
- Sovereignty by **Hazel/Cedar Troost**
- An Immodest Proposal by **Heather Corinna**

If you want to read more about Media Matters, try:

- Offensive Feminism: The Conservative Gender Norms That Perpetuate Rape Culture, and How Feminists Can Fight Back by **Jill Filipovic**
- The Fantasy of Acceptable "Non-Consent": Why the Female Sexual Submissive Scares Us (and Why She Shouldn't) by **Stacey May Fowles**
- In Defense of Going Wild or: How I Stopped Worrying and Learned to Love Pleasure (and How You Can, Too) by **Jaclyn Friedman**

CHAPTER TEN

Offensive Feminism: The Conservative Gender Norms that Perpetuate Rape Culture, and How Feminists Can Fight Back

By Jill Filipovic

"Rape, ladies and gentlemen, is not today what rape was. Rape, when I was learning these things, was the violation of a chaste woman, against her will, by some party not her spouse. Today it's simply, 'Let's don't go forward with this act.'"
—Tennessee State Senator Doug Henry, February 2008

Senator Henry is right: Rape today is not what it once was. Raping your wife is now a criminal offense. A rape survivor's sexual history cannot be used to discredit her in court. Acquaintance rape (or date rape) has gained greater visibility, and the stranger-in-the-bushes model of sexual assault is no longer the only one we recognize. And feminist activism around sexual assault has been phenomenally successful—rape crisis centers have been built, laws have been changed, and men's assumption of power over women has been challenged. As a result, sexual assault rates have steadily decreased, and survivors have greater resources.

But there remain creeping challenges even to the modest gains that anti-rape activists have achieved. The most effective—and perhaps the least visible, at least where rape is concerned—is the right-wing offensive on female autonomy. While religious conservatives are obvious foot soldiers in the War on Sex and in the anti-abortion and anti-contraception movements, their role in maintaining and even promoting rape culture is too often overlooked. In truth, the organized religious right—which, to be clear, is not the same thing as individual religious or conservative Americans—is waging a culture war that is about much more than which god you pray to or whether you value fetal life over reproductive choice. It is a war over the most basic of values: the human rights to bodily autonomy and self-determination, the role of women in society, and the construction of the family. And while abortion and same-sex marriage are the hot-button political issues, rape is smack dab in the middle of the battle. The conservative status quo is most threatened not just by traditional anti-rape laws, but by putting the onus on men *not* to rape, and by a feminist model of enthusiastic consent, in which women are viewed as autonomous actors empowered to request *or* decline sex—a model where "no" is respected and "yes" is an equally valid response.

THE GOOD OLD DAYS

> *"We have forgotten that before we began calling this date rape and date fraud, we called it exciting."*
> —Warren Farrell, men's rights activist and
> author of *The Myth of Male Power*

Under old English and American law, "Husband and wife are one, and that one is the husband."[1] Coverture laws required that a woman's legal rights were merged with her husband's; even long after those regulations were obsolete, women still lacked equal rights in marriage, as they were required to be sexually available to their husbands—with no laws against marital rape, husbands could demand (or force) sex with no legal repercussions. A woman's place as a personal servant for her husband in exchange for financial Feminism security was enshrined into law. According to family historian Stephanie Coontz:

> *"Even after coverture had lost its legal force, courts, legislators, and the public still cleaved to the belief that marriage required husbands and wives to play totally different domestic roles. In 1958, the New York Court of Appeals rejected a challenge to the traditional legal view that wives (unlike husbands) couldn't sue for loss of the personal services, including housekeeping and the sexual attentions, of their spouses. The judges reasoned that only wives were expected to provide such personal services anyway.*
>
> *As late as the 1970s, many American states retained 'head and master' laws, giving the husband final say over where the family lived and other household decisions. According to the legal definition of marriage, the man was required to support the family, while the woman was obligated to keep house, nurture children, and provide sex. Not until the 1980s did most states criminalize marital rape. Prevailing opinion held that when a bride said, 'I do,' she was legally committed to say, 'I will' for the rest of her married life."[2]*

These ideas are not nearly obsolete. In practice, many American couples have fairly egalitarian, progressive marriages—including conservative and religious couples. But a small yet incredibly powerful minority of conservative extremists is unhappy with the shift toward gender equality and the idea that a woman maintains her bodily integrity even after there's a ring on her finger. Arguments for "traditional marriage" still rely on opposite-sex partners and an assumption of complementary roles—and those "complementary" roles assume that the man is in charge and the woman complements him. Regressive gender roles (and the need for complementary relationships) are among the most common arguments against marriage equality.[3] And old ideas about the requirement of female sexual availability are far from dead. Anti-feminist activist Phyllis Schlafly—who has made a highly lucrative career out of telling other women to stay home—told students at Bates College, "By getting married, the woman has consented to sex, and I don't think you can call it rape."[4]

This ideology isn't limited to a few wacky conservatives, either; we teach it in public schools. According to a report by U.S. Representative Harry Waxman that evaluated the most widely used abstinence-only curricula, girls are regularly described as dependent and submissive, and are even discussed as objects to be purchased or otherwise attained:

> *In a discussion of wedding traditions, one curriculum writes: "Tell the class that the Bride price is actually an honor to the bride. It says she is valuable to the groom and he is willing to give something valuable for her."*[5]

> *And religious events like Purity Balls involve daughters pledging their virginity to their fathers until their wedding day, when 'I give myself as a wedding gift to my husband.' The father pledges, 'I, [daughter's name]'s father, choose before God to cover my daughter as her authority and protection in the area of purity.'*[6] *This hymenal exchange is represented by a 'promise ring' that a father gives his daughter, which she wears until it is replaced by a wedding ring. The religious, abstinence-promoting groups that organize Purity Balls are bankrolled by the federal government—the Bush administration funds abstinence initiatives to the tune of $200 million a year."*[7]

Central to the right-wing family ideal is the position of women as servants and helpmeets, not autonomous actors or individuals in their own right. The very concept of individualism is a threat. Opposition to individualism and female bodily autonomy are crucial components to the so-called "pro-family" movement—even as most American families embrace the very values and achievements that conservative groups seek to dismantle.

THE FEMALE PROBLEM

The biggest threat to the conservative traditional ideal? Women. Time and again, when women have the ability to plan their families, they do. When women have the right to open their own checking accounts, to make their own money, to go to school, to have sex without fearing pregnancy, to own property, to have children when they want, to marry whom they want, *they do*. When you extend human rights to women, they act like human beings with individual needs, ambitions, and desires—just like men.

A lot of women also have sex "like men"—that is, for pleasure. Ninety-seven percent of Americans will have sex before marriage, and 95 percent of American women will use contraception at some point in their lives. The average American woman spends about three decades trying to prevent pregnancy. Clearly, women like sex—and they like it on their own terms and for recreation, not just for baby making.

And therein lies the problem. Sex, in the conservative mindset, is essentially a bartering tool and a means to an end: A woman maintains her virginity until it can be exchanged for a wedding ring. After that, the family economy is simple: Women give sex, housework, and reproduction in exchange for financial security and social status, and sex is purely for reproductive purposes. The idea that women might want to have sex for pleasure without having to carry a pregnancy for nine months afterward and then raise a child is quite contrary to conservative values. So is the idea that a woman might have the right to say no to sex within marriage. Bodily autonomy doesn't figure into the scheme because, as the conservative group Focus on the Family says on its website, "It's Not My Body."

While right-wing groups certainly don't come out in *support* of rape, they do promote an extremist ideology that *enables* rape and promotes a culture where sexual assault is tacitly accepted. The supposedly "pro-family" marital structure, in which sex is exchanged for support and the woman's identity is absorbed into her husband's, reinforces the idea of women as property and as simple accoutrements to a man's more fully realized existence. And the traditional gender roles so exalted by conservative groups—roles that envision women as passive receptacles and men as aggressive deviants—further excuse and endorse sexual assault.

MANLY MEN AND PASSIVE WOMEN

"To resist rape a woman needs more than martial arts and more than the police; she needs a certain ladylike modesty enabling her to take offense at unwanted encroachment."

—Harvard Professor Harvey Mansfield,
author of the book *Manliness*

At the heart of the sexual assault issue is how mainstream American culture constructs sex and sexualities along gendered lines. Female sexuality is portrayed as passive, while male sexuality is aggressive. Sex itself is constructed around both the penis and male pleasure— male/female intercourse begins when a man penetrates a woman's vagina with his penis, and ends when he ejaculates. Penetration is the key element of sex, with the man imaged as the "active" partner and the woman as the passive, receptive partner. And sex is further painted as something that men *do to* women, instead of as a mutual act between two equally powerful actors.

But the myth of passivity is not the only cultural narrative about female sexuality. Women are simultaneously thought of as living in inherently tempting bodies, and using those bodies to cause men to fall.[8] These two myths—the passive woman and the tempting woman—have been used to justify the social control of half the population for centuries. The biblical fall was caused by a woman, and her punishment was painful female sexuality and suffering in reproduction.[9] We have hardly seen reprieve since. In Western societies, women have been cloistered away, been deemed alternately "frigid" or "hysterical,"[10] undergone clitoridectomies as girls to "cure" chronic masturbation,[11] been barred from accessing contraception and even information about pregnancy prevention,[12] been the legal property of men, been forcibly and nonconsensually sterilized,[13] and been legally forced to continue pregnancies they did not want.[14] The ideas of the female body (and, specifically, female sexual organs and reproductive capacity) as public property and as open to state control persist today, as abortion and contraception remain hot-button issues and the anti-choice right promotes policies that would give a fetus rights that no born person even has.[15] The message is simple: Women are "naturally" passive until you give them a little bit of power—then all hell breaks loose and they have to be reined in by any means necessary. Rape and other assaults on women's bodies—and particularly infringements and attacks on women's reproductive organs—serve as unique punishments for women who step out of line.

Male sexuality, and maleness in general, are socially enforced by requiring men to be Not Women. Men who transgress and exhibit characteristics that are traditionally associated with femaleness—passivity, gentleness, willingness to be sexually penetrated—have their masculinity questioned. The most obvious example is gay men, who are routinely characterized as "effeminate" for transgressing the boundaries of gender and of the act of sex itself.

Aggression is such a deeply entrenched characteristic of maleness that it is often justified through references to nature and evolutionary biology. It further bleeds over into the sexual sphere, wherein men are expected to be aggressive sexual actors attempting to "get" sex from passive women who both hold and embody sex itself.

In the ongoing effort to paint men and women as opposites, men take on the role of sexual aggressor and women are expected to be sexually evasive. While virginity until marriage is practiced by very few women, deeply held standards of female virtuousness remain, and women are rarely taught how to say yes to sex, or how to act out their own desires. Rather, we are told that the rules of sexual engagement involve men pushing and women putting on the brakes.

While this clearly compromises women's sexual subjectivity, it also handicaps men and prevents them from connecting with their own desires. Men are as well versed in the sexual dance as women are, and when they are fully aware that women are expected to say no even when they mean yes, men are less likely to hear "no" and accept it at face value. When society equates maleness with a constant desire for sex, men are socialized out of genuine sexual decision making, and are less likely to be able to know how to say no or to be comfortable refusing sex when they don't want it. And the "boys will be boys" sexual stereotype makes it much easier for date rapists to victimize women and simply argue that they didn't *know* they were raping someone—sure, she said no, but it's awfully easy for men to convince other men (and lots of women) that "no" is just part of the game.

THE FEMINIST CHALLENGE

Feminism and anti-rape activism challenge the dominant narrative that women's bodies aren't our own, they insist that sex is about consent and enjoyment, not violence and harm, and they attack a power structure that sees women as victims and men as predators. Feminists insist that men are not animals. Instead, men are rational human beings fully capable of listening to their partners and understanding that sex isn't about pushing someone to do something they don't want to do. Plenty of men are able to grasp the idea that sex should be entered into joyfully and enthusiastically by both partners, and that an absence of "no" isn't enough—"yes" should be the baseline requirement. And women are not empty vessels to be fucked or not fucked; we're sexual actors who should absolutely have the ability to say yes when we want it, just like men, and should feel safe saying no—even if we've been drinking, even if we've slept with you before, even if we're wearing tight jeans, even if we're naked in bed with you. Anti-rape activists further understand that men need to feel empowered to say no also. If women have the ability to fully and freely say yes, and if we established a model of enthusiastic consent instead of just "no means no," it would be a lot harder for men to get away with rape. It would be a lot harder to argue that there's a "gray area." It would be a lot harder to push the idea that "date rape" is less serious than "real" rape, that women who are assaulted by acquaintances were probably teases, that what is now called "date rape" used to just be called "seduction."

But building that model requires us to dismantle traditional notions of female sexuality and femininity itself. Doing that poses a direct threat to male power, and the female subordination it relies on.

A CULTURE OF FEAR

So why *do* some conservative extremists—and even some regular folks—want to maintain a culture that enables and promotes rape? Quite simply, because women pose a threat to entrenched power structures, and the constant threat of rape keeps both men and women in line.

The social construction of rape suffers from a marked disconnect from the reality of rape. Sexual assault is routinely depicted along the stranger-rape storyline, despite the fact that 73 percent of sexual assaults are committed by someone the victim knows.[16] Further, rape victims are almost always depicted as female, despite the fact that one in thirty-three men will survive sexual assault.[17] Prison populations are especially at risk, and especially invisible—while statistics are hard to come by, conservative estimates suggest more than three-hundred thousand men are sexually assaulted behind bars every year.[18] Assaults on male inmates are seen as somehow not as wrong as the stranger-rape of women, perhaps because we have little sympathy for convicted criminals (a significant proportion of whom are not violent, thanks to punitive drug laws), or because men of color make up a disproportionate percentage of prison populations and the experiences of incarcerated brown and black men are generally deemed unimportant. Men, then—even men who are likely to be assaulted—are left out of the narrative of fear that women live. The one aspect of the rape narrative that actually reflects reality is the fact that 99 percent of rapes are perpetrated by men.[19]

Unlike other forms of assault or even murder, rape is both a crime and a tool of social control. The stranger-rape narrative is crucial in using the threat of sexual assault to keep women afraid, and to punish women who step out of the traditionally female private sphere and into the traditionally male-dominated public one. Portraying rape as something that happens outside of a woman's home enforces the idea that women are safe in the domestic realm, and at risk if they go out.

There exists a long history of conflating female exodus from the home with female sexual availability—for quite a long time, the "public woman" was a prostitute. The defining feature of the "common woman" sex worker was "not the exchange of money, not even multiple sexual partners, but the public and indiscriminate availability of a woman's body."[20] Public and outspoken women today are still routinely called "whores" as a way of discrediting them. Street harassment remains a widespread method of reminding women that they have less of a right to move through public space than men do. And rape serves as the ultimate punishment for women who move through public space without patriarchal covering.

While the threat of rape has hardly kept women indoors, it does keep women fearful. If a woman is raped by a stranger, her decisions are immediately called into question—why was she walking alone, why was she in that neighborhood, why did she drink so much? If she is raped by someone she knows, her actions are similarly evaluated, and the question of whether it was "really" rape is inevitably raised—why did she go out with him if she didn't want sex, why did she invite him up to her room, why did she go to a frat party, why did she drink wine at dinner, why did she consent to some sexual activity if she didn't want to consent to all of it?

Men are 150 percent more likely to be the victims of violent crimes than women are.[21] Men are more likely to be both victims and perpetrators of crimes. Men are more likely to be assaulted, injured, or killed when alcohol is involved. Men are more likely to be victimized by a stranger (63 percent of violent victimizations), whereas women are more likely to be victimized by someone they know (62 percent of violent victimizations). Women are more likely to be victimized in their home or in the home of someone they know, whereas men are more likely to be victimized in public.[22]

And yet it is women who are treated to "suggestions" about how to protect themselves from public stranger assaults: go out with a friend, don't drink too much, don't walk home alone, take a self-defense class. Well-meaning as they may be, such suggestions send the false message that women can prevent rape. Certainly, on an individual basis, self-defense and other trainings do help women to protect themselves. But while these trainings are invaluable for the women they assist, they place all of the responsibility on the individual women who use them—in other words, they are not the answer to dismantling rape culture.

The focus on the victim's behavior, rather than the perpetrator's, sends the message that a woman must be eternally on guard, lest she bring sexual assault onto herself. This message adds to a broader view of women as vulnerable, keeping women fearful and justifying paternalistic and sexist laws and customs. As media critic Laura Kipnis writes:

> *"Given the vast number of male prison rapes and the declining number of female nonprison rapes, it seems as though the larger social story about sexual vulnerability is due to be altered. It is, after all, a story upon which a good chunk of gender identity hinges, including a large part of what it* feels *like to be a woman: endangered."*[23]

The "if only she had …" response to rape serves the valuable psychological purpose of allowing other women to temporarily escape that sense of endangerment. If we convince ourselves that we would never have done what she did, that her choices opened her up to assault and we would have behaved differently, then we can feel safe.

But it's a strategy that is bound to fail. The threat of rape holds women—all women—hostage. Obviously, women and men need to take common-sense measures to avoid all sorts of victimization, but the emphasis on rape as a pervasive and constant threat is crucial to maintaining female vulnerability and male power. That narrative, though, does more than just paralyze women—it privileges men. The benefits that stem from the simple ability to *not live in fear* are impossible to quantify. Certainly many, if not most, men have no desire to keep women afraid, but there are some whose goals necessitate a fearful and compliant female population. How else will they justify keeping women under their thumbs under the guise of "protection"?

Conservative "pro-family" activists envision a world in which men are in control, both in the public realm and at home. But the natural desire for freedom and autonomy exists in women, and has always been nearly impossible to smother with bribery (the carrot of the wedding and the family and the home) alone. The stick also has to come out, and that's where the pervasive threat of rape (or otherwise losing one's "virtue") comes into play. Certainly, the threat of rape as a tool of social control was not created by anti-feminist conservatives; that threat, however, is an important weapon in the culture war they are waging against equality.

A FEMINIST RESPONSE TO SEXUAL ASSAULT

An improved response to rape requires a broad-based approach, and involves challenging the entire right-wing agenda: the wars on sex, on women's bodies, on the poor, on people of color. Sexual assault simply cannot be removed from its broader context, and as long as powerful people continue to promote a worldview that requires women to be second-class citizens—and as long as that view is bolstered by policies that literally subjugate women's bodies and by social codes that render women passive and men aggressive—women will not be safe.

A second crucial prong of anti-rape activism must simply be teaching men not to rape. Ridiculous and simplistic as it may sound—after all, criminals will commit crimes, and would anyone consider lowering the murder rate by "teaching men not to murder"?—sexual assault is more caught up in gender stereotypes and intimate relationships than most other violent crimes are. The "teach men not to rape" method will admittedly be entirely unsuccessful in combating stranger rape. It will certainly not eradicate acquaintance rape or intimate-partner rape, either, but it very well might decrease it.

Teaching men not to rape involves addressing the disconnect between men who commit sexual assault and men who self-identify as rapists. It is both a social and an institutional process that requires accurately representing the reality of sexual assault (dismantling the stranger-rape and the women-should-be-fearful narratives), developing positive masculinities, and teaching boys (in sex education classes and through legal standards) that forcing a woman to have sex with you *is rape*. If we are to bridge the divide between how women experience rape and how some men define it—and how they define it as something apart from sexual activities that may be ordinary parts of manhood—we need to eliminate the idea that rape must involve extreme violence. Instead, we need to recognize that rape is unique because it takes a natural and usually pleasurable act and turns it into an act of violence. Context, as much as the act itself, matters.

We must also take broader steps toward gender equality. As feminism has seen greater and greater success, the sexual assault rate has decreased. Sexual assault is not only a crime of violence and power, but also one of entitlement. So long as men feel entitled to dominate and control women's bodies, sexual assault will continue. While issues like reproductive justice may initially seem unrelated to sexual assault, they are a crucial aspect of women's bodily autonomy and integrity—legally forcing a woman to carry a pregnancy for nine months and give birth against her will and without her consent, or coercing certain kinds of "unfit" women into not reproducing, are deeply troubling uses of women's bodies to serve the needs, ideologies, and desires of others. Allowing women a full range of reproductive freedoms affirms the fact that women's bodies are private property, and that their sexual and reproductive choices should not be forced or coerced.

We must work with women, too, but not in the traditional way of warning women away from moving through public space and engaging in normal social behaviors like drinking or going to bars and parties. Rather, we must emphasize a pleasure-affirming vision of female sexuality, wherein saying yes and no are equally valid moral decisions in many sexual contexts—and wherein women not only are answering the question, but also feel equally entitled to ask for and initiate sex when they want it and their partner agrees.

We need to situate sexual assault within the greater cultural battles over women's bodies, and recognize that anti-rape activism cannot be separated from action for reproductive freedom, anti-racism, LGBT rights, and broader gender equality; and that the opponents of those movements are the same people who have an interest in maintaining rape culture.

Eradicating rape may very well be impossible. But as long as we continue to view it as a crime committed by an individual against another individual, absent of any social context, we will have little success in combating it. Women must feel fully entitled to public engagement and consensual sex—and if conservative and anti-feminist men continue to argue that women's very public presence enables men to assault them, then perhaps they're the ones who should be pressured to stay home.

If you want to read more about Media Matters, try:

- A Woman's Worth by **Javacia N. Harris**
- How Do You Fuck a Fat Woman? by **Kate Harding**
- The Fantasy of Acceptable "Non-Consent": Why the Female Sexual Submissive Scares Us (and Why She Shouldn't) by **Stacey May Fowles**

If you want to read more about The Right Is Wrong, try:

- Toward a Performance Model of Sex by **Thomas Macaulay Millar**
- Purely Rape: The Myth of Sexual Purity and How It Reinforces Rape Culture by **Jessica Valenti**

CHAPTER ELEVEN

Introduction to Human Trafficking: Definitions and Prevalence

By Mary C. Burke

The purpose of this chapter is to introduce the reader to the complex issue of human trafficking. A definition is offered and trafficking in its various forms is explained. Characteristics of victims are described, and the right to work is provided as a context in which to understand the relationships between poverty, migration and trafficking in persons. The extent to which human trafficking occurs is discussed as well as some of the limitations related to relevant data. The process of trafficking people is reviewed and the chapter closes with an introduction to the issue as it exists in the United States.

CHAPTER LEARNING OBJECTIVES

- Be able to define human trafficking according to the Protocol to Prevent, Suppress and Punish Trafficking in Persons, Especially Women and Children of the United Nations Convention against Transnational Organized Crime and the US Trafficking Victims Protection Act of 2000 (TVPA).
- Understand the differences between human trafficking and other related phenomena such as immigration, emigration, and smuggling.
- Understand the underlying causes of human trafficking.
- Understand the ways in which human trafficking constitutes a violation of fundamental human rights.
- Understand the difference in viewing human trafficking as an issue of human rights, crime, migration, and labor.

Human trafficking has received increased attention over the past 10 to 15 years, both in political and public arenas. "Human trafficking" or "trafficking in persons" and "modern slavery" are terms often used interchangeably to refer to a variety of crimes associated with the economic exploitation of people. Human trafficking has been associated with transnational organized crime groups, small, more loosely organized criminal networks and local gangs, violations of labor and immigration laws, and government corruption (Richard, 1999; US Government Accountability Office, 2006; Vayrynen, 2003). At the international level, the United Nations Convention against Transnational Organized Crime, which was adopted by UN General Assembly resolution 55/25, is the primary legal instrument used to combat transnational organized crime.[1] The Convention is supplemented by three Protocols, each of which focuses on specific types of organized crime and are as follows: the Protocol to Prevent, Suppress and Punish Trafficking in Persons, Especially Women and Children; the Protocol against the Smuggling of Migrants by Land, Sea and Air; and the Protocol against the Illicit Manufacturing of and Trafficking in Firearms, their Parts and Components and Ammunition. Article 3 of the Protocol to Prevent, Suppress and Punish Trafficking in Persons, Especially Women and Children defines human trafficking as follows:

> Trafficking in persons shall mean the recruitment, transportation, transfer, harboring or receipt of persons, by means of the threat or force or other forms of coercion, of abduction, of fraud, of deception, of the abuse of power, or of a position of vulnerability or of the giving or receiving of payments or benefits to achieve the consent of a person having control over another person, for the purpose of exploitation. Exploitation shall include, at a minimum, the exploitation of the prostitution of others or other forms of sexual exploitation, forced labor or services, slavery or practices similar to slavery, servitude or the removal of organs.
>
> (Europol, 2005, p. 10)

The definition of trafficking noted above was intended to facilitate convergence in approaches to the issue by member states of the United Nations around the world. The hope was to enhance international cooperation in addressing trafficking in a manner that would support the end goal of the protocol: to end human trafficking as it exists today. While there have been disagreements about and variations on the definition of human trafficking among practitioners, scholars, activists and politicians (Laczko and Gramegna, 2003; Richard, 1999), this definition is commonly used and has indeed provided the foundation for a legal framework for dealing with the issue. For the purpose of this text the definition above will be used.

The definition comprises three essential parts: recruitment, movement, and exploitation, all of which point to critical aspects of the trafficking process. It is important to note that it is not necessary for "movement" to include crossing from one country into another; an individual can be trafficked within the borders of her or his own country or town and can even be trafficked from the home in which she or he lives, in which case movement is not even relevant. As an example of an in-country situation, it is not uncommon for a girl or woman to be trafficked from the rural areas of Costa Rica to the coastal regions where the commercial sex industry is thriving. Also critical to understanding human trafficking is understanding what is meant by coercion. The term "coercion" in this context specifically refers to (a) threats of harm to or physical restraint against any person; (b) any scheme intended to cause a person to believe that failure to perform an act will result in harm or physical restraint against any person; or (c) the abuse or threatened abuse of the legal process. However, it is essential to take other factors into consideration with regard to coercion, in particular when working with victims of sex trafficking and prostitution, such as whether the individual had any legitimate alternatives to support her basic needs (Hernandez, 2001) when approached by the pimp (trafficker). If not, then the thinking is that desperation to perform responsibilities such as support a child, and feed and keep one's self safe, can be a form of coercion.

Technically, people are trafficked into a slavery-like situation, however, that distinction is not often made in reference to these terms, meaning the terms human trafficking and slavery are sometimes used interchangeably. This leads to an incomplete and therefore inaccurate representation of human trafficking. Coercive and sometimes forcible exploitation of one human over another has occurred in a variety of forms throughout history, as you will learn more about in Chapter 2 of this text. The primary characteristics of this phenomenon have remained the same over time and include one person exercising fear and sometimes violence based control over another for economic gain. What is typically different in the twenty-first century is that it is far less expensive to purchase or otherwise secure a person today than previously. For example, costs as low as 10 US dollars have been reported in places like South East Asia, with the average cost for a person being 90 US dollars (Free the Slaves, 2010). A second difference is that the relationship between the trafficker and the victim is shorter in duration. This is primarily a consequence of the large number of individuals vulnerable to trafficking (i.e., available to be exploited) and the care and health care costs associated with a lifelong or longer-term relationship (i.e., it's easy and less costly to find a healthy replacement). A trafficker would rather purchase another person for 90 US dollars than invest hundreds or thousands of dollars into maintaining the health and profitability of a victim.

FORMS OF HUMAN TRAFFICKING

Categorization of trafficking by the nature of the work performed is a common although misleading practice. Categories of labor and sex trafficking are most often used, however concerns have been raised that this separation may serve to make invisible the sexual exploitation that occurs for most women in this situation, even if they are involved in what might be described as a labor trafficking situation. In other words, a woman may be trafficked primarily for domestic servitude, however it is likely that she will be forced to engage in sex acts as well. This speaks to the unique vulnerabilities of women and girls, which Chapter 5 explores in more detail.

While the type of labor performed by victims is varied (both with regard to labor and sex trafficking), some of the most common *forms* of human trafficking are noted below.

Bonded labor or **debt bondage** is a form of human trafficking that most closely parallels slavery, in which a person takes or is tricked into taking a loan. The person must then work to repay the loan; however, the nature of the work and the amount of time necessary to repay the loan are undefined and often remain that way. Individuals in debt bondage may receive food and shelter as "payment" for work, and in some cases victims will not be paid monetarily at all and their debt may increase to account for costs associated with food and shelter. A debt can be passed down for generations, which means that the child or grandchild of the person originally taking the loan is left to pay off the debt. It is important to note that not all instances of work-based debt are human trafficking, as someone may willingly enter into this type of arrangement and actually be fairly compensated for her or his labor.

Chattel slavery is characterized by ownership of one person by another and individuals in this form of slavery are bought and sold as commodities. It is the least common form of human trafficking today; however, it was the most prevalent in the United States until the 1865 passage of the Thirteenth Amendment to the United States Constitution.

Early and forced marriage primarily affects girls and women who are married to men without any choice. They then live as servants to the men and often experience physical and/or sexual violence in the home environment.

Forced labor is characterized by an individual being forced to work against her or his will, without compensation, with restrictions on freedom, and under violence or its threat. This term is also sometimes used in reference to all forms of human trafficking.

Involuntary domestic servitude is a form of forced labor in which an individual performs work within a residence such as cooking, cleaning, childcare and other household tasks. This becomes trafficking when the employer uses force, fraud and/or coercion to maintain control over the individual and to cause the worker to believe that she or he has no other options but to continue in the position. This type of environment puts the individual at increased risk because she or he is isolated and authorities are not able to easily gain access to inspect the workplace.

Sex trafficking is an extremely traumatic form of human trafficking in which a commercial sex act is induced by force, fraud, or coercion; or a sex act in which the person induced to perform is under 18 years of age. Victims of sex trafficking can be girls, boys, women, or men—although the majority are girls and women. It is not uncommon for traffickers to employ debt bondage as an attempt to legitimize their confiscation of the victim's earnings. Sex traffickers use a variety of methods to control and "break-in" victims, including confinement, physical abuse, rape, threats of violence to the victim's family, forced drug use and more. Victims of this form of trafficking face numerous psychological and physical health risks, which are covered in depth in later chapters.

Slavery by descent occurs when individuals are born into a socially constructed class or ethnic group that is relegated to slave status.

Child trafficking involves displacing a child for the purpose of economic exploitation. In the case of children, force, fraud and coercion do not need to be demonstrated. It is estimated that 1.2 million children are trafficked each year (ILO, 2002).[2] Like adults, children are trafficked for the purpose of labor and sexual exploitation.

Worst forms of child labor is a term that refers to child work that is seen as harmful to the physical and psychological health and welfare of the child. The International Labour Conference in 1999 adopted Convention No. 182 concerning the Prohibition and Immediate Action for the Elimination of the Worst Forms of Child Labour. The sale and trafficking of children is noted in this convention as one of the "unconditional" worst forms of child labor.

Other unconditional worst forms noted in the Convention include "the use, procuring or offering of a child for prostitution, for the production of pornography or for pornographic performances" and "the use, procuring or offering of a child for illicit activities."

Child soldiering is a form of human trafficking that involves the use of children as combatants; it may also involve children forced into labor or sexual exploitation by armed forces. In this case, traffickers may be government military forces, paramilitary organizations, or rebel groups. In addition to being used directly in armed conflict, children may be used for sexual purposes or forced to work as servants, cooks, guards, messengers, or spies.

THE TRAFFICKED PERSON

In popular stereotypes victims of human trafficking are often portrayed as innocent young girls who are lured or kidnapped from their home countries and forced into the commercial sex industry (Bruckert and Parent, 2002). While this is not necessarily an erroneous depiction, girls are by no means the only victims of trafficking. Women, men, and children of all ages can be trafficked for sex and labor. Those at risk of trafficking most often come from vulnerable populations including undocumented migrants, runaways and at-risk youth, females and members of other oppressed or marginalized groups, and the poor. Traffickers target individuals in these populations because they have few resources and work options. This makes them easier to recruit through deception or force and they tend to be easier to control.

At-risk youth and runaways are targeted by traffickers and by pimps for labor exploitation, begging, and very often for commercial sex (Finkelhor and Ormrod, 2004). Pimps and sex traffickers manipulate child victims and are known to make use of a combination of violence and affection in an effort to cultivate loyalty in the victim, which can result in Stockholm syndrome, a psychological phenomenon wherein hostages experience and express empathy and positive feelings for their captors. This is more likely to develop with children than with adults. This psychological manipulation reduces the victim's likelihood of acting out against the trafficker.

A combination of factors make undocumented immigrants extremely vulnerable to being trafficked (Human Rights Watch, 2012). Some of these factors include lack of legal status and related protections, poverty, few employment options, immigration-related debt, limited language skills and social isolation. It is not uncommon for undocumented immigrants to be trafficked by those from a similar ethnic or national background, which may play into the victims trust in a way that makes her or him more easily deceived.

Regions impacted by political instability and war create an environment that fosters trafficking. In particular, long-term military occupation as well as the presence of "peace keepers" feed the commercial sex industry in these areas and facilitate the sex trafficking of women and girls (Mendelson, 2005). Another situation that promotes trafficking is that of natural disaster. Natural disasters can destroy communities in a matter of minutes and create physical and economic insecurity. Children can be separated from their caregivers, making them prime targets for traffickers. The December 2004 Indian Ocean earthquake and ensuing tsunami is an example of one such natural disaster, where the lives of close to a million children were placed in jeopardy. In this situation, seemingly for the first time, a concerted effort was made to stop human trafficking before it could begin. Another example, although with a bleaker outcome, is the 2007 severe drought in Swaziland during which ECPAT International (End Child Prostitution and Trafficking) found increases in trafficking of children; specifically there were reports of parents trading the bodies of their children for food and water. Natural disasters not only impact children, they increase adult vulnerability to trafficking as well. The kind of devastation imposed by disasters of this type can create extreme poverty and make it very difficult to meet basic needs. This, for example, may lead to immigration that, as demonstrated above, can lead to victimization at the hands of a trafficker.

GLOBALIZATION, THE RIGHT TO WORK, AND HUMAN TRAFFICKING

Globalization has had an enormous impact on the trade in people, widening the gap between rich and poor and making it easier for traffickers to recruit and move victims. In fact, it can be said that those involved in transnational crime have benefited significantly from globalization. Current global conditions have created increased demand for cheap labor, thereby increasing migration and consequently human trafficking and smuggling (Naim, 2006). Increased supply of individuals vulnerable to exploitation is present because globalization has contributed to an increase in economic disparities between more developed and developing countries. Tourism has also grown because of globalization, which made it easier for consumers of the sex industry to travel and engage in sex tourism.

The right to work is the concept that every human has the right to work and to be fairly compensated. The term was coined by French socialist leader Louis Blanc in the early nineteenth century. The right to work is articulated in the Universal Declaration of Human Rights (1948) and elaborated upon in the International Covenant on Economic, Social and Cultural Rights (1976). The right to work is also recognized in international human rights law. Article 23.1 of the Universal Declaration of Human Rights states: *"Everyone has the right to work, to free choice of employment, to just and favourable conditions of work and to protection against unemployment."*

Despite Article 23.1 in the Declaration, millions of people around the world work in inhumane conditions for little or no compensation. Corporations from countries with more developed economies intentionally produce goods in countries with fewer resources because it's better for their bottom line. Products that are commonly used, ranging in value from goods such as coffee and chocolate to cell phones and televisions, are too often made by people who are struggling to survive. By utilizing these workers, corporations are exploiting the low cost of labor and lack of environmental and community protections that are characteristic of developing countries. Workers, including children, pay the price by toiling long hours, often in unsafe environments, for wages that barely afford the basic necessities, or in slavery conditions for no compensation at all. The result is corporations and consumers who reap the benefits of this unlawful "employment."

The disproportionate availability of resources worldwide creates conditions of vulnerability to labor exploitation and slavery. Before addressing this issue, it is important to understand the nuances of the different terms involved. The term **migration** is used to describe the movement of people from one country to another. **Immigration** is when a person moves *to* a country and **emigration** is when a person moves from a country. The primary reasons for immigration remain constant—immigration is typically fueled by the need to escape poverty, political instability, or warfare. The possibility of finding work that will better enable one to be self-sufficient and meet the basic needs of family members is also a driving force. Human smuggling is one method by which a person may immigrate to a country. According to the US Department of State (2006), **human smuggling** is the facilitation, transportation, attempted transportation, or illegal entry of a person across an international border. This usually refers to crossing an international border either secretly, such as crossing at unauthorized locations; or deceptively, such as with the use of falsified or counterfeit documents. Human smuggling is generally a voluntary act, with the person being smuggled paying a significant amount of money to the smuggler (also known as a "coyote"). An individual being smuggled may be subjected to unsafe conditions during the smuggling process including physical and sexual violence. It is not uncommon for the smuggled person to be held by the smuggler until her or his debt is paid off by someone (often a family member) in the destination country. It is important to note that at any point in the smug -gling process, the person may become a trafficking victim.

Table 11.1. Human Trafficking Compared to Migrant Smuggling

	HUMAN TRAFFICKING	MIGRANT SMUGGLING
Action	Recruitment, transportation, transfer, harboring or receipt of a person by means of threat or use of force, fraud, coercion	Facilitation of illegal entry of a person into a country of which the person is not a citizen or legal resident
Transnational Border Crossing	Not required	Required
Consent	If other elements of definition present, consent not relevant Not relevant for minors	Required
Outcome	Economic exploitation of the individual, which may include sexual exploitation and/or forced labor	Illegal border crossing

Traffickers who actively recruit victims use traditional immigration as a way to conceal their criminal intentions. With the false promise of compensated work in another country, traffickers are more easily able to get people to cooperate with illegal border crossing. For example, a woman may knowingly agree to be smuggled into a country to work in the sex industry or as a nanny, but she may be unaware that the traffickers will keep all of the money she makes, restrict and control her movement, and subject her to physical and sexual violence. In other instances, an individual may migrate on her or his own, legally or illegally, identify a work opportunity upon arriving in the destination country and become a victim of trafficking due to the illegal practices of an employer.

It has been suggested that more stringent border entry regulations force migrants to use illegal channels more often which can increase their risk of being exploited (Salt, 2000). Another perspective is that there is a need for additional anti-trafficking legislation and that the enforcement of the laws that are in place is inconsistent across points of entry, thereby reducing the effectiveness of these anti-trafficking laws.

PREVALENCE AND PROFITS

According to the United Nations Office on Drugs and Crime (2000), human trafficking is the fastest-growing criminal industry in the world and one of the most profitable (Haken, 2011; Interpol, 2002). However, despite its magnitude, there are a variety of reasons why this crime and its included human rights violations are so difficult to quantify. Some reasons include variation in the operational definitions used by researchers, methodological flaws such as those related to sampling techniques, and the difficulty and potential risks involved for researchers wishing to engage in primary versus secondary research. Also, and perhaps most challenging in the quest to obtain accurate statistics on the prevalence and geography of human trafficking, is that traffickers work to keep their crime undetected. Victims are difficult to identify since they often work in businesses or homes or behind the locked doors of a factory.

Case Study 11.1: Thailand farm Workers

A recruiting agency in Thailand was looking for men to work in the United States as farmers through the H2A visa program. The men were to pay recruiting fees totaling 20,000 US dollars, an amount that, if repaid in the Thai economy, would take approximately three generations to eliminate. Many of the men secured high-interest loans using their family home and land as collateral. They believed that being paid 9.42 US dollars hourly (as specified in their contract) would mean that they could make the loan money within a year and spend the next two years earning enough money to bring their families out of poverty. However, when the men arrived in the US, things were quite different to their expectations. Their passports and visas were taken by the traffickers. They lived in a rural area and had no access to transportation or to US citizens. Forty-four men were housed in one 5-bedroom, 2-bathroom house. There were not enough beds in the house so some of the men slept on the floor. They woke each morning at 4 a.m. so that there was time for everyone to shower. They were driven to work at 6 a.m. in a produce truck with a vertical sliding door and no windows. They had inconsistent access to food. They were not paid the hourly wage they were promised and oftentimes they were not paid at all.

Question: Was this a case of smuggling or human trafficking?

Answer: The men in this situation were victims of human trafficking. They were transported for the purposes of labor exploitation through the use of fraud and coercion, which resulted in their being subjected to involuntary servitude. Confiscation of their passports by the trafficker led the workers to believe that they had no other choice but to stay with the company.

They are closely monitored by the traffickers and often not permitted in close proximity to those who may be of assistance. These and other similar factors make human traffick -ing particularly difficult to accurately quantify and describe. Therefore, all reports regarding prevalence should be inter preted with caution. What follows are popular estimates in the field today.

- According to the International Labour Organization (ILO 2005, 2009) there are at least 12.3 million people in forced labor (including sexual exploitation) worldwide.
- Data suggest that women and girls comprise 80 percent of the individuals trafficked across international borders (US Department of State, 2010).
- Approximately 70 percent of victims are trafficked for commercial sexual exploitation (US Department of State, 2010).
- UNICEF estimates that 158 million children between the ages of five and 14 are engaged in child labor. This is equal to one in six children worldwide (UNICEF, 2011).
- In countries with the fewest resources, 29 percent of all children are engaged in child labor that often interferes with their education, robs them of childhood pleasures, and has a negative impact on their physical and psychological (UNICEF, 2011).
- ILO estimates that 246 million children and youth between the ages of 5 and 17 are presently involved in some type of debt bondage or forced labor (ILO, 2009).
- Research by Bales (1999) indicates that 27 million people are enslaved worldwide at any given time.
- Farr (2005) reports that 4 million people are enslaved worldwide.

It is similarly as difficult to assess profits as it is to assess forced labor and human trafficking. Globally, it is estimated that annual profits from forced labor are equal to 31.6 billion US dollars, of which 15.5 percent and 9 percent are generated in industrialized countries and countries in economic transition, respectively. It is further estimated that of the 31.6 billion US dollars, 30.6 percent is generated in Asia and the Pacific, 4.1 percent is generated in Latin America and the Caribbean, 5 percent is generated in Sub-Saharan Africa and 4.7 percent is generated in the Middle East and North Africa (Besler, 2005).

THE TRAFFICKING PROCESS

The business of human trafficking is carried out by individuals, small, loosely organized criminal networks, or by traditionally organized crime groups. It includes both small "mom-and-pop" type operations, as well as larger well-organized businesses that operate in a competitive international arena. Some involved in trafficking may assist with a single border crossing while others may work in an ongoing manner with a larger trafficking organization. These larger trafficking organizations often function on a more permanent basis and are involved in the entire trafficking enterprise from the recruitment of victims to the selling and reselling of victims to employers. **Organized crime groups or criminal organizations** are local, national, or transnational groupings of centralized enterprises with the purpose of engaging in illegal activity for financial gain. **Transnational organized crime** refers to the planning and execution of unlawful business ventures by groups or networks of individuals working in more than one country (Reuter and Petrie, 1995). Those involved in both national and transnational organized crime systematically use violence and corruption to achieve their goals (Albanese, 2004). Transnational organized crime undermines democracy and impedes the social, political, economic, and cultural development of societies around the world (Voronin, 2000). It is multi-faceted and can involve a variety of different illegal activities including drug trafficking, trafficking in firearms, migrant smuggling and human trafficking. In addition to human trafficking being carried out by organized crime groups, it is also carried out by more loosely organized **criminal networks**. These criminal networks are decentralized and less hierarchical, and according to international securities expert Phil Williams, they can be as effective as and more difficult to detect than traditional organized crime groups (2001).

The processes through which people are trafficked are varied. Because trafficking is a money-making endeavor for the trafficker, all exchanges are made in an effort to maximize financial gain while minimizing costs and financial loss. Traffickers engage in numerous individual and small group transactions, the characteristics of which are situation-dependent. Common roles traffickers assume in the process are described below; keep in mind that not all roles are relevant for all trafficking situations.

Trafficker Roles

Recruiter: The recruiter identifies, makes contact with and brings the victim into the first phase of the trafficking process. Depending on the situation, the recruiter sells the victim either directly to the employer (e.g., brothel owner) or to the broker. The recruiter does not always know that the person she or he recruited is going to be enslaved. Some common recruitment methods include:

- use of the internet to advertise for employment opportunities, study abroad, or marriage;
- in-person recruitment in public places such as bars, restaurants, and clubs;

- in-person recruitment through community and neighborhood contacts including families and friends;
- purchase of children from their parents or legal guardians.

Broker (agent): The broker is the middle person between the recruiter and the employer.

Contractor: The contractor oversees all of the exchanges involved in the trafficking of the victim.

Employment agent: The employment agent takes care of securing "employment" for the victim; this sometimes includes making arrangements for identification paperwork such as visas and passports.

Travel agent: The travel agent arranges for the transport of the victim from her or his point of origin to the destination. This can mean arranging for travel within one country or across country borders.

Document forger/thief: The document forger/thief secures identification documents for cross-border travel. In some instances, this may include creating false documents and in others it may mean illegally modifying actual government documents.

Transporter: The transporter actually accompanies the victim on the journey from point of origin to destination. Transportation may be via boat, bus, car, taxi, train, plane, or on foot. Delivery of the victim is made either to the broker or directly to the employer.

Employer (procurer): The employer purchases and then sells or otherwise exploits the human trafficking victim.

Enforcer ("roof" or guard): The enforcer is responsible for ensuring victim compliance, protecting the business and, at times, for ensuring that outstanding debt is paid by the customer (e.g., payment by a john in a sex trafficking situation).

Pimp: A pimp is a sex trafficker who directly or indirectly controls a person who is prostituted. He or she takes the profit made from the sex act and may or may not dole out a portion of this to the person being prostituted. The notion exists that the pimp provides protection for those being prostituted; however, the pimp himself often presents the most danger to the individual through threats, physical abuse, rape and the introduction or maintenance of drug use by the person being prostituted.

In order for human trafficking to work, the traffickers either have to force or somehow convince victims to leave their homes and to accompany the trafficker to the destination point. While coercion was defined above, what follows are common means of ensuring victim compliance with departing from her or his point of origin:

- abduction or kidnapping;
- purchasing of a child from her or his parents or legal guardians;
- deception through the promise of legitimate employment and/or entry into a country;
- deception about working conditions;

- deception about compensation and other benefits (e.g., school attendance for children);
- deception through a seemingly intimate/romantic relationship (i.e., trafficker pretends to be romantically interested in the victim).

Traffickers will use a combination of methods to control victims. Methods used depend on a variety of factors including, for example, the personality of the trafficker, the culture of the group in which they are working, the gender and age of the victim, and the behaviors of the victim while in the situation. Examples of control methods follow:

- violence (including rape and murder) and the threat of violence against the victim and her or his family;
- depravation of agency or the sense of control over self;
- isolation;
- confiscation of identification and/or travel documents;
- religious beliefs and practices (e.g., threat to use voodoo to harm the family member of a victim whose religious beliefs include voodoo).

Also, a commonly employed strategy of control is for traffickers to tell victims that law enforcement and immigration officials are not trustworthy or will treat them harshly if they are discovered. Obstacles to seeking assistance on the part of the victim are many, for example, in many instances of international trafficking, victims are unaware that they have rights and often do not know that contracts they may have signed are not legally binding. Other obstacles to seeking assistance can be related to family loyalty (i.e., desire to protect family from the trafficker), cultural practices, language barriers and political suppression in countries of origin.

SNAPSHOT OF INTERNATIONAL EFFORTS TO END TRAFFICKING

Non-governmental organizations and activists assumed a grass-roots role in the fight against human trafficking and have been instrumental in bringing the issue to the attention of governments around the world. At the international level and largely consequent of international agreements reached at the UN, the United Nations Global Initiative to Fight Human Trafficking (UN.GIFT) was initiated in March 2007 to support the global fight on human trafficking.

The Global Initiative is based on the idea that the crime of human trafficking is of such magnitude that it requires an approach to eradication that is implemented globally and by a variety of relevant stakeholders. In order for this to happen according to UN.GIFT, stakeholders must "coordinate efforts already underway, increase knowledge and awareness, provide technical assistance; promote effective rights-based responses; build capacity of state and non-state stakeholders; foster partnerships for joint action; and above all, ensure that everybody takes responsibility for this fight."[3] UN.GIFT sees its role as that of facilitator of coordination and to "create synergies among the anti-trafficking activities of UN agencies, international organizations and other stakeholders to develop the most efficient and cost-effective tools and good practices."[4] Efforts to address human trafficking are further addressed in Chapter 13 of this text.

UN.GIFT

United Nations Global Initiative to Fight Human Trafficking

FIGURE 11.1. United Nations Global Initiative to Fight Human Trafficking Logo

HUMAN TRAFFICKING IN THE UNITED STATES

Like most countries with well-developed market economies, the United States plays a role in fueling the international trade of people. Also, as is the case with most if not all countries affected by human trafficking, the United States is faced with the trafficking of its own citizens within country borders. Sex trafficking of women and children, in particular girls, is the most significant form of domestic trafficking in the United States. Children targeted in these situations by traffickers, who are commonly referred to as "pimps," are most often runaways or homeless youth. Labor trafficking is also an issue within the United States, however many of these cases involve individuals trafficked into the country to perform a variety of what are characterized as low-paying jobs. An example of labor trafficking of US citizens appears in the textbox below.

At the federal level in the United States, Congress passed the Victims of Trafficking and Violence Protection Act (TVPA) of 2000 (P.L. 106-386), the Trafficking Victims Protection Reauthorization Act of 2003 (H.R. 2620), the Trafficking Victims Protection Reauthorization Act of 2005 (H.R. 972), and the Trafficking Victims Protection Reauthorization Act of 2008 (H.R. 7311). Prior to the passing of the TVPA in 2000, no comprehensive federal law existed to address human trafficking in the United States.

Case Study 11.2: A Federal Case of Domestic Labor Trafficking

Labor camp owners recruit homeless African-American addicts form shelters throughout the Southeast, including Tampa, Miami, Orlando, and New Orleans, to work at labor camps, promising food and shelter for only $50 a week. The camp owners picked up prospective workers in vans and transported them to isolated labor camps in North Florida and North Carolina. Once on site, the workers were supplied with crack cocaine. The cost of the drug was deducted from their pay checks. Every evening camp owners gave workers the opportunity to buy crack, untaxed generic beer and cigarettes from the company store. Most workers spiraled into debt. On average, workers were paid about 30 cents on the dollar after decuations. The case broke in 2005 after a Federal raid on the North Florida camp. Advocates were stunned that the camps could so easily exploit American citizens.

Source: *Naples Daily News*, September 23, 2006.

In the United States TVPA severe forms of trafficking in persons are defined as:

(a) Sex trafficking in which a commercial sex act is induced by force, fraud, or coercion, or in which the person induced to perform such act has not attained 18 years of age; or

(b) The recruitment, harboring, transportation, provision or obtaining of a person for labor services, through the use of force, fraud, or coercion for the purpose of subjection to involuntary servitude, peonage, debt bondage, or slavery.

(8 U.S.C. §1101)

Much like the United Nations trafficking Protocol, the TVPA focuses on the "three Ps" of trafficking to guide antislavery efforts: *prevention* of the crime, *prosecution* of the trafficker, and *protection* for victims. Recently, a fourth "P" standing for "*partnerships*" was added to the framework. Partnerships are intended to take place across all levels of society—local, regional, national, and international—and are to involve both government and civil society organizations. In addition to providing a comprehensive definition of human trafficking, this legislation gave law enforcement tools to enhance the extent to which traffickers are prosecuted and punished. The TVPA also called for the establishment of a global Trafficking in Persons (TIP) Report, which is published annually and the President's Interagency Task Force to Monitor and Combat Trafficking in Persons.

The TIP Report documents and evaluates the anti-trafficking efforts of foreign governments. Countries are ranked in tiers depending on the extent to which they are compliant with minimum standards established by the TVPA. Countries on the lowest tier may be subject to economic sanctions enacted by the United States. While the TIP Report is thought to be a useful tool, it has been criticized for presenting incomplete information, for not including evaluation of the United States and for being biased and "politicized." Three primary concerns are as follows: how the minimum standards are applied; what methods are used to justify tier placements; and how information for the report is collected and analyzed. Recently, efforts have been made to address some of these concerns, the most visible of which is the inclusion of analysis of US efforts in the 2010 publication of the report.

Under the TVPA, the US Department of Health and Human Services can "certify" international human trafficking victims as such in the eyes of the law. After being certified, victims are then qualified for physical and psychological health services, housing, food stamps, educational and vocational programs, as well as support for legal services. Victims of international trafficking may also be granted a T-Visa, which allows them to live and work in the US for up to three years after which application for permanent resident status may be made. Criticisms of the TVPA have included that eligibility requirements for the T-Visa are too rigid and enforcement is deficient, leaving many deserving victims unprotected. Others have noted that there are unnecessary barriers to obtaining the benefits afforded through the TVPA. These include victim identification, difficulty qualifying as a "severe trafficking" victim, and the time it takes to certify a victim. Victims are often left for long periods of time waiting for assistance to meet the most basic of needs such as shelter, food, and clothing. Communities in which grass-roots anti-trafficking coalitions are established often step in to provide support at this critical time. The TVPA has been most strongly criticized by victims' rights activists and social service providers for its requirement that victims participate in prosecution of the trafficker prior to releasing funding in support of their basic needs (e.g., shelter, food, clothing, access to health care and counseling). This requirement is tantamount to requiring a rape victim to press charges against her rapist before giving her access to medical attention and counseling.

As of August 2011, most states have developed laws that address trafficking; the number of states with sex trafficking offenses is 45 and 48 have labor offenses. The Polaris Project, a nonprofit agency working against trafficking nationally, has a rating process through which it tracks the presence or absence of 10 categories of state statutes they deem essential to a comprehensive anti-trafficking legal framework.

While the United States has made progress with regard to the extent to which trafficking is addressed, there is still much to be done. Within this text, Chapter 13 in particular explains some ways in which anti-trafficking efforts can be augmented both in communities and nationally.

TO THE PROFESSOR

In addition to the discussion questions below, there are examination questions to supplement the book. For those interested in copies of the examination questions please contact saleshss@taylorand-francis.com.

DISCUSSION QUESTIONS

1. How is human trafficking defined by the United Nations Protocol to Prevent, Suppress and Punish Trafficking in Persons, Especially Women and Children?
2. What are the differences between human trafficking and other related phenomena such as immigration, emigration, and smuggling?
3. What are some of the underlying causes of human trafficking?
4. Name some of the ways in which human trafficking constitutes a violation of fundamental human rights.

NOTES

1. It was signed by member states of the UN at a conference in Palermo, Italy, on December 15, 2000 and was entered into force in 2003 on September 29 (www.unodc.org/unodc/en/treaties/CTOC/index.html).
2. The ILO still stands by the estimate to which this reference refers. See United Nations (2009) *Improving the Coordination of Efforts Against Trafficking in Persons*. Available at: www.un.org/ga/president/63/letters/SGbackgroundpaper.pdf (accessed February 22, 2013).
3. See www.ungift.org/knowledgehub/en/about/index.html.
4. Ibid.

CHAPTER TWELVE

Female Sex Trafficking:
Defining the Nature and Size of the Problem

By Vidyamali Samarasinghe

Human trafficking in the form of slavery has being a part of history as evidenced in the ancient empires of Egypt, Babylon, Greece and Rome. Later, the transatlantic slave trade that spanned nearly four and a half centuries captured and transported thousands of able-bodied men, women and children from the African continent across the Atlantic to the Americas. Even after the abolition of slavery in 1838, the use of 'indentured' labor, transported from the Asian continent by the colonial powers to work in plantations in South America and Asia, had broad similarities to slavery (Tinker, 1974). All or most of the characteristics associated with slavery are also played out in the contemporary human trafficking. Modern forms of trafficking are a flourishing international business involving a chain of people, which includes the victims, local recruiters, corrupt officials, business interests, governments and global syndicates of organized crime.

Trafficking in human cargo, whether the victims are females or males, adults or children, involves the movement of people internally or internationally for some form of work, which may be legal or illegal, and under highly exploitative working conditions. Today, women, men and children are trafficked across borders and domestically for farm work, factory work, domestic servitude, camel jockeys, begging, forced marriage, mail-order brides and forced prostitution and also for harvesting human organs. A fundamental issue in the discourse of trafficking is that while the trafficker is well aware of all the ramifications, the trafficked victims have at best partial information, and at worst none at all. Trafficking basically caters to a demand, created by a scarcity often stemming from the illegal nature of the work and the social stigmatization of the type of work demanded. However, trafficking is also triggered by the need to use cheap labor in order to maximize profits from a range of certain goods and services produced for the market. In all cases, profiteering from the use of bodies, labor and the time of the victims motivates the traffickers.

DEVELOPING THE DISCOURSE ON FEMALE SEX TRAFFICKING

Female sexual exploitation accounts for a significant proportion of the current global flows of trafficking. Female prostitution, separated for the most part from the morally accepted norm of female chastity, has been a global phenomenon since the time of recorded history. Lerner's scholarship on the *Creation of Patriarchy* illustrates that while commercial prostitution was seen as a social necessity for meeting the sexual needs of men, it was also used as a distinguishing marker between chaste women and immoral prostitutes. For example she notes that the Assyrian legal code established that while all chaste women who go out in the streets should veil themselves, "… [H]arlot must not veil: her head must be uncovered." (Lerner, 1987:137). The moral structures of any society are shaped by different socio-behavioral elements, which are perceived to be appropriate or inappropriate by that particular society. Madonnas and whores are thus created to uphold the binary opposites, i.e., respectability and decency of the Madonnas in contrast to the immorality and indecency of the whores. Hence, female sexuality has to be controlled in order to maintain the sanctity of marriage, the legitimacy of children and, by extension, the stability of society. At the same time prostitution is implicitly accepted since the controlled female sexuality within marriage and other stable forms of cohabitation inhibits males, whose sexual demands are expected to go beyond the restricted spaces dictated by stable forms of cohabitation. As Emma Goldman stated in 1917 "… [S]ociety considers the sex experience of a man as attributes of his general development, while similar experiences in the life of a woman are looked upon as a terrible calamity. A loss of honor and all that is good and noble in a human being. The double standard of morality has played no little part in the creation and perpetuation of prostitution" (Goldman, 1917/1970:25). What is embedded as a constant throughout human history is that prostitution is perceived to be immoral and that those who engage in prostitution should be shunned by decent society. Yet it continues to be sought out by a section of the male population creating a space for a thriving clandestine activity. In modern society, where laws are encoded to uphold moral strictures, prostitution is illegal or restricted to specific locations in an overwhelming majority of countries, but the demand for prostitutes seems to be increasing. Thus, given the immorality and illegality of prostitution and social acceptance of the male need for sex outside stable co-habiting relationships, trafficking of women and girls becomes the *modus operandum* of obtaining the supply to meet the demand.

The contemporary discourse on trafficking in women may be traced to the latter part of the nineteenth century when Europe was caught up in the intermingled discourses on prostitution and 'white slavery'. The Contagious Diseases Acts (CDA) enacted in England between 1864 and 1869 was an attempt to subject prostitutes to a set of regulations, including mandatory medical examinations for sexually transmitted diseases and to impose restrictions on prostitutes' freedom to move. The 'Abolitionist' movement spearheaded by Josephine Butler waged a successful campaign to abolish the Act on the premise that regulating prostitution gave it legitimacy and exposed the "official recognition of the 'double standard' of sexual behavior of men and women" (Doezema, 2000:30). Abolitionists noted that when the state regulates or legalizes prostitution, it leads to its acceptance as a social institution and as a legitimate form of work. In that context the state would not have to concern itself with whether or not women are trafficked or coerced (Barry, 1995:237). Early abolitionists equated prostitution of women to their victim-hood as exploited human beings.

In the last decade of the nineteenth century, the International Society for the Suppression of the White Slave Trade was formed and covered conferences periodically from 1899–1913. Member countries signed agreements to maintain surveillance at ports, repatriate women and criminalize the acts of abduction and trafficking (Tambe, 2001). The term 'white slavery' was formally used at the 1902 Paris Conference where representatives of several governments met to draft an international instrument for the suppression of white slave traffic. While initially the term was meant to distinguish the practice from the nineteenth century black slavery, it immediately assumed a racial, gendered image of innocent 'white women' outraging the sensibilities of white racist segments of society (Barry, 1979). This social outrage over 'white slavery' was greatly influenced by the social purist movement and supported by the abolitionists, although some of the abolitionists challenged the often repressive aspects of the social purists (Walkowitz, 1980). The anti-trafficking 'white slavery' campaign had an explicit racial overtone. Grittner explains 'white slavery' as "the enslavement of white women or girls by means of coercion, tricks or drugs by nonwhite or non-Anglo-Saxon men" (Grittner, 1990:5). The emphasis was on the purported transportation of innocent white females for purposes of sexual exploitation by non-whites, and not on prostitution in general. The anti-white slavery campaign withered away in the early twentieth century.

The International Conference of 1921 recommended that the term 'white slavery' be dropped and replaced with "traffic in women and children" (Lazarsfeld, 1938: 437). This new term was also adopted by the League of Nations, which began focusing on trafficking in women after 1921. Prostitution remained the cornerstone of Conventions on trafficking proposed by the League of Nations. Its 1921 Convention raised the age of consent of women from 20 to 21 years, and the convention of 1933 made all trafficking, even of adult women, a criminal activity (Tambe, 2001). The U.N Convention of 1949 on the Suppression of Traffic in Persons and the Exploitation for the Prostitution of Others in effect had adopted as its foundation the abolitionists' perspectives on anti-prostitution. The preamble to the 1949 Convention declares[1] that prostitution and trafficking in persons are incompatible with the dignity and worth of human persons and endanger the welfare of the individual, the family and the community. It called upon nations to close brothels and punish those who procure for and promote prostitution (Barry, 1995:120). However, although the U.N. Convention of 1949 uses the word 'trafficking' in its title, it did not specifically define the concept of trafficking.

The issue of trafficking is specifically addressed in the 1979 U.N. Convention on the Elimination of All forms of Discrimination Against Women (CEDAW).[2] Article 6 of the Convention directs state parties to take all appropriate measures, including legislation to suppress all forms of traffic in women and exploitation of women for the purpose of prostitution. Children's rights were addressed by the 1989 Convention on the Rights of the Child[3], in which Article 35 directs the states to take appropriate national, bilateral and multilateral measures to prevent the abduction and sale of or traffic in children for any purpose or in any form. A new urgency for a comprehensive and a stronger commitment to combat slavery-like practices and transnational criminal activity has resulted in a series of new and expanded protocols to address the issue of global human trafficking. The complete set of commitments made by member states regarding human trafficking are embedded in the *U.N. Convention Against Transnational Crime; The Protocol to Prevent, Suppress and Punish Trafficking in Persons, Especially Women and Children*, which supplements the *U.N. Convention and Interpretive Notes on the Trafficking Protocol*.[4] Taken together (hereafter referred to as the *U.N. Trafficking Protocol*), these three documents comprise a set of international obligations, which specifically address the issue of human trafficking (Jordan, 2002). The 1990 International Convention on the Protection of the Rights of All Migrant Workers and Members and Their Families, in force only since July 2003 also addresses the issue of trafficking.

The main thrust on human trafficking during the past century and half has been primarily focused on female prostitution. Spurred on by the powerful campaigns of the abolitionists and the social purists the emphasis was on 'rescuing' the female from immoral sexual behavior. Female prostitution was considered as an involuntary activity and women who became prostitutes were thus by definition deemed to be 'trafficked'. This assertion of necessary victim-hood of female prostitutes has since been challenged by different anti-trafficking advocates who argue that some women may choose to become prostitutes and hence cannot be categorized as trafficked. The main thrust of the current trafficking discourse is still focused primarily on the issue of prostitution, which continues to be perceived, by and large, as an exercise based on sexual exploitation of women and girls.

While the supply of trafficked women that outraged Europeans and led to the anti-trafficking campaigns at the turn of the twentieth century came mainly from white Anglo-Saxon societies, the current global female sex trafficking pattern illustrates a shift of the supply lines to developing countries of Asia, Africa and Latin America and the former socialist countries of Eastern Europe and the Soviet Republic. Furthermore, while Anglo-Saxon women no longer play a significant part in the supply side of female sex trafficking, there is a blurring of 'skin colors' of trafficked women since all major racial categories are caught in the web of female sex trafficking flows. Both internationally and intra-nationally, relatively richer and more developed areas demand the supply of trafficked women and a higher premium is placed on lighter skinned women and young virgins. The supply and demand structure of female sex trafficking clearly illustrates the nature of commodification of the trafficked female.

THE NUMBERS GAME

A serious concern of policy makers, donor agencies, NGOs, advocates and scholars who are involved in analyzing the trafficking situations and formulating and implementing empirically grounded anti-trafficking initiatives is the serious lack of accurate statistics on sex trafficking. U.S Government estimates on trafficking of human beings, as reported in the U.S State Department annual Trafficking in Persons Reports (TIP), demonstrate the underlying problems in getting accurate data on trafficking in human beings. All numbers quoted by the U.S. Government are estimates and furthermore, there has been a gradual reduction of global human trafficking estimates over the past four years. In 2002 the estimate was 700,000 to 4 million people, reduced to 800,000 to 900,000 people in 2003, and 600,000 to 800,000 in 2004. The 2005 estimate of trafficked persons globally is the same as for 2004 (U.S State Department, 2002, 2003, 2004, 2005). Among them eighty percent of the cases of trafficking concerned sexual exploitation. Of the cases where women were reported to be victims of trafficking, eighty-five percent were said to be trafficked for sexual exploitation, two percent for other types of forced labor and thirteen percent for both types of exploitation (Kangaspunta, 2003).

The United Nations Office of Drug Control and Crime Prevention (UNODC), whose databases on monitoring global trends, routes and volumes of trafficking in persons and the smuggling of migrants are used extensively by organizations engaged in anti-trafficking initiatives derives its statistics of traffic flows mostly from estimates. Unfortunately, once published, the initial estimate is often cited by other publications and becomes credible. Lin Lean Lim notes that since the estimates range so widely they should be treated with caution. For instance, she points out that the figure of 800,000 Thai child prostitutes has been seriously questioned by other sources familiar with the situation in

Thailand. The estimate was based on a sample of just one brothel and extrapolated to the 60,000 brothels found in Thailand (Lim, 1998:9). Similarly, Sanghera and Kapur (2000) observe that the common belief that 5,000–7,000 Nepali girls are trafficked across borders to India each year, and that currently 150,000–200,000 women and girls are in various Indian cities, were disseminated in an article published in 1986 and has remained unaltered over the past 18 years.[5] While this is not to say that all estimates are gross exaggerations, fabrications or dated, my own field visits to countries of Asia have shown that trafficking numbers are indeed significant and in some instances, numbers quoted appear to be underestimates. The problem seems to be in the flawed methodology used, especially the difficulty of tracing the estimate back to the methods (Steinfatt, Baker and Beesey, 2002).

While accurate numbers of trafficking could be obtained best from good field-based methods, several inter-related factors inhibit this process. The most significant road block is the illegality of trafficking, hence its clandestine nature and the intimate, private activity of sexual relationships, compounded by the stigma attached to prostitution. The serious lack of anti-trafficking legislation and law enforcement mechanisms makes the already vulnerable women and girls who become victims reluctant to report trafficking incidents to the authorities. In fact, until very recently, indifference or apathy on the part of the policy makers to the issue of trafficking in women and girls was the rule rather then the exception. Victims of sex trafficking mostly belong to the poorer segments of society who are usually ignored by decision-making political groups in society.

As Tyldum and Brunovskis have shown, two main issues inhibit accurate counting of trafficking victims. First is the problem of a common 'conceptual identification' of a trafficked victim. The second is the 'practical identification' of trafficked victim-of "being able to say this is a victim of trafficking" (Tyldum and Brunovskis, 2005:20). While new international anti-trafficking instruments have constructed more expanded definitions of trafficking, continuing lack of clarity in defining female sex trafficking leads to confusion, both at the theoretical as well as at practical levels (Gallagher, 2001, GPAT, 2003). Indeed, in practice identification of trafficked victims becomes a difficult task since they are enclosed within a 'hidden population' (Heckathorn, 1997), one that refuses to cooperate or gives unreliable responses to questions in order to protect itself since her/his activities are socially stigmatized and/or illegal. Blurred boundaries between smuggling/immigration/trafficking also not only demonstrate problems in conceptual clarity, they pose practical problems in clearly identifying a trafficked victim.

Most governments do not give priority to research and data collection on trafficking numbers or patterns. One gets the impression that any new efforts in this direction, particularly among developing countries, is at the behest of donor agencies which are increasingly pushing anti-trafficking initiatives as a segment of development aid. A significant feature of the U.S. *Trafficking in Persons Act of 2000* is that the U.S. Government reserves the right to impose mandatory non-emergency sanctions on those governments which, according to the annual survey conducted by the U.S. State Department, do not make a significant effort to combat trafficking (US Department of State, 2001). Such policies by major aid donor countries compel developing countries to undertake statistical surveys in order to formulate anti-trafficking strategies.

Apart from structural and systemic problems faced in obtaining accurate numbers of female sex trafficking, the trafficking discourse itself carries with it certain practical problems in identifying a clearly distinct category of trafficking. Firstly, the ideological debate on prostitution between the anti-legalization/abolitionists and pro-legalization advocates would give different numbers of trafficking victims. While the anti-prostitution abolitionists would consider all prostitutes as trafficking victims, the pro-prostitution would want to separate those adult women who enter prostitution voluntarily from women who are forced into commercial sex sector and all child sex workers. Second, there is a more practical difficulty of separating trafficking statistics from migration statistics, and especially in terms of migrant smuggling. 'Smuggling' and 'trafficking', which are often used interchangeably, confuse the issue of separating the numbers between the two categories of human flows. Third, there is also confusion in pinpointing the difference between legitimate migration and trafficking. For instance, women who migrate to Japan for work from the Philippines or Thailand may have official travel papers and employment/fiancée contracts. However, once they reach their destination some of them are forced into sexual exploitation. In such cases, while their mobility as a primary dimension of trafficking is legal, would they be deemed to be trafficked victims since the final outcome of their migration is sexual exploitation? Fourth, there is an element of danger in gathering trafficking data for two reasons. First, some of the female sex trafficking is known to occur in conflict zones, where any type of data gathering on sex trafficking becomes difficult. Second, the increasing control exercised by criminal groups on the sex industry in general makes the efforts of data gathering dangerous for a researcher. Finally, trafficking is generally not incorporated into the national agendas in most countries. Consequently, there are very few state coordinated mechanisms to research or gather trafficking data. Citing a successful anti-trafficking initiative started in 2003 by the Government of Norway, Tyldum and Brunovskis (2005) state that law enforcement bodies were given more resources and were instructed to give higher priority to trafficking for sexual exploitation. The number of cases identified had increased dramatically, although the overall numbers still remained rather low. The question was whether the low numbers were the tip of the iceberg or an accurate number of all cases of trafficking. The researchers also bring up the issue of bias of law enforcement or rehabilitation organizations which could distort the numbers of trafficked persons.

Indeed, while data gathered directly as numbers would give a clearer picture of the volume of trafficking flows, it is obviously an elusive goal. Estimates of sex trafficking, derived through extrapolation is useful in understanding the direction and the nature of trafficking and gives us an idea of the magnitude of the problem faced by the global community. The global network of female sex trafficking flows show that no part of the world is completely free of sex trafficking (Mattar, 2005).

DISCUSSION QUESTIONS

1. How did the international understanding of female sex trafficking develop?
2. How would you define human trafficking? How would you try to identify trafficking victims?
3. Why is it difficult to obtain an estimate of the number of trafficking victims?

NOTES

1. Convention for the Suppression of the Traffic in Persons and of the Exploitation of the Prostitution of Others, adopted by the General Assembly in its resolution 317 (1V).
2. General Assembly resolution 34/180 (A/RES/34/180).
3. Convention on the Rights of the Child, adopted by the General Assembly in its resolution 44/25 (A/RES/44/25).
4. The UN Convention Against Transnational Organized Crime entered into force on September 29, 2003, after it received its fortieth ratification in July 2003, nearly three years after its adoption by the UN General Assembly in

November 2000. The UN Protocol to Prevent, Suppress and Punish Trafficking in Persons, Especially Women and Children Entered into Force on December 25, 2003, with 45 countries ratifying.

5. The article that first published these statistics was written by Dr. I.S. Gilada of the Indian Health Association in Mumbai, India, and presented in a workshop in 1986. Subsequently a version of this article was published in the *Times of India*, January 2, 1989 (quoted in Sanghera and Kapur, 2002).

REFERENCES

Barry, Kathleen. 1979. *Female and Sexual Slavery*. New York: New York University Press.

Barry, Kathleen. 1995. *Th e Prostitution of Sexuality*. New York: New York University Press.

Doezema, Joe. 2000. "Loose Women or Lost Women? The reemergence of the Myth of 'White Slavery' in Contemporary Discourse on Trafficking in Women." *Gender Issues* 18 (1):23–50.

Gallagher, Ann Theresa. 2001. The International Legal Response to Human Trafficking. Paper read at Technical Consultative Meeting on Anti-trafficking Programs in South Asia: Appropriate Activities, Indicators and Evaluation Methodologies. Katmandu, Nepal. September 11–13.

Goldman, Emma. 1917/1970. *Traffic in Women and Other Essays on Feminism*, (2nd ed.). New York: Mother Earth Publishing Association.

Global Program Against Trafficking in Human Beings (GPAT). 2003. Coalition Against Trafficking in Human Beings in the Philippines: Research and Action Final Report. Vienna: United Nations.

Grittner, F.K. 1990. *White Slavery: Myth, Ideology and American Law*. New York and London: Garland Press.

Heckathorn, D.D. 1997. "Respondent-driven Sampling: A New Approach to the study of Hidden Populations." *Social Problems* 44 (2):174–198.

Hugh, Tinker. 1974. *A New System of Slavery: the Export of Indian Labor Overseas 1830–1890*. London: Oxford University Press.

Jordan, Ann. 2002. *The Annotated Guide to the Complete UN Trafficking Protocol*. Washington, D.C.: International Human Rights Law Group.

Kangaspunta, Kristiina. 2003. Mapping the Inhuman Trade: Preliminary findings of the Human Trafficking Database. *Forum on Crime and Society* 3 (1–2):81–103.

Lazarsfeld, Sofi. 1938. *Women's Experience of the Male*. London: Encyclopedic Press.

Lerner, Gerder. 1987. *The Creation of Patriarchy*. London: Oxford University Press.

Lim, Lin Lean. 1998. "The Economic and Social bases of Prostitution in Southeast Asia." In Lin Lean Lim (ed.) *The Sex Sector: The Economic and Social Bases of Prostitution in Southeast Asia*. Geneva, Switzerland: International Labour Organization, 1–28.

Sanghera, Jyoti. 2000 and R. Kapur. *An Assessment of Laws and Policies for Prevention and Control of Trafficking in Nepal*. Kathmandu: The Asia Foundation and New Delhi: Population Council/Horizons.

Steinfatt, Thomas M., Simon Baker and Allan Beesey. 2002." Measuring the number of trafficked women in Cambodia." Paper presented at The Human rights Challenge of Globalization in Asia-Pacific-US: The Trafficking in Persons, Especially Women and Children. Honolulu, Hawaii. November 13–15.

Tambe, Ashwini. 2001. Codes of Misconduct: The Regulation of Prostitution in Colonial Bombay, 1860–1947. Ph.D Thesis. American University, Washington, D.C.

Tyldum, Guri and Anette Brunovskis. 2005. "Describing the Unobserved Methodological Challenges in Empirical Studies on Human Trafficking" In Frank Laezko and Elzbieta Gozdiek.eds. *Data and Research on Human Trafficking: A Human Survey*. IOM. 17–34.

USDS. 2001. Trafficking in Persons Report 2001. Washington, D.C.: U.S. State Department.

USDS. 2002. Trafficking in Persons Report 2002. Washington, D.C.: USDS.

USDS. 2003. Trafficking in Persons Report 2003. Washington, D.C.: USDS.

USDS. 2004. Trafficking in Persons Report 2004. Washington, D.C.: USDS.

USDS. 2005. Trafficking in Persons Report 2005. Washington, D.C.: USDS.

Walkowitz, J. 1980. *Prostitution and the Victorian Society: Women, Class and State*. Cambridge, UK: Cambridge University Press.

CHAPTER THIRTEEN

When Sexual Autonomy Isn't Enough: Sexual Violence Against Immigrant Women in the United States

By Miriam Zoila Pérez

WOMEN CROSSING BORDERS

The most common way for immigrants coming from Latin America to enter the United States is by crossing at some point along the approximately two-thousand-mile U.S./Mexico border. Immigrants cross on foot, in vehicles, in trunks of cars, by wading through the Rio Grande. They have to avoid checkpoints, border patrols, fences, and barbed wire. Female immigrants taking on this increasingly dangerous journey face an added risk during the crossing: sexual assault and rape. In a 2006 *Boston Globe* article, Julie Watson wrote, "Rape has become so prevalent that many women take birth control pills or shots before setting out to ensure they won't get pregnant. Some consider rape 'the price you pay for crossing the border,' said Teresa Rodriguez, regional director of the UN Development Fund for Women."[1]

Many of us who work in reproductive health in cities with large Latina populations see the effects of these abuses firsthand. Women arrive here with untreated sexually transmitted infections that they were given while crossing, as well as with unintended pregnancies. Women are often abused by everyone from the *coyotes* they hire to take them across the border, to other men in their groups, to officials they encounter along the way.

A May 2008 *Chicago Tribune* series on immigration addressed this violence: "Sometimes female migrants are sold by gangs along the border, used as lures to attract male migrants, or raped, say officials at Grupo Beta, the immigrant protection service in Nogales, Mexico, on the Arizona border. 'Women are used like meat on a hook [by the smugglers] to attract more men to their groups,' says Dr. Elizabeth Garcia Mejia, the head of Grupo Beta in Nogales."[2]

While there are invariably connections between the sexual abuses immigrant women face and the wider rape culture within the United States, there are also very different things at stake. What would a world free from sexual violence look like for immigrant women? Do the strategies employed by mainstream U.S. feminists to combat rape serve immigrant women?

Traditional attempts to combat rape in the United States have taken an individualized educational approach: Teach women to avoid "risky" behaviors (wearing skimpy clothing, drinking alcohol, walking alone), empower them to say no, and encourage men to respect boundaries. Newer, more feminist attempts have focused on reclaiming women's sexual autonomy and pleasure as a way to combat rape. For immigrant women whose bodies are being turned into a commodity, both of these methods fall short. Their bodies are a commodity to be exchanged in return for passage across the border, primarily because of their socioeconomic vulnerability. This is true at the U.S./Mexico border, as well as the Mexico/Guatemala border. Women who are raped while crossing or sexually assaulted by immigration officials (or while in custody) are not protected by these preventative measures. On top of it all, immigrant women have a particularly hard time speaking out about the abuses. First of all, reporting abuses they suffered while crossing the border without documents carries with it the obvious and understandable fear of deportation or criminal penalty. Additionally, much of the time women who report are asked to cooperate in the prosecution of their abusers, both for their sexual assaults and for their smuggling activity. They fear retribution on the part of the *coyotes* and other individuals involved in border crossing—and for good reason. Immigrant women in these situations are in one of the most powerless of circumstances, and few, if any, people are advocating on their behalf. The traditional individualistic efforts to combat rape fall way short when the abuses against immigrant women occur in part because of their position in the larger structures of poverty and racism. Even the efforts to empower women and ensure their sexual autonomy, which are obviously important, won't serve immigrant women until we work to correct the larger class imbalances that force them into these vulnerable positions.

When we take a step back from the experiences of individual immigrants crossing into the United States, we can see a complex institutional structure that aids and abets these forms of sexual violence. First, there is the racist and classist U.S. immigration policy. Based on a quota system, the number of visas available to immigrants from Latin America is severely limited, making it difficult to gain access legally. U.S. foreign economic policies like the North American Free Trade Agreement (NAFTA) have worsened the economic situation in Latin America, creating that much more demand to enter the United States.[3] In response, a large black market has developed for helping immigrants cross without documents.

Things have only worsened in recent years as the Bush administration has led an immigration crackdown. Primarily, this has involved militarizing certain sections of the border, planning for a U.S./Mexico border fence, and increasing border patrol along highly trafficked areas. It has been documented that rather than stemming the flow of people across the border, these actions serve only to increase the likelihood of deaths from border crossings, by pushing the immigrants to less trafficked and more dangerous parts of the border.[4] This militarization also increases immigrants' reliance on *coyotes* and other smugglers, who charge huge fees and often sexually abuse the women in their charge.

HUMAN TRAFFICKING AND SEXUAL ABUSE

These abuses are not limited to women crossing the U.S./Mexico border. Female immigrants from all over the world face different forms of exploitation in the United States The Human Trafficking and Asian

Pacific Islander Women fact sheet published by the National Asian Pacific American Women's Forum (NAPAWF) reveals that human trafficking has become a large black-market industry in the United States—46 percent of human-trafficking victims are forced into different forms of sex work, and Asian Pacific Islander (API) women represent the largest group of women trafficked into the United States.[5] This trafficking can take on many forms, including women's being brought into this country without documentation and held captive by their traffickers, forced to work for little or no money and in substandard conditions; international marriages (also known as bride trafficking), where women are paired up via international marriage broker agencies and then abused by their American partners; and women's being brought from their country of origin as domestic workers, and then mistreated by their employers.

The common link between of all these trafficking cases is that the women are dependent on their abusers for their immigration status. It is the ultimate form of control, as their ability to be in the United States is connected to their relationship (personal, romantic, or business) with their sponsor. This creates the power imbalance that facilitates these abuses and makes it extremely difficult for women (and all people) to escape these situations without facing the threat of deportation. If a woman marries a U.S. citizen, her immigration status is dependent on their relationship. If a woman comes to the United States to serve as a domestic worker or childcare provider with an American family, her visa is contingent on her employment with them. All of these circumstances leave women extremely vulnerable to abuse and exploitation. U.S. immigration policies are partially to blame, as well as the foreign countries that do not do a sufficient job of protecting women in these situations and educating them about their rights. Once again, we see how immigrant women are particularly vulnerable to rape and sexual abuse because of their socioeconomic position, an issue that current strategies for combating rape do not address directly.

CONTROLLING REPRODUCTION: ANOTHER FORM OF SEXUAL VIOLENCE AGAINST IMMIGRANT WOMEN

A 2006 *Ms.* magazine exposé on sweatshop labor in garment factories in the Commonwealth of the Northern Mariana Islands (CNMI) found that some women employed there were coerced into having abortions for fear of losing their jobs: "According to a 1998 investigation by the Department of Interior Office of Insular Affairs, a number of Chinese garment workers reported that if they became pregnant, they were 'forced to return to China to have an abortion or forced to have an illegal abortion' in the Marianas."[6]

This is not the only attempt at institutional control over immigrant women's reproduction. In the early 1970s, medical students and community activists at the USC–Los Angeles County hospital uncovered that hundreds of Mexican-origin women in the U.S. had been sterilized without their consent. Most of the women were sterilized shortly after delivering by cesarean section. This coercion took various forms, from the women's being asked to sign consent forms in English (when most spoke only Spanish), women's being told that the procedure was reversible, or women who were offered the operation while in labor.[7] Because of the way they impact and manipulate women's sexual and reproductive lives, coercively ster-ilizing women, forcing them through economic incentives (like the threat of being fired) to terminate pregnancies, and offering them long-term birth control at no or low cost are all forms of sexual violence against immigrant women. Racist population-control philosophies are behind these policies and practices, from the myth about immigrant women using "anchor babies" to stay in the United States to misconceptions and fears about overpopulation among certain racial and ethnic groups.

MOVING FORWARD: FIGHTING BACK AGAINST THE ABUSE OF IMMIGRANT WOMEN

When the International Marriage Broker Restriction Act (IMBRA) was first introduced in the United States, its sponsors wanted to name it the Anastasia King Bill, after an Eastern European immigrant woman who was murdered in 2000 by her American husband. For years, Asian Pacific Islander women had been abused and exploited in these international marriages—there were even two very high-profile murders of Filipina women in Washington state in the 1990s.[8] It is no coincidence that in spite of this history, the sponsors wanted to name it after a white immigrant—or that the bill was introduced after Eastern European women were brought into the international marriage market. In the end, the API community mobilized against the naming of the bill, and it was changed to IMBRA. These acts of sexual violence against immigrant women, while invariably very much connected to issues of gender and inequality, are also inseparable from issues of class and race.

The National Coalition for Immigrant Women's Rights (NCIWR) is a coalition—led by the National Latina Institute for Reproductive Health (NLIRH), the National Asian Pacific American Women's Forum (NAPAWF), and the National Organization for Women (NOW)—that puts the needs of immigrant women at the center of the immigration-reform debate. While in recent years the percentage of female immigrants coming into the United States has amplified tremendously, debates continue to center on this profile of the immigrant: a single Latino male, coming over to work in agriculture and construction, who sends money home to his native country. In reality, women and children are crossing the border as well in higher and higher numbers, and their needs are distinctly different from those of single men.

In addition to advocating for national, state, and local policy changes, organizations like NLIRH and NAPAWF also work to place immigrant women themselves at the center of organizing for reproductive justice. NLIRH works with groups of women around the country, particularly in larger immigrant communities (like those near the Texas/Mexico border), to ensure that their voices and needs are part of these immigration-reform discussions. NAPAWF's "Rights to Survival and Mobility: An Anti-Trafficking Activist's Agenda" provides a tool for grassroots activists to use to combat trafficking in their communities. The guide outlines the complexities of human trafficking and the API community, a broad-based anti-trafficking agenda, and steps for activists to take in organizing in their communities. Tools like these take complex issues and attempt to educate and spread awareness about the abuses immigrant women face, while leading individuals toward action. It is crucial that work that prioritizes immigrant women has their voices and perspectives at its center.

A number of laws have been passed that also attempt to protect immigrant women from abuse. Organizations like the American Civil Liberties Union (ACLU) and those mentioned above have been an important part of the process of passing this legislation. The Violence Against Women Act (VAWA) and the Trafficking Victims Protection Act (TVPA) try to protect immigrant women from abuses by offering them a path to citizenship if they are victims of intimate-partner violence or trafficking. IMBRA attempted to regulate the international bride industry and protect women entering into those agreements. Federal sterilization guidelines passed in 1979 as a direct result of organizing around the sterilization abuses Mexican-origin women in Los Angeles faced have also tried to protect immigrant women (and all women) from coercive ster-ilization by mandating informed-consent procedures. While these pieces of legislation are an important tool in the arsenal to combat violence against immigrant women, they alone are not enough to protect women, many of whom do not know about these laws or have access to the legal services needed to use them.

Community activists have also long been involved in the work to stem abuses against immigrant women. As part of labor movements, nationalist movements, and immigration-reform efforts, grassroots activists have been fighting against the abuses that immigrant women face. The U.S./Mexico border has been a particularly active site of resistance and organizing, on both sides of the border. Women in Ciudad Juárez have been speaking about the murders of countless numbers of women there, as have organizations and activists in California and Texas. A group of domestic workers in Maryland has been organizing against abuses by diplomats in conjunction with CASA de Maryland, providing support and resources to women in these domestic-worker arrangements. Bloggers of color have also been writing and speaking publicly about these abuses to draw attention to them. Blogger Brownfemipower[9] has written about immigration abuses in the Latina community for the last three years, as have a slew of other writers, including The Unapologetic Mexican[10] and numerous reporters and organizations.

What does a world without rape look like for immigrant women? These forms of sexual violence are inextricably linked to issues of race, class, and gender. Immigrant women will not be free from rape until we see economic justice, until all people have access to living-wage jobs, education, healthcare services, and safe living environments. Activist movements are restructuring the frameworks we use to organize to emphasize this intersectionality and the need for cross-movement work. The reproductive justice movement (led by organizations like Asian Communities for reproductive justice, the National Latina Institute for Reproductive Health, National Asian Pacific American Women's Forum, SisterSong Reproductive Justice Collective, and others) focuses on how all of these aspects of a woman's life are intertwined and must be taken into account in order to effect change.

Reclaiming female sexual power means reclaiming immigrant women's position within the larger social institutions. Movements of sex-positivity—particularly those that have gained popularity among U.S. feminists—aren't enough to combat this type of sexualized violence against immigrant women. These movements do not have the same resonance in immigrant communities, nor necessarily the same efficacy, for reasons of cultural differences as well as race and class dynamics. Sexual autonomy, respect for one's body, embracing sexual pleasure, and diversity are all well and good but do not serve women in economically vulnerable situations, who do not have the freedom to make decisions for themselves, who face the obstacles of oppression from various fronts. We have to combat the forms of institutionalized violence that facilitate these abuses; we have to work to place the most marginalized populations at the center of our organizing and move beyond overly individualistic strategies.

If you want to read more about Fight The Power, try:

- Invasion of Space by a Female by **Coco Fusco**
- The Not-Rape Epidemic by **Latoya Peterson**
- Who're You Calling a Whore?: A Conversation with Three Sex Workers on Sexuality, Empowerment, and the Industry by **Susan Lopez, Mariko Passion, Saundra**

If you want to read more about Race Relating, try:

- Queering Black Female Heterosexuality by **Kimberly Springer**
- What It Feels Like When It Finally Comes: Surviving Incest in Real Life by **Leah Lakshmi Piepzna-Samarasinha**
- When Pregnancy Is Outlawed, Only Outlaws Will Be Pregnant by **Tiloma Jayasingh**

CHAPTER FOURTEEN

Prostitution: The Gendered Crime

By Jody Raphael and Mary C. Ellison

Prostitution is the ultimate gendered crime. Although there are boys and men who sell sex, demand for girls' and women's bodies fuels the very lucrative world-wide sex trade industry. Until recently, the criminal justice system has pursued a gendered approach to prostitution, with no or few penalties for male buyers as compared to harsh sanctions for female sellers. In fact, in 1962 the American Law Institute enshrined this unequal treatment in its influential Model Penal Code, which specified a misdemeanor penalty with jail time for women in prostitution, but only a minor infraction with a fine for the customer. The Institute justified the unequal treatment on the fact that the women receive money from the activity, making their crime more serious, deserving of harsher penalties (Lefler, 1999).

This gendered pattern has recently been disrupted by new facts coming forward about the trafficking of women and girls into prostitution, which forces a consideration of the women as victims rather than as criminals. They can be considered victims of violence and degradation from customers, and victims of coercion and violence from pimps and traffickers as well.

Until recently in the United States prostitution was *ipso facto* legal, because laws in every state other than Nevada criminalizing prostitution were rarely enforced, typically and only when law enforcement officials were under pressure to clean up newly gentrified neighborhoods. Within the last five years, however, government policy in the United States has undergone a major change. Due to new concerns about sex trafficking, law enforcement officials have stepped up efforts to apprehend customers buying sex from minors, have begun to develop procedures to identify and rescue trafficked women and girls, and have started to prosecute the men and women who have recruited, controlled, and abused them for profit. In the United States, the government has recently taken a new look at prostitution, viewing the young girls supplying the demand as victims of coercion, violence, and abuse, and not as offenders or perpetrators, a development that has not been mirrored in Europe or other countries around the world.

As law enforcement and state legislators are revising laws and practices on prostitution in response to these new facts, a hotly contested debate has arisen. Viewing prostitution as sex between consenting adults, some commentators take great pains to differentiate prostitution from sex trafficking, which involves fraud, violence and coercion, often along with relocation to obtain access to a particular market. Arguing for decriminalization of prostitution, they look upon women in prostitution as those who have freely chosen to participate and abusive customers to be in the minority (Weitzer, 2010). Others (Jeffreys, 2009) believe that increased demand for women's bodies in prostitution, especially in venues like Germany where prostitution is legal, make trafficking, violence, and coercion inevitable as an adequate quantity of volunteers to meet this new demand is unavailable. They worry about the implications of so many uneducated poor women of color without economic opportunities supplying this demand. Is participation truly voluntary? How does this power differential affect customer behavior? And, as the majority of women in prostitution begin regularly as teens, is consent a meaningful term in this context?

It would be helpful if facts could settle this dispute about the nature of prostitution and its acceptability, but the clandestine nature of the sex trade industry makes constructing representative samples for research impossible. Research cannot give us any real sense of the number of girls and women currently active in the sex trade on any given day and their race and ethnicity. Nor can research help determine the number of individuals trafficked for the sex trade.

For example, estimates are bandied about by governmental and nongovernmental groups about the prevalence of trafficking for the sex trade. Supporters of decriminalization rightfully point out that the number of trafficked individuals in the United States often put forward by the State Department is just an estimate not resting on any sound research base (Weitzer, 2010), and in this they are entirely correct. Over the past few years, the number of trafficking cases identified by law enforcement in the United States has been low; only about 2,515 suspected incidents of human trafficking were identified for investigation between January 2008 and June 2010 by 45 federally funded task forces (Banks and Kyckelhahn, 2011). It is interesting to note, however, that the number of trafficking cases investigated and charged has risen appreciably during the past five years in the United States, presenting much useful information about how victims are recruited and controlled, and the manner in which the business is structured and managed. And since 2007, the National Human Trafficking Resource Center hotline has identified 4,904 potential human trafficking victims (Polaris Project, 2011a).

Given the difficulty of identifying or discovering trafficking victims, who are always deeply hidden, these data cannot in and of themselves dictate a definitive conclusion about the extent of sex trafficking in the United States. But from cases investigated by law enforcement during the past few years and research with samples of women and girls in the sex trade industry in the United States, much is beginning to emerge that has heavily influenced law enforcement to view women and girls in the sex trade industry as victims rather than perpetrators. This chapter will explore relevant research findings as well as new criminal justice responses to these data in the United States.

PROSTITUTED GIRLS AND WOMEN IN THE UNITED STATES

Childhood Sexual Assault

Although most childhood sexual abuse survivors do not engage in prostitution, the large majority of women in prostitution in the United States have been victims of incest and other forms of sexual abuse. Two recent studies of women in street prostitution found that half had been sexually abused as children (Kramer and Berg, 2003; Surratt, Inciardi, Kurtz and Kiley, 2004). Research with women who had all been involved in prostitution before age 18 found that 91 percent had a child abuse history (Nixon, Tutty, Downe, Gorkoff and Ursel, 2002), and interviews with 13 girls who were victims of sex trafficking in Toledo, Ohio found that 91 percent had experienced child abuse in their homes (Williamson and Prior, 2009). In a sample of more than 1,000 women in the Cook County Jail (Chicago) between 1991 and 1993, detainees who had experienced childhood sexual abuse had substantially higher rates of ever being involved in prostitution (44 percent), compared with 28.5 percent for detainees with no history of abuse. Childhood sexual assault nearly doubled the odds of entry into prostitution during the lifetime of the respondent (McClanahan, McClelland, Abram and Teplin, 1999).

Childhood sexual assault teaches girls that sexual favors are a commodity to be exchanged both for survival and for developmental needs like intimacy and sense of importance. In addition, prostitution appears to be a mechanism assisting girls and women to cope with distressing violation and loss of control; by exchanging sex this time for money, they achieve a sense of missing empowerment by controlling the circumstances under which someone can sexually penetrate their bodies (Campbell, Ahrens, Seft and Clark 2003). Because they have stayed in the sexual arena to try to reclaim missing power, women and girls in prostitution, already victims of unimaginable violence, become enmeshed in survival strategies that, as we shall see, can put them in danger from both customers and pimps and traffickers.

Age of Entry

Due to our inability to construct a representative sample of women and girls in prostitution, determining the average age of entry into the sex trade in the United States is impossible. We neither know the total number of girls and women involved, nor their race and ethnicity, and given the clandestine nature of the sex trade industry, we will never be able to determine them. In addition, computations of average age of entry depend on the ages of the girls and women in any given research sample. For example, with a group of almost 50 women who entered prostitution before age 18, two-thirds began their involvement when they were 15 years of age or less (Nixon et al., 2002), a low age because everyone in the sample had, by definition, begun by age 18. And with a sample of 100 young girls up to age 25, all of whom were controlled by a pimp at the time of the interview, the median age of entry was 16, with 33 percent entering between 12 and 15 years of age (Raphael and Reichert, 2008). However, it is entirely possible that pimp-controlled girls enter prostitution at ages earlier than others.

Research with different samples of women and girls in prostitution in North America, however, consistently finds that the majority enter the industry on a regular basis before age 18. Women of color appear to start in prostitution earlier and stay in longer than white women (McClanahan et al., 1999; Nixon et al., 2002). Researchers speculate that minority girls are more often homeless than white girls, accounting for earlier prostitution entry as a survival strategy (Kramer and Berg, 2003).

Pathways to Prostitution

Determining the pathways of girls and women into the sex trade should help inform humane and effective criminal justice system responses. Yet until recently this issue has received very little attention.

Prostitution as the "Family Business"

When prostitution is "the family business," girls can find themselves coerced into selling their bodies as part of the family enterprise. In two recent research samples, 10–12 percent said they were forced to participate in the family business (Kennedy, Klein, Bristone, Cooper and Yuille, 2007; Raphael, Reichert and Powers, 2010). Accounts from girls "put out" by family members reveal a particularly virulent form of child abuse, like "Linda," whose mother prostituted her as early as age 6:

> My mother was my first pimp. She used to sell me to the landlord and other men who wanted a young girl. She was a junkie. We lived in sleazy hotels where everyone was doing it. My mom was very abusive and she used to beat me if I didn't do what she wanted me to do so she could sell me to her male friends. Sometimes she would hit me so hard and put marks on my face and body that she had to stop letting me go to school.

Linda ran away when she was 15 years old and landed a job selling sex in a massage parlor. Some days she slept in the massage parlor and the manager asked her to watch the desk a couple of times. He told Linda that if she could recruit girls she could run the spot herself as long as she covered each shift with at least three to four girls. Linda accepted the deal.

> I have been pimped all my life, used by my family, and sold to any Johnny-come-lately. I was tired of selling my own body. It wasn't my idea at first, but I knew all the ropes and the girls trusted me. I guess it was being in control of the same situation, I gave orders, and the girls depended on me.
>
> *(Raphael and Myers-Powell, 2010)*

Another young woman told a researcher she had been sold by her father at the age of 10 to a man at a truck stop. At age 12, her father injected her with cocaine and she was forced to prostitute herself on the streets to support their joint drug habits (Kennedy et al., 2007). Coerced prostitution can also be an aspect of domestic violence. In a research project with homeless women, 35 percent had been involved in the sex trade. Of these, all had been coerced into selling sex by their partners, abusive and violent men (Harding and Hamilton, 2009). In Chicago in 2010 prosecutors brought charges against a man who forced his girlfriend to prostitute herself for his financial gain by beating and strangling her and threatening to make false complaints to the child protective service about her young child (*Chicago Sun Times*, 2010). The man took the victim to bars and forced her to solicit men to have sex with her in exchange for money. Although her partner continued to threaten to kill her, she finally found a way to escape and contacted the authorities.

Recruitment By Pimps

Another hotly debated topic is the prevalence of pimps recruiting and managing women and girls in prostitution in North America. Recent research with a Chicago sample of 100 currently pimp-controlled girls found that 71 percent said they were actively recruited into the sex trade, many under conditions meeting the federal definition of trafficking. Thirty-five percent were recruited by someone serving in a role of a boyfriend who in fact was a pimp living off the sale of the young women's bodies (Raphael, Reichert and Powers, 2010). The study documented the ways that the boyfriend pimps "turn women out" by first providing them with attention, protection, and love and a sense of belonging, and then later, building on the sense of indebtedness for gifts and money, asking them to financially help out by selling their bodies, methods documented by other research studies (Kennedy et al., 2007; Williamson and Prior, 2009). At the time of recruitment many of the girls in this study were entirely vulnerable; they were homeless or needed to leave home due to ongoing sexual assault, drug abuse, or domestic violence in the household.

Monica's account shows how needy girls can become involved in prostitution. A pimp helped the 15-year-old run away from home because her mother's boyfriend was abusing her. "He was sleeping with me and no one would believe me, so I was out of there," she said. "We ran out of money while on the road and he showed me how to work the truck stops." Eight years later, she is still with her pimp/boyfriend, having sex with nine customers a day on the street and in hotels. Yet she has no plans to leave him, "I am okay with what I have and do," she explained. "It's better than where I came from" (Raphael and Reichert, 2008).

Over time, however, coercive control and violence were needed to keep the girls and women involved in the industry; after recruitment the girls in the 2008 Chicago sample were more than three times as likely to be pinched or kicked, twice as likely to be punched, kidnapped, or to have clothing ripped, and more than twice as likely to be forced to have sex with their pimps. At the time of the interview, almost 50 percent said they were subjected to punching and sexual assault from their pimps. Girls were also more likely to be transported to customers and the number of customers increased from an average daily of six to ten. They were attacked with hammers and screwdrivers, subjected to suffocation with pillows, and thrown into the trunks of cars. Most doubted their ability to safely exit the sex trade (Raphael and Reichert, 2008). Rachel Lloyd (2011), a survivor of pimp-controlled prostitution, describes the effects of this exploitation:

> In addition to their strategies of control and their paternalistic rationalizations, the other thing that pimps have in common, regardless of who they are, are the damaged lives they leave in their wake. To a girl who's been beaten because she didn't make her quota, or put out on the street after a rape and told, "There's nothing wrong with your mouth," it doesn't really make that much difference whether her pimp was a sociopath or not, if he had one girl or ten, if he ever felt bad about what he was doing, if he wished he could do something else with his life. The humiliation, the physical and emotional pain, the trauma, the nightmares all feel the same. The damage is done.

After receiving an anonymous tip, police officers in Chicago went undercover in 2010 posing as customers in a brothel. There they found the young woman who had called in, as well as five others, one of whom was a 16-year old girl who was picked up from high school several times a week. The girls said they were lured in under false pretenses of legitimate work and held in the brothel servicing customers because of death threats from the madam. "The defendant made threats that this is not the kind of business that you can quit and something terrible would happen to the victims or their families," the prosecutor explained. "One victim was told that something would happen to her daughter, and the other was told that she would turn up dead in an alley" (Walberg and Sweeney, 2010).

Information from interviews with pimp-controlled girls and women and from case files of trafficking cases, while providing important facts about the lives of some girls and women in the sex trade, cannot help us determine how many others are currently pimped and trafficked. Thus the question of just how many girls and women in the sex trade in North America are pimp-controlled and could be said to be victims of trafficking remains unanswered. Indeed, also unknown is just how many juveniles are involved in prostitution in the United States.

The most commonly used estimate of juvenile involvement in the United States comes from Estes and Weiner (2001), who in a highly publicized report stated that about 326,000 children were "at risk for commercial sexual exploitation." The Crimes Against Children Research Center (Stransky and Finkelhor, 2008) convincingly demonstrates that this frequently cited figure cannot even be called an estimate because of the highly speculative nature of its methodology. The Center's own research with law enforcement found 1,450 arrests or detentions in cases involving juveniles in prostitution from police records in 2005. Interestingly, in 57 percent of these cases, a pimp/exploiter was involved, most often a male (85 percent). Of these cases, 59 percent involved pimps with little commercial or organizational sophistication. Only 3 percent of the exploiters were family members (Mitchell, Finkelhor and Wolak, 2009). And in research in 2007 (Gragg, Petta, Bernstein, Eisen and Quinn, 2007), a sample of New York City and Upstate agencies identified 2,652 actual cases of child sexual exploitation in a one-year period. Fifty-eight percent of the children in New York City and 32 percent Upstate had force used to coerce their participation in the sex trade. Finally, in New York City, the majority (43 percent) were between the ages of 14 and 15 at the time of their first exploitation, while in Upstate 43 percent were between the ages of 10 and 11 (Gragg et al., 2007).

The high percentage of pimp exploiters in these juvenile samples leads to a hypothesis that a large number of the youth in prostitution are controlled by pimps and traffickers, pointing the way toward viewing youth in the sex trade industry as victims of commercial sexual exploitation as opposed to delinquents or criminals. Anecdotal information also confirms this supposition; law enforcement officials in San Diego and the Chicago metropolitan area, believing that pimping has become more lucrative and less dangerous than selling drugs, assert that more and more needy young girls like Monica are being recruited over the Internet, through schools, or on the street, lured with money, material items, and love (Lowrey, 2011).

Violence from Customers

That prostituted girls and women on the streets experience violence from customers is not contested. The common occurrences include being beaten, being threatened with a weapon, and being raped or gang raped (Surratt et al., 2004). Women and girls report extreme measures to escape this violence, jumping from cars or running away, often without their clothes or with torn clothing. Every girl and woman selling sex on the street has experienced this scenario and probably more than once:

> They violated me in every way possible. And I just remember trying to hold back the tears and how much pain I was in and how they laughed and thought it was funny … . Like I remember everything that happened, but at that moment I was not there. Like you leave your body … that [the rape] lasted about a good three or four hours. And when they were done with me, threw more dope in my face and left me in the room.
>
> *(Williamson and Prior, 2009)*

Supporters of decriminalization of prostitution allege that indoor prostitution venues do not present similar risks. However, the evidence is mounting that women and girls in escort services are frequently subjected to terrifying acts of violence, most often involving rapes forced with weapons (Church, Henderson, Barnard and Hart, 2001; Raphael and Sha-piro, 2004). The existence of panic buttons in brothel rooms points to the reality of assaults from customers (Jeffreys, 2009). In strip clubs, which all now feature customer contact through lap dancing, women and girls have their genitals licked and men's fingers poked into both orifices (Maticka-Tyndale, Lewis, Clark, Zubick and Young, 2000).

Alcohol and Drugs

For many girls and women in the sex trade, addictions become a way of life, compromising their own safety and their ability to leave the sex trade. Almost 100 percent of samples of women and girls participating in street prostitution are found by researchers to be addicted to alcohol and drugs (Dalla, 2000; Raphael and Shapiro, 2002). Some girls and women turn to prostitution to secure money to supply their addictions, but others already in the sex trade begin to use alcohol and drugs to help them cope or dissociate while in prostitution. Research studies have found equal numbers for both scenarios, cautioning against a single conclusion (Miller, 1995; Raphael and Shapiro, 2002). In fact, drugs and prostitution are inter-related. As one woman in prostitution explained, "I do this work to earn the money to buy gear and I take the gear to block out the work I'm doing" (Coy, 2012).

One research study found a relationship between serious drug addiction and male violence. Women on the streets of New York were likely to experience more physical abuse from customers if the women used cocaine or injected heroin. These women may be less able to protect themselves from violent customers or, alternatively, might be targets for violent men who know they will be less able to resist (El-Bassel, Witte, Wada, Gilbert and Wallace, 2001). As one drug-addicted woman selling sex on the street explained:

> Prostitution, drugs, and violence go hand in hand; it's all in one palm, OK? And because the prostitute is out there to get drugs and because she has an addiction and whether it be violence from the date or violence from the dope boy, either way we're looking at it, there's still violence involved.
>
> *(Surratt* et al., *2004)*

Nor is drug and alcohol addiction limited to women and girls in the streets; drugs and alcohol appear to be prevalent among girls and women in strip clubs and escort services as well (Maticka-Tyndale et al., 2000; Raphael and Shapiro, 2002). An escort service owner interviewed by one researcher said she knew that some of her employees broke her rules prohibiting drug use. Most, she thought, used sedatives that customers were less able to detect (Norton-Hawk, 2003).

Olivia, a survivor of 19 years in the sex trade, describes her use of alcohol and drugs in a Chicago strip club to dissociate:

> I became someone different, it was a whole fantasy thing for me in the club. If customers got rough, or whatever would happen, I would pretend it didn't happen, and not face it at all.

It is kind of like you are out of your body watching someone else do this. At the time, you don't feel, but the next day, always before I reached for that first drink, I would get glimpses of whatever it was that happened, and right away I would want that drink.

(Raphael, 2004)

Customers

Again, the impossibility of constructing a representative research sample makes generalizations about customers impossible. Interviews with samples of customers, however, do present some useful information about some buyers of sex. In an unpublished paper, Martin Monto describes his interviews with 1,636 men in a court-sanctioned voluntary diversionary program, nearly all of whom had propositioned female police officers posing as women in prostitution in the streets of three US cities. When Monto asked the men a series of questions about their sexual preferences, more than half indicated they liked to be in control when having sex and enjoyed being with a woman who likes "to get nasty." They were excited by the idea of approaching a woman in the sex trade and they saw prostitution as positive for women. High frequency of prostitution encounters was strongly associated with these factors.

Only 1 percent reported threatening force to get sex and a mere 11 said they had used force to obtain sex. These men answering "yes" to force were among the frequent users of women in prostitution. Certainly this research is limited because many men may be unwilling to admit to violence or may not view their activities as falling within the rubric of "using force to obtain sex." Nevertheless, the small number of violent men in the sample may account for most of the violence against women, as these men buy sex frequently. One could speculate that as the number of men introduced to sex through prostitution as a social rite of passage has declined, a decrease in the proportion of customers interested in sex and a proportionate increase in the number of violent buyers interested in power and cruelty results.

Some of the comments of a group of 113 Chicago male buyers of sex, recruited as volunteers over the Internet for interviews between 2006–2007, support this hypothesis (Durchslag and Goswami, 2008). Forty-eight percent of interviewees said they wanted to obtain sex acts they either felt uncomfortable asking of their partner or which she refused to perform, including anal and oral sex, group sex, sadomasochism, and domination. Said one:

I want to pay someone to do something a normal person wouldn't do. To piss on someone or pay someone to do something degrading who is not my girlfriend.

Explained another: "It was in Las Vegas—it was a threesome of me and my play bro … we came on her face at the same time, like in the porn movies." And a third stated:

She feels a lot of force between her legs, because I'm not going to be lenient. I'm going to give her everything I've got. You can pound them, she don't mind.

Forty-three percent of interviewees stated that if men pay for sex, the women should do anything they ask: "she gave up her rights when she accepted my money." Similar comments were collected by researchers who interviewed 137 men through newspaper advertisements in East London around the same time (Coy, Horvath and Kelly, 2007). Women were viewed as commodities but not exactly as humans: "A prostitute is a piece of meat;" and "I don't have to ask or think, 'No, is that too dirty for her?' or—like I don't really have to be as respectful as if it was my girlfriend or my wife or partner" were two of the typical responses.

Normalization of Prostitution

As a result of this customer research experience, the London researchers conclude that prostitution has now been positioned as a legitimate service industry with prostituted women the commodity that is consumed. Now a multi-billion dollar worldwide enterprise, the sex trade is marketed as socially acceptable entertainment meeting men's rightful needs. And this message, propagated by television, movies, magazines, and the Internet, has gained widespread acceptance, the exploitation of girls and women in the industry is not widely known.

The strip club boom in the United States reflects the new acceptability of prostitution. In 2005 in the United States, there were an estimated 3,000 clubs employing 300,000 women, with customers said to spend $15 billion a year at these venues (Jeffreys, 2009). Corporations think it a legitimate business practice to take customers, potential customers, and employees to these clubs, all of which feature lap dancing and other opportunities for customer contact in back rooms (Juettner, 2011). In the UK former Prime Minister Margaret Thatcher was a guest at a Tory Party fundraiser in a London strip club, and Prince Harry as well as the son of the then Prime Minister Blair were spotted at other strip clubs (Jeffreys, 2009). Parties of male college athletic teams feature strippers, as in the Duke lacrosse case, as do pre-wedding stag party celebrations, which now can involve out-of-state or even out-of-country trips. On the Internet companies advertise sex tours to locations such as Costa Rica, Thailand, and Amsterdam, where the industry is said to be worth a substantial proportion of Gross National Product (Jeffreys, 2009). The over three million annual visitors to Atlanta, Georgia conventions are handed advertisement cards for discounts at area strip clubs, with the cards also distributed at sporting events. One major hotel's courtesy guest shuttle was observed providing transportation for guests to a strip club (Jeffreys, 2009).

Another manifestation of the acceptance of the sex trade industry in the United States is the current admiration of pimps and prostitutes as sexy players, as evidenced by high sales of pimp and prostitute adult Halloween costumes and pimp and prostitute costume balls on Halloween, even in toddler sizes (Harris, 2004). The circumstances under which girls and women supply their bodies to meet the entertainment needs of men and their experiences while doing so are totally ignored, and no more so than the disregard for the self-confessed exploitative role of pimps. That the Oscar for best original song in 2006 went to "It's Hard Out Here for a Pimp" was a matter of amazement to many, as was the performance of the number on the televized award program, featuring men dressed as pimps and women in the hot pants and rabbit furs of streetwalkers, while the song lyrics were chanted: "That's the way the game goes, gotta keep it strictly pimpin / Gotta have my hustle tight, makin change off these women, yeah." (Thomas-Lester, 2006).

Survivor Rachel Lloyd (2011) is outraged by the idolization of pimps:

> Right now, the pendulum has swung so far in favor of pimps that it's critical to bring it back to the reality of their crimes, the damage that they do, the callousness with which they treat girls' and women's lives. We don't have to demonize them. Stopping the glorification would be enough for now.

Another factor in the normalization of the sex trade industry has been Craigslist's Erotic Services Forum. Maintaining over 30 million new classified Internet advertisements and viewed over 9 billion times every month, Craigslist is in ninth place among web sites in the United States with estimated revenues at $80 million a year (AIM group, 2010). In September 2003 Craigslist began to accept prostitution advertisements, complete with revealing photographs. During a one-month period, one study examined eight American cities, finding that the erotic services sections consistently garnered the highest number of individual visitors, almost twice as many as the next ranking category, averaging 260,000 per city (Bagg, 2007). Advocacy groups considered the web site to be one of the largest sources for prostitution in the country, efficiently facilitating linkage of the buyer and the seller. But more importantly, Craigslist is a mainstream web site normally used by consumers wishing to buy or sell automobiles or furniture, with the result that buyers of sex achieve a sense of comfort using Craigslist to make assignations. Advertisements for escort services and massage parlors can also be found in newspaper sports pages and in the classified sections of alternative newspapers in large cities.

Empowerment or Exploitation?

Contributing to this cultural acceptance of prostitution has been a split between feminists about the value of participation in the sex trade industry for women and girls. A small but vocal minority insists that involvement is empowering for women (Jeffreys, 2009). Those females who sell sex, they aver, are socially transgressive, openly defying the roles (home and family) that patriarchal society has given them. Thus laws against prostitution are viewed as the state's interference with a person's sexual freedom and autonomy. Furthermore, they believe that women in prostitution are empowered, controlling the male customers and taking their money, and do not want to regard them as victims:

> With men the suckers, and women pocketing the cash, the striptease becomes a reversal of society's conventional male/female roles. Striptease is, at its core, a form of role reversal in which women are "clearly in charge."
>
> *(Jeffreys, 2009)*

In the main, persons putting forth these views are focusing on feminist theory; facts about violence and coercion do not appear to affect them. Those who do admit to some violence in the sex trade attribute all of it to the fact of prostitution's criminalization, as the outlawing of the sex trade enshrines into law the view that the women are bad women, and thus legitimate targets for abuse. Organized groups of "sex workers" fight initiatives for arresting customers and advocate instead for safer workplaces. By airbrushing the harms that girls and women suffer in the sex trade industry, feminists advocating legalization of prostitution have aided in its cultural normalization and acceptance.

In her interviews with almost 20 current and former strippers Jennifer Wesely (2002) did learn about the sense of power the women felt at the customers' attention and adulation. But at the same time she discovered the frequent vulnerability and exploitation when the dancers lost control of their own bodies while stripping, as customers viewed the women merely as sexual objects and acted accordingly. Although the dancers made efforts to stay in control, their attempts were constantly undermined by customer assumptions of entitlement, indicating that the experiences of women and girls in the sex trade industry are more varied and nuanced than those put forward by feminists who have embraced participation as empowering.

Other researchers have documented the long-term psychological effects on women as they participate in the industry. Coy (2012) found that women moved from feelings of agency and autonomy to being depersonalized commodities and they internalized the belief, becoming dehumanized, disembodied selves:

> The contamination experienced by women is therefore not just about being viewed as worthless by societies and communities, but the treatment of the disembodied self as valueless except for sexual gratification. Women thus appear to absorb a sense of being disposable and devalued through social perception *as well* as the actions of sex buyers for whom they are interchangeable outlets for sexual release.

A pro sex industry stance, other feminists assert, ignores the reality of today's sex trade industry, with its huge demand for women's bodies and the phenomenon of trafficking, which undermine the viability of concepts of consent and agency. They also maintain that some feminists are blind to the fact that the entire sex trade industry is organized around male domination and men's rights to be sexually serviced, which totally ignore women's rights and sexual needs (Jeffreys, 2009).

This spirited battle between groups of feminists continues to rage with no relief in sight. What is new, however, is that law enforcement officials and the criminal justice system have recently accepted the view that women and girls in the sex trade industry should more properly be thought of as victims of exploitation and violence.

US CRIMINAL JUSTICE SYSTEM RESPONSES

Arrests of Women and Girls

Although all states except Nevada have laws penalizing prostitution for both buyers and sellers, arrests for prostitution have generally remained low because of law enforcement's higher priorities such as drug sales and gun crime. In 2009, for example, there were only 48,281 arrests nationwide for prostitution and commercial vice (Federal Bureau of Investigation, 2010), but these data do not enable us to determine how many were for prostitution as opposed to commercial vice; nor can the numbers be broken down between buyers and sellers. Most often, however, those arrested are the sellers. In 2009, for example, in Chicago Police Department arrests for prostitution-related offenses twice the number of women were arrested as were men (1,150 men and 2,259 women) (Chicago Police Department, 2009). This discrepancy reflects an historical bias of demonizing and punishing the seller of sex (female) as opposed to the buyer, as was demonstrated in the case of New York State Governor Eliot Spitzer, who was caught, as part of another investigation altogether, employing an escort service for multiple assignations in violation of his own state's laws. Spitzer was never prosecuted, but Manhattan Madam Kristin Davis, who arranged his appointments, served four months in a New York City jail on prostitution charges, in addition to five years probation (Weber, 2010).

As much as 80 percent of prostitution may now occur indoors, making arrests of either buyer or seller impossible without law enforcement officials employing sting methods in which they pose as customers; to arrest buyers, police have to impersonate prostituted women. Resources for these activities in the past have been scarce.

Arrests of women and girls in prostitution can be seen as penalizing individuals who are already violence victims and who may be under control of a pimp and unable to leave prostitution safely. Nor, until recently, does arrest do anything to bring needed services to these girls and women. Furthermore, given the demand for girls and women in prostitution, their very arrest creates a situation that causes *more* girls and women to be recruited to take their places.

The American approach has been diametrically opposite to that in Europe during the past ten to 15 years, where prostitution has been decriminalized or decriminalized in part and regulated. These initiatives were thought to promote better health and safety for the girls and women as well as preventing their arrest, incarceration, and stigmatization. However, in these countries demand for women and girls in prostitution has increased exponentially, and with that has come increased trafficking of young girls to meet these additional needs (Jeffreys, 2009). As a result, these countries must confront the difficulty of fighting pimping and trafficking within the context of public policy that has legalized prostitution.

The Campaign Against Craigslist

In the United States law enforcement officials had the opportunity to learn about the trafficking of local girls and women as these individuals came to their attention through hotline calls and use of the Internet for prostitution stings. As awareness of trafficking and pimping grew, police officers and sheriffs began to ask arrestees how they were transported to the site and whether they were controlled by another person. Sometimes they heard shocking accounts that ultimately led to arrests of traffickers.

Throughout the country, sting operations using Craigslist advertisements demonstrated that the Internet site was indeed a hub for child prostitution. At a news conference in March 2009, Cook County Sheriff Tom Dart announced that between 2007 and 2009 his officers arrested traffickers and pimps through Craigslist, many of whom had pimped girls as young as 14. On one occasion, the Sheriff's officers responded to a Craigslist post that featured a nude photograph of a 16-year-old girl, who said she was forced into prostitution by two men who were later arrested and charged. Eventually, 43 state attorney generals called upon Craigslist to shut down its Erotic Services Forum. In November 2008 their negotiations resulted in Craigslist's promises of implementation of a screening system to prevent the posting of advertisements of juveniles as well as better monitoring of the site (Saletan, 2010). Craigslist, however, continued to argue that federal law provided it with immunity for the content of the advertisements placed by others on its site. It also maintained that the site provided a valuable service to law enforcement by providing a method of catching pimps and traffickers through stings (Saletan, 2010). During the campaign against Cragislist, two young women, whose pimps put up their pictures on Craigslist, provided information about how they had been sold on the Internet site at ages as young as 11 (McGreal, 2010). In March 2009 Cook County Sheriff Tom Dart filed a case in the US district court in Chicago against Craiglist, seeking an injunction against the site as well as damages.

Sheriff Dart lost his lawsuit in October 2010 when the district judge ruled that federal law immunized Craigslist from liability for the content of Craigslist advertisements, even if they were promoting illegal activities. He did, however, win the war when Craigslist shut down its Erotic Services Forum the month before. However, Backpage.com, operated by Village Voice Media, appears to have seen a 17.5 percent increase in the number of its online prostitution listings within a few months and attention has now turned toward shutting down that web site (AIM group, 2010). But importantly, the information law enforcement gleaned from its undercover activities with Craigslist's advertisements has helped build the case that there is enough of a serious problem with pimping and trafficking of local girls and women, especially minors, to warrant new laws, policies, practices, and priorities.

New Legal Approaches

Although new laws and policies have emerged in the last decade, the struggle to reconcile the fundamental fallacy that one can be both criminal defendant and crime victim simultaneously remains embedded and embodied in the laws of the United States related to prostitution and sex trafficking, including the sex trafficking of minors. This fact both necessitates and greatly complicates efforts to create new laws and policies to protect sex trafficking victims and to prosecute purchasers of commercial sex.

When the Trafficking Victims Protection Act (TVPA) was enacted in 2000, Congress attempted to resolve the long-standing issue of whether one may simultaneously be both criminal defendant and crime victim. In the TVPA sex trafficking is defined as "the recruitment, harboring, transportation, provision, or obtaining of a person for the purpose of a commercial sex act" (21 USC § 7102 (9)). The TVPA also defines severe forms of trafficking in persons as "sex trafficking in which a commercial sex act is induced by force, fraud, or coercion, or in which the person induced to perform such act has not attained 18 years of age" (21 USC § 7102 (8)). A commercial sex act is "any sex act on account of which anything of value is given to or received by any person" (21 USC § 7102 (3)).

As of October 2011, 45 states have sex trafficking criminal offenses, many of which follow the federal definition of sex trafficking. All states prohibit the prostitution of minors under state laws predating the enactment of the federal anti-trafficking law. Twenty-five states provide for a lower burden of proof for sex trafficking of minors that does not mandate evidence of force, fraud, or coercion (Polaris Project, 2011b).

Given these definitions, it should be clear that a sex trafficked individual under 18 who is recruited, harbored, transported, provided or obtained for prostitution is a crime victim of the severe form of trafficking in persons, and therefore not a criminal defendant. It also stands to reason that an adult forced, defrauded, or coerced into prostitution is a crime victim of the severe form of trafficking in persons, and therefore not a criminal defendant. Furthermore, an adult recruited, harbored, transported, provided or obtained for prostitution is a crime victim of sex trafficking and therefore not a criminal defendant.

Despite these seemingly logical conclusions, the criminal justice system in the United States often treats sex trafficking victims as criminal defendants to be arrested, detained, charged, convicted, and incarcerated. In fact, the system misplaces its focus on the victims rather than on purchasers of commercial sex. Only a few states have faced the fundamental fallacy head-on by developing, passing, and enacting legislation to ensure that the criminal justice system treats both adult and minor victims of sex trafficking as the crime victims they are rather than as criminal defendants.

Some states allow adult victims of sex trafficking to raise a specific affirmative defense to the charge of prostitution by demonstrating they are victims of sex trafficking under either federal or state law (Alabama, Connecticut, Iowa, Minnesota, New Hampshire, New Jersey, Oklahoma, Oregon, Rhode Island, Vermont, and Wisconsin). In other states, sex trafficking victims may raise the general defenses of duress, necessity, justification, or choice of evils if accused of crimes incident to the sex trafficking situation. Adult sex trafficking victims may apply to vacate prostitution convictions incident to their sex trafficking in New York (2010), Maryland (2011), Nevada (2011), and Illinois (2011). These types of laws enable trafficking victims to avoid criminal convictions or to erase those criminal records, an important first step addressing the fundamental fallacy and shifting the paradigm.

Minor victims of sex trafficking may find "safe harbor" in an innovative and relatively recent type of law aimed at protecting children from being treated as criminals and rather treating them as crime victims. As of 2011, seven states had enacted forms of "safe harbor" laws: Connecticut (2010), Illinois (2010), Minnesota (2011), New York (2008), Tennessee (2011), Vermont (2011), and Washington (2010). Although each of these states has approached the idea of protecting sex trafficked minors differently, they have signaled that policymakers, law enforcement, and the criminal justice system should shift their response from one of criminalization to restoration.

As the first state to recognize the need for restoration of sex trafficked children, New York legally recognized that children engaged in prostitution need specialized services and protection due to their status as victims of a brutal form of sexual abuse, exploitation, and in fact, human trafficking. New York defines a "sexually exploited child" as "any person under the age of eighteen who has been subject to sexual exploitation because he or she: is a victim of the crime of sex trafficking" (New York Statute § 447-a (2008)). The New York "Safe Harbor for Exploited Children Act" also mandates child welfare services provide for sexually exploited children by placing them in shelter, providing crisis intervention and community-based programming (New York Statute § 447-b (2008)). The law presumes that an individual under 18 arrested for prostitution is a sex trafficking victim and allows for a child protection response rather than a juvenile delinquency response (New York Statute § 311.4 (2008)).

Laws to protect minor victims of sex trafficking should strive to include the following general principles: (1) Prevent minor victims of sex trafficking from being prosecuted for prostitution including immunity for individuals under 18 from prosecution for prostitution; define trafficked children as victims of abuse and neglect; and divert arrested children to child protection rather than juvenile delinquency proceedings; (2) Ensure that knowledge of age and coercion are not required to prosecute sex trafficking of children, including penalizing child traffickers without proof of force, fraud, or coercion; and hold purchasers of children for commercial sex acts accountable with strong penalties and without the option of raising the "mistake of age" defense; and (3) Protect minor victims of sex trafficking by providing them with specialized services.

In implementing these general principles, states tend to fall along one or more continua. One continuum determines the approach taken by the criminal justice system, while another continuum determines the degree of services provided to sex trafficked children. Yet another continuum determines the level of accountability for purchasers of commercial sex, which typically has not been addressed contemporaneously with "safe harbor" laws.

The first continuum ranges from an approach which presumes that an individual under 18 arrested for prostitution is a sex trafficking victim (New York and Washington), but only diverts her (him) temporarily from prosecution, to one which grants immunity from prosecution to an individual under 18 arrested for prostitution (Illinois, Tennessee, and Vermont). A second ranges from an approach without services (Connecticut), to services phased in over time (Minnesota and New York), to one that provides comprehensive and near-term services to sex trafficked children (Illinois and Vermont). The third ranges from an approach which does not penalize purchasers appropriately given their status as statutory rapists, to one which creates suitable penalties and disallows defenses such as the "mistake of age" defense.

At least ten states still allow purchasers of commercial sex acts from minors to assert the defense that he or she reasonably believed the person was of the age of consent at the time of the act (Arizona, Arkansas, Illinois, Indiana, Kentucky, Maine, New York, Washington, West Virginia, and Wyoming). In 2011, several state legislatures considered legislation to increase penalties for purchasing sex from minors or habitually from adults. Many states have passed laws that increase the penalties for procuring or purchasing prostitution (Colorado, Georgia, and Tennessee), procuring or seeking to procure the sexual services of a minor (California), or habitual solicitation of prostitution (Hawaii). New York also sent a bill to the Governor that would create a separate offense with increased penalties for patronizing a prostitute within a school zone. Oregon legislators approved increased criminal penalties and mandatory fines for customers who patronize minors who have been exploited through prostitution. Although the passage of such laws signals an increasing interest in holding sex purchasers accountable, whether the laws will be implemented remains to be seen in light of the fact that trafficked and prostituted individuals frequently bear the brunt of law enforcement efforts.

Alternative penalty schemes for purchasers of adults, known as "john's schools," provide men with education about the realities of the commercial sex industry, harm to the prostituted and trafficked individuals, and the effect on families and communities, based on the model used by Standing Against Global Exploitation (SAGE) in California, Breaking Free in Minnesota, and many other organizations. Such programs fill the need of educating purchasers, but do not meet the imperative of educating boys and men about the harm in purchasing sex prior to commission of the act.

CONCLUSION

As it is the huge demand for women's bodies in the sex trade industry itself that produces trafficking, the attempt to differentiate prostitution from sex trafficking is one doomed to failure. In 2007 in the United States alone, revenue from the sale of women and girls enslaved in sex trafficking netted traffickers and exploiters $581 million (Kara, 2009). Given the profitability of the sale of women, men, and children, the only way to end their exploitation is to alter purchasers' behavior through legal risk, while at the same time increasing the legal risk to traffickers, and simultaneously continuing to shift from criminalizing the victims to providing protection and services. Such an approach eliminates the gender discrimination inherent in law enforcement's traditional approach to prostitution, while at the same time dismantling the industry that exploits women an girls.

REFERENCES

AIM group (2010, October 19). *Backpage replaces Craigslist as prostitution-ad leader.* Aimgroup.com/blog/2010/10/19/backpage-replaces-craigslist-as-prostitution-ad-leader.

Bagg, S. (2007). *Craigslist's dirty little secret.* Blog at *completepulse*, April 6, http://blog.compete.com/2007/04/05/craigslist-popular-categories.

Banks, D. and Kyckelhahn, T. (2011). *Characteristics of suspected human trafficking incidents, 2008–2010.* Washington, DC: Office of Justice Programs, U.S. Department of Justice.

Campbell, R., Ahrens, C., Sefl, T. and Clark, M. (2003). The relationship between adult sexual assault and prostitution: An exploratory analysis. *Violence and Victims, 18,* 299–317.

Chicago Sun Times (2010, December 22). Chicago man accused of sex trafficking girl friend.

Chicago Police Department (2009). *Arrests by offense classification, age and gender.* Chicago, IL: Chicago Police Department Annual Report.

Church, S., Henderson, M., Barnard, M. and Hart, G. (2001). Violence by clients towards female prostitutes in different settings: Questionnaire survey. *British Medical Journal, 322,* 524–5.

Coy, M. (2012). "Sometimes I'm just a hole for men to use": Women's accounts of the psychosocial harms of prostitution. In M. Coy (ed.), *Prostitution, harm and gender inequality.* London: Ashgate.

Coy, M., Horvath, M. and Kelly, L. (2007). *It's just like going to the supermarket: Men buying sex in East London.* London: London Metropolitan University, Child Woman Abuse Studies Unit.

Dalla, R. (2000). Exposing the "pretty woman" myth: A qualitative examination of the lives of female streetwalking prostitutes. *Journal of Sex Research, 37,* 344–53.

Durchslag, R. and Goswami, S. (2008). *Deconstructing the demand for prostitution: Preliminary insights from interviews with Chicago men who purchase sex.* Chicago, IL: Chicago Alliance Against Sexual Exploitation.

El-Bassel, N., Witte, S. S., Wada, T., Gilbert, L. and Wallace, J. (2001). Correlates of partner violence among female street-based sex workers: Substance abuse, history of childhood abuse, and HIV risks. *AIDS Patient Care and STDs, 15,* 41–51.

Estes, R. and Weiner, N. (2001). *The commercial sexual exploitation of children in the U.S., Canada, and Mexico.* Philadelphia, PA: University of Pennsylvania School of Social Work.

Federal Bureau of Investigation (2010). *Crime in the United States, 2010.* www.fbi.gov/about-us/cjs/ucr/crime-in-the-u.s./2010.

Gragg, F., Petta, F., Bernstein, H., Eisen, K and Quinn, L. (2007). *New York prevalence study of commercially sexually exploited children.* Rensselaer, NY: New York State Office of Children and Family Services.

Harding, R. and Hamilton, P. (2009). Working girls: Abuse or choice in street-level sex work? A study of homeless women in Nottingham. *British Journal of Social Work, 39,* 1118–37.

Harris, R. (2004). Pimp costumes ill-fitting? Some see popular Halloween garb as more trash than flash. *Seattle Times* October 30. Retrieved from: community.seattletimes.nwsource.com/archive/? date=20041030+slugspimps30.

Jeffreys, S. (2009). *The industrial vagina: The political economy of the global sex trade.* New York: Routledge.

Juettner, J. (2011, May 25). German prostitutes speak out: "Corporate sex parties are commonplace." *Spiegel Online,* www.spiegel.de/international/business/0,1518,764830,00.html.

Kara, S. (2009). *Sex trafficking: Inside the business of modern slavery.* New York: Columbia University Press.

Kennedy, M. A., Klein, C., Bristowe, J. T. K., Cooper, B. S. and Yuille, J. C. (2007). Routes of recruitment: Pimps' techniques and other circumstances that lead to street prostitution. *Journal of Aggression, Maltreatment & Trauma, 15,* 2–19.

Kramer, L. and Berg, E. (2003). A survival analysis of timing of entry into prostitution: The differential impact of race, educational level, and childhood/adolescent risk factors. *Sociological Inquiry, 73,* 511–28.

Lefler, J. (1999). Shining the spotlight on johns: Moving toward equal treatment of male customers and female prostitutes. *Hastings Women's Law Journal, 10,* 1–35.

Lloyd, R. (2011). *Girls like us: Fighting for a world where girls are not for sale, an activist finds her calling and heals herself.* New York: Harper.

Lowrey, B. (2011). Oceanside: Targets shift in prostitution law enforcement. *North County Times.*

Maticka-Tyndale, E., Lewis, J., Clark, J. P., Zubick, T. and Young, S. (2000). Exotic dancing and health. *Women & Health, 31,* 87–108.

McClanahan, S. F., McClelland, G. K., Abram, K. H. and Teplin, L. A. (1999). Pathways into prostitution among female jail detainees. *Psychiatric Services, 50,* 1606–13.

McGreal, C. (2010). Craigslist is hub for child prostitution, allege trafficked women. *Guardian,* August 8. Retrieved from http://www.guardian.com.co.uk/technology/2010/August/08/craiglist-underage-prostitution-allegations.

Miller, J. (1995). Gender and power on the streets: Street prostitution in the era of crack cocaine. *Journal of Contemporary Ethnography, 23,* 427–52.

Mitchell, K. J., Finkelhor, D. and Wolak, J. (2009). Conceptualizing juvenile prostitution as child maltreatment: Findings from the national juvenile prostitution study. *Child Maltreatment, 15,* 18–36.

Monto, M. (n.d.). Conceiving of sex as a commodity: A study of arrested clients of female street prostitutes. Unpublished manuscript.

Nixon, K., Tutty, L., Downe, P., Gorkoff, K. and Ursel, J. (2002). The everyday occurrence: Violence in the lives of girls exploited through prostitution. *Violence against Women, 8,* 1016–43.

Norton-Hawk, M. A. (2003). Social class, drugs, gender and the limitations of the law: Contrasting the elite prostitute with the street prostitute. *Studies in Law, Politics, and Society, 29,* 115–31.

Polaris Project (2011a). *Human trafficking legislative issue brief: Sex trafficking of minors andn"safe harbor."* www.polarisproject.org/what-we-do/policy-advocacy/legislative-toolbox.

——(2011b). *How does your state rate on human trafficking laws?* www.polarisproject.org/what-we-do/policy-advocacy/state-policy/current-laws.

Raphael, J. (2004). *Listening to Olivia: Violence, poverty, and prostitution.* Boston, MA: Northeastern University Press.

Raphael, J. and Myers-Powell, B. (2010). *From victims to victimizers: Interviews with 25 ex-pimps in Chicago.* Chicago, IL: DePaul University College of Law.

Raphael, J. and Reichert, J. (2008). *Domestic sex trafficking of Chicago women and girls.* Chicago, IL: Illinois Criminal Justice Information Authority and DePaul University College of Law.

Raphael, J., Reichert, J. and Powers, M. (2010). Pimp control and violence: Domestic sex trafficking of Chicago women and girls. *Women & Criminal Justice, 20,* 89–104.

Raphael, J. and Shapiro, D. (2004). Violence in indoor and outdoor prostitution venues. *Violence Against Women, 10,* 126–39.

——(2002). *Sisters speak out: The lives and needs of prostituted women in Chicago.* Chicago, IL: Center for Impact Research.

Saletan, W. (2010). Craigslist shuts its "adult" section. Where will sex ads go now? www.slate.com.

Stransky, M. and Finkelhor, D. (2008). *How many juveniles are involved in prostitution in the U.S.?* Durham, NH: Crimes against Children Research Center.

Surratt, H., Inciardi, J., Kurtz, S. and Kiley, M. (2004). Sex work and drug use in a subculture of violence. *Crime & Delinquency, 50,* 43–59.

Thomas-Lester, A. (2006). Oscar winner hits angry chord. *Washington Post.* Retrieved from www.washingtonpost.com/wp-dyn/content/article/2006/03/06/AR2006030601461.html.

Walberg, M. and Sweeney, A. (2010, November 24). Woman charged with human trafficking. *Chicago Tribune.* Retrieved from http://www.articles.chicagotribune.com/2010-11-24/news/ct-met-underage-prostitution-20101124_1_humantraffiking-task-force-underage-girls-prostitution.

Weber, C. (2010). Ex-madam Kristin Davis protests Eliot Spitzer's TV show, runs for governor. www.politicsdaily.com/2010/06/24/ex-madam-kristin-davis-protests-eliot-spitzers-tv-show-runs-for-governor.

Weitzer, R. (2010). The movement to criminalize sex work in the United States. *Journal of Law and Society, 37,* 61–84.

Wesely, J. K. (2002). Growing up sexualized: Issues of power and violence in the lives of female exotic dancers. *Violence Against Women, 8,* 1186–1211.

Williamson, C. and Prior, M. (2009). Domestic minor sex trafficking: A network of underground players in the Midwest. *Journal of Child & Adolescent Trauma, 2,* 1–16.

TOPICAL BOX 14.1

Human Trafficking

By Rebecca J. Macy

Human trafficking is a horrific problem affecting children, men and women worldwide. The United States' 2000 Trafficking Victims Protection Act defines the problem as both: "sex trafficking in which a commercial sex act is induced by force, fraud, or coercion, or in which the person induced to perform such an act has not attained 18 years of age;" and "the recruitment, harboring, transportation, provision, or obtaining of a person for labor or services, through the use of force, fraud, or coercion for the purpose of subjection to involuntary servitude, peonage, debt bondage, or slavery" (U.S. Department of State, 2010, p. 8). Thus, trafficking takes many forms, including bonded and forced labor, child soldiers, debt bondage, involuntary domestic servitude, as well as sex trafficking. Forced labor is one of the more common forms of human trafficking (U.S. Department of State, 2010). Often but not always, trafficking involves movement of persons from one location to another. Such movement can cross national borders. However, human trafficking also occurs within countries (U.S. Department of State, 2010). For example, homeless and runaway youth are especially vulnerable to trafficking within the United States (Clawson, Dutch, Solomon and Grace, 2009).

National and worldwide data about trafficking victims and trafficking law enforcement activities are limited. Trafficking research is challenging to conduct because it involves investigating "hidden populations" (Tyldum and Brunovskis, 2005, p. 18). People are "hidden" in a research context for two reasons. First, there are few data sources (e.g., survey records) in which these persons can be found, unlike other crime, health and social issues. For sources that do exist, many are fraught with data collection limitations and measurement bias (Tyldum and Brunovskis, 2005). Consequently, the statistics produced by such sources cannot be considered rigorous or reliable. Second, trafficking involves politicized issues (e.g., immigration, sex work), illegal activities, and stigmatizing circumstances (e.g., undocumented immigration, prostitution) (Cwikel and Hoban, 2005; Tyldum and Brunovskis, 2005). Thus, trafficking victims, perpetrators and those who use the services of trafficking victims have reasons to remain concealed. Nonetheless, estimates suggest that globally 12.3 million adults and children are human trafficking victims (U.S. Department of State, 2010).

Little research and information exists on trafficking perpetrators, as well as those who use trafficking victims' services (e.g., those who pay for sex with trafficking victims and those who employ trafficking victims as domestic workers) (Cwikel and Hoban, 2005; Schauer and Wheaton, 2006). However, there is preliminary information about trafficking victims. People who live in communities and countries where there is conflict and war, gender inequality, law enforcement corruption, political corruption, serious crime problems, and significant poverty are at higher risk of trafficking relative to people who do not live in such circumstances (Clawson et al., 2009). In addition, children and young people, unemployed people, people with physical and mental health problems, and people who have been previously victimized are also at heightened risk (Clawson et al., 2009). Both males and females are vulnerable to trafficking. Globally just over half (56 percent) of trafficking victims are female (U.S. Department of State, 2010).

The needs of trafficking victims are considerable. Victims will always need safety and protection. Depending on their circumstances, location and the form of trafficking that they were forced to endure, victims might also need education and job training, interpretation and translation, legal and immigration advocacy, life skills training, physical and mental health care, shelter and housing, and substance abuse treatment (Clawson et al., 2009; Macy and Johns, 2011).

In 2000, the United Nations developed the "Palermo Protocol" to address the problem of human trafficking globally. The protocol called on nations to criminalize trafficking and prosecute traffickers, as well as to prevent trafficking and protect victims. Thus, prevention, policy and service attention to trafficking has been increasing. Nevertheless, the level of attention given to trafficking varies considerably by country and is uneven worldwide. Further, no country has yet to develop a comprehensive and effective strategy to address human trafficking (U.S. Department of State, 2010).

Divergent perspectives about sex trafficking in relation to voluntary prostitution and voluntary sex work further complicate research on and intervention in sex trafficking specifically (Cwikel and Hoban, 2005; Kaufman and Crawford, 2011). Not all adult women who engage in prostitution and sex work are trafficking victims. However, the coercion that brothel owners and pimps use to initiate and maintain women in prostitution and sex work may be subtle (e.g., "mundane pressure, control, and veiled threats" Cwikel and Hoban, 2005, p. 309). Research on how women enter into and remain in prostitution and sex work, as well as research on how victims are coerced into and forced to stay in sex trafficking, has been encouraged to help clarify the nuances among these issues (Cwikel and Hoban, 2005).

Fortunately, there are emerging practices and policies to address both labor and sex trafficking. Promising policy strategies include special protections for child victims and immigration relief for all victims (U.S. Department of State, 2010). Likewise, there are emerging recommended practices for sheltering, protecting and serving trafficking victims (e.g., Clawson and Dutch, 2008; Macy and Johns, 2011). Such practices emphasize that all trafficking responses should be "victim-centered," meaning that victims' needs, protection and wishes should always be the foremost consideration (U.S. Department of State, 2010). Unfortunately, little research attention has been brought to bear on these emerging practices and policies (Kaufman and Crawford, 2011). Thus, the helpfulness of emerging strategies to prevent trafficking, prosecute traffickers and protect victims has yet to be determined. The dearth of evidence-based practices and policies is a serious problem because it is unclear when current efforts might do more harm than good for victims (Kaufman and Crawford, 2011). Solutions to prevent and address human trafficking will likely require cooperative, interdisciplinary and international strategies. Such strategies should include anti-poverty, criminal justice, educational, health and social welfare efforts.

Consequently, extensive work is needed worldwide to address human trafficking. In particular, practice, policy and research attention is needed: (a) to determine the incidence and prevalence of trafficking; (b) to investigate trafficking perpetrators and those who use trafficking victims' services; (c) for aftercare services and protection for trafficking victims; (d) for trafficking education and training for criminal justice, health, human service, and law enforcement personnel worldwide; (e) toward developing effective multi-disciplinary and international partnerships to address trafficking; and (f) for trafficking prevention interventions. Given the complex and dynamic nature of this problem, addressing human trafficking will be a considerable challenge for our global community. Nonetheless, given the horrific nature of this problem, this is a challenge we must address successfully.

REFERENCES

Clawson, H. J. and Dutch, N. (2008). *Addressing the needs of victims of human trafficking: Challenges, barriers, and promising practices*. U.S. Department of Health and Human Services, Office of the Assistant Secretary for Planning and Evaluation. Retrieved from http://aspe.hhs.gov/hsp/ 07/HumanTrafficking/Needs/ib.shtml.

Clawson, H. J., Dutch, N., Salomon, A. and Grace, L. G. (2009). *Human trafficking into and within the United States: A review of the literature*. U.S. Department of Health and Human Services, Office of the Assistant Secretary for Planning and Evaluation. Retrieved from http://aspe.hhs.gov/hsp/07/HumanTrafficking/ LitRev/index.shtml.

Cwikel, J. and Hoban, E. (2005). Contentious issues in research on trafficked women working in the sex industry: Study design, ethics, and methodology. *Journal of Sex Research, 42*(4), 306–16.

Kaufman, M. R. and Crawford, M. (2011). Sex trafficking in Nepal: A review of intervention and prevention programs. *Violence Against Women, 17,* 651–65.

Macy, R. J. and Johns, N. (2011). Aftercare services for international sex trafficking survivors: Informing US service and program development in an emerging practice area. *Trauma, Violence & Abuse, 12*(2) 87–98.

Miller, J. (2011). Grounding the analysis of gender and crime: Accomplishing and interpreting qualitative interview research. In D. Gadd, S. Karstedt, and S. F. Messner (eds), *The Sage handbook of criminological research methods* (pp. 49–62). London: Sage.

Schauer, E. J. and Wheaton, E. M. (2006). Sex trafficking into the United States: A literature review. *Criminal Justice Review, 31*(2), 146–69.

Tyldum, G. and Brunovskis, A. (2005). Describing the unobserved: Methodological challenges in empirical studies on human trafficking. *International Migration, 43*(1/2), 17–34.

U.S. Department of State. (2010). *Trafficking in persons report*. Retrieved from http://www.state.gov/documents/ organization/142979.pdf.

BIOGRAPHICAL BOX 14.1

By Jody Miller

My primary research agenda involves investigating the relationships of gender and inequality with offending and victimization, at the situational, interactional, and micro-organizational levels. I use qualitative research methods—primarily in-depth interviewing techniques—to examine the social organizational facets of gender within offender networks and neighborhoods, and the impact of gendered meaning systems on offending and victimization. In doing so, I gear my research to two primary purposes: to contribute to the refinement of feminist theoretical developments in criminology; and to speak to non-feminist audiences in criminology, with the goal of demonstrating *why* gender matters to the uninitiated, unconcerned, or unconvinced. Simply, it makes good scholarly sense to investigate gender inequality within criminology because gender remains a primary organizing structure within and across societies; this is clearly reflected in patterns of crime, victimization, and social control.

How my particular set of theoretical, methodological, and epistemological commitments came about reaches back to my days as a university student. I was a photojournalism major as an undergraduate, and as I made the transition to academic sociology and criminology, I did so embedded within two influential contexts. First, I was at the time blending my interest in photography with my growing concerns about gender, inequality, and crime. Over two summers in my early twenties, I taught photography at a residential facility for delinquent girls. Many of the girls I worked with had very troubled histories; a number had been in and out of such facilities throughout much of their young lives, and most had been victimized and involved in crime. Yet, I found them to be passionate, vivacious, and sometimes downright fun to be around.

At the same time, I was working toward my master's degree in women's studies. This was an intellectually exciting time in the early 1990s when feminist scholars had very much begun to take up questions about the relationships between victimization, agency, and resistance, as well as the intersections of gender with inequalities of race, class, age, and sexuality. Two works in particular—Sandra Harding's edited collection *Feminism and Methodology*, and Elizabeth Spelman's *Inessential Woman*—led me to think critically about the philosophical underpinnings and politics of our research. Combined, these critical insights and my work with girls whom I found to be resilient against many odds led to my primary scholarly emphasis on teasing out the gendered nuances and complexities of situations. For a variety of reasons (see Miller, 2011), I found qualitative interview research the best means for me to accomplish this.

Perhaps not surprisingly, much of my work has remained focused on the experiences of adolescent girls, as illustrated by my two research monographs, *One of the Guys: Girls, Gangs and Gender* and *Getting Played: African American Girls, Urban Inequality, and Gendered Violence.* In these and other works, I routinely push for scholarly attention to processual, organizational, and symbolic facets of gender and gender inequality, and the intersection of gender with other social positions of inequality; and I challenge scholars to look beyond the all-too-common—but often implicit—conceptualization of gender as merely an individual-level attribute. I seek explanations for gender differences in the social world, and also carefully attend to often overlooked similarities across gender. Over the past 20 years, I have seen tremendous growth in the field with regard to approaching gender in these more sociological ways. And yet, androcentrism certainly remains; and as feminist scholars, we also must remain ever vigilant in thinking about how we study women's (and men's) lives and to what consequence.

REFERENCE

Miller, J. (2011). Grounding the analysis of gender and crime: Accomplishing and interpreting qualitative interview research. In D. Gadd, S. Karstedt and S.F. Messner (eds), *The Sage handbook of criminological research methods* (pp. 49–62). London: Sage.

CHAPTER FIFTEEN

Male Prostitution

By Ronald Weitzer

Traditionally, scholars have focused their attention on female prostitution and have ignored male and transgender prostitution, despite the fact that males and transgenders comprise a substantial percentage of the prostitutes in many cities (Weitzer 1999). In the past decade, however, a growing body of literature has examined male sex workers. Most male prostitutes sell sex to other men.

MALE PROVIDERS, MALE CUSTOMERS

There are some basic similarities as well as some important differences between male and female prostitution. For instance, there is a similar hierarchy in each—stratified by whether the worker sells sex on the street, in a bar or a brothel/club/massage parlor, through an escort agency, or as an independent call boy. Like female street workers, young men on the street often enter the trade as runaways or to support a drug habit, and they engage in "survival sex." Like upscale female workers, call boys and escorts possess social skills that allow them to relate to educated, upper-class customers, and they may develop emotional attachments to some of their regular clients (Smith *et al.* 2008; van der Poel 1992). And, like female workers in the mid-and upper-level tiers, similarly situated males are more likely than street workers to hold positive views of their work and themselves (Koken *et al.* 2010; West 1993). Interviews with 185 male prostitutes in three Australian cities found that two-thirds felt good about being a sex worker (Minichiello 2001). A study of male escorts reported that, as a result of being generously paid for sex, the escorts felt desired, attractive, empowered, and important; they also developed greater self-confidence and more positive body images over time (Uy *et al.* 2007). As a male brothel worker stated, it was "so wonderful to have love made to me by so many wealthy and socially elite men" (Pittman 1971: 23).

Economic motives are central for both male and female sex workers, but some males are also motivated by the potential for sexual adventure that prostitution may offer (van der Poel 1992). Differences in the ways male and female prostitutes experience their work are evident in the following areas. Males tend to be:

- involved in prostitution in a more sporadic or transitory way, drifting in and out of prostitution and leaving the trade earlier than women (Aggleton 1999; Weinberg *et al.* 1999);
- less likely to be coerced into prostitution, to have pimps, and to experience violence from customers (Aggleton 1999; Weinberg *et al.* 1999; West 1993);
- in greater control over their working conditions, because few have pimps (West 1993);
- more diverse as to their sexual orientation: some self-identify as gay; others as bisexual; and others insist that they are heterosexual despite engaging in homosexual conduct, an identity–behavior disparity typically not found among female prostitutes (Aggleton 1999);
- less stigmatized within the gay community (Aggleton 1999; Koken *et al.* 2010) but more stigmatized in the wider society because of the coupling of homosexuality and prostitution.

Like female sex workers, males draw boundaries around the services they are willing to perform. Some limit their activity to oral sex; some engage in penetrative but not receptive oral or anal sex; and others engage in all types. Some limit their encounters to sexual exchanges, while others are open to more comprehensive interactions, including cuddling, massage, and conversation. This has come to be known as the "boyfriend experience," a quasi-romantic, yet paid, encounter.

Although most research focuses on street prostitution, a thriving indoor market has been studied by some researchers. Male brothels are fairly rare, though a few have been studied (Pittman 1971). One hybrid brothel–escort agency, a business that provided services to about 200 clients per month, was studied by Smith, Grov, and Seal (2008). Most of the sexual encounters took place outside the agency, but some were "in-call," occurring in a designated room at the agency. Some of the workers even lived at the agency. When not working, some of the men engaged in social activities with other men at the agency, including the manager and friends of their fellow escorts. The manager served as a mentor to the escorts and was well liked by them. Like madams in female brothels, the manager screened clients and sought to ensure a safe and pleasant working environment for his employees. The benefits of working for this agency were that it provided a "sense of community" for the workers, "shielded escorts from potential stigma," and was "a source of positive support" for their work and lifestyle (Smith *et al.* 2008: 206, 208).

Most escort agencies do not double as brothels, resulting in much more social distance between the employees. Salamon's (1989) study of an escort agency in London that did not provide in-call services reported very little social interaction between the manager and the workers, and few workers knew any of the others.

Research on street prostitution offers a picture of a very different world—more risky for the workers but also potentially exciting. McNamara's (1994) ethnographic study of male street prostitutes in Times Square, New York, in the early 1990s found a community involved in selling sex on the street and at peep shows, gay bars, the bus terminal, and hotels. Most were Hispanic youths, and most of the clients were white men. The sex trade was remarkably well ordered: "very few problems occur either between the hustlers and the clients or among the boys themselves. In the vast majority of cases, the activities are completed without incident" (McNamara 1994: 62). The police generally left the prostitutes alone unless there was a disturbance.

Although most of the research on sex tourism centers on female prostitutes and foreign male clients, sometimes men travel abroad to meet and pay for sex with other men. Padilla's (2007) ethnographic study in the Dominican Republic provides a unique window into gay male sex tourism. Many of the workers do not self-identify as gay—in fact, many are married—and they service men simply because they comprise a much larger market than female sex tourists who are willing to pay for a sex encounter. Many sex tourists eroticize this, as it seems to accord with the fantasy of having gay sex with a heterosexual male. While some male prostitutes aim to avoid long-term or serial relationships with particular clients, due to the potential emotional risks involved, others cultivate long-term clients, develop affectionate feelings toward them, and await their next visit. The latter put a premium on meeting customers who will continue to send money or gifts after they return home. Padilla found a connection between the material and emotional aspects of these relationships: workers who received the most economic rewards were most likely to develop affectionate feelings toward a customer. Older clients were more likely to seek stable and more intimate relationships with a specific worker, while younger clients sought sex with multiple partners.

MALE PROVIDERS, FEMALE CUSTOMERS

Relatively little is known about male prostitutes who sell sex to women, and the few studies on this topic all center on tourist destinations. A handful of studies have examined contacts between affluent Western female tourists and young Caribbean men, who meet at clubs and on beaches (Phillips 1999; Sanchez Taylor 2001, 2006). There are some basic similarities between female sex tourism and male sex tourism (e.g., economic inequality between buyer and seller) as well as some differences (e.g., female sex tourists rarely act violently against male prostitutes). There is a profound economic inequality between the buyer and seller, and this gives the buyer a similar level of control over the worker, whether the latter is female or male. Like male sex tourists, female sex tourists use their economic power to buy intimate relations with local men, and during these encounters they assert control over the men. One study in the Caribbean concluded:

> The kind of control exercised in their relationships with local men is actually very similar to that exercised by male sex tourists in sexual economic relationships with local women ... They are able to use their economic power to limit the risk of being challenged or subjugated.
> *(Sanchez Taylor 2006: 49–50)*

Female customers may become long-term companions or benefactors to the men, and in some cases this can lead to marriage.

Many of the female sex tourists do not define themselves as "customers" who buy sex from local men. Instead, they construct the encounters as "holiday romances" or "real love," and almost none describe their affairs as "purely physical" (Sanchez Taylor 2001: 755). The women do not see themselves as sex tourists and the men do not see themselves as prostitutes. However, the latter do receive material rewards for the time they spend with foreign women, including meals, lodgings, gifts, and money. According to Sanchez Taylor, these relationships therefore have all the hallmarks of sex tourism, irrespective of whether they are short or long term or whether money is exchanged, provided that the man receives at least some material benefits. Similarly, Phillips (1999: 191) argues that these transactions can be "easily fitted under the umbrella of prostitution," even though both the tourist and the provider do not perceive their liaison as such.

The "host club" in Japan is another example of male sex work involving female clients. Similar to the hostess clubs where women entertain male customers, host clubs are locations where women go to enjoy themselves in the company of attractive male hosts, which may include sexual encounters. Such bars have flourished in the past decade, with approximately 200 now operating in Tokyo alone. The hosts serve exorbitantly expensive alcoholic drinks to their clients and lavish praise, compliments, and advice upon the specific women to whom they attach themselves. The nature of this phenomenon is captured in the concept of "commodified romance" (Takeyama 2005), which involves nonsexual intimacy but may also include sexual services.

Why do women seek out these paid encounters? An ethnographic study of host clubs revealed that "customers claim that there are few other places in Japan's male-centered entertainment world where women can safely enjoy romantic excitement" (Takeyama 2005: 204). According to this study, the vast majority of hosts have had sex with at least some of their customers, although they prefer to avoid sexual intercourse in order to keep the woman coming back to the club and paying the high prices (the host gets a cut). Some hosts sleep with their customers without having sex with them.

CONCLUSION

Further research on male sex workers who service women will help address the question of whether the customer's gender influences the character and subjective meaning of the encounter. To what degree, if at all, is gender inequality or domination present in exchanges between female customers and male workers? Do female customers engage in less objectification of the workers, or is objectification evident irrespective of the customer's gender? Do female customers expect more emotional involvement from sex workers than is true for male customers? When the customer is a woman, is there less likelihood of violence from either party? These questions have yet to be investigated, but such research would be invaluable in answering the theoretical question of whether prostitution has certain "fundamental" or "essential" qualities, irrespective of the gender of the worker and the customer, or whether it varies significantly according to the actors involved. To answer these questions, we need systematic examinations of male prostitutes who service men in comparison with those who service women, and of male and female prostitutes working in the same tier, such as the comparative studies by Koken *et al.* (2010) and Weinberg *et al.* (1999).

REFERENCES

Aggleton, P. (ed.) (1999) *Men Who Sell Sex*, Philadelphia, PA: Temple University Press.
Koken, J., Bimbi, D., and Parsons, J. (2010) "Male and female escorts: a comparative analysis," in R. Weitzer (ed.) *Sex for Sale: Prostitution, Pornography, and the Sex Industry*, 2n edn, New York: Routledge.

McNamara, R. (1994) *The Times Square Hustler: Male Prostitution in New York City*, Westport, CT: Praeger.

Minichiello, V. (2001) "Male sex workers in three Australian cities: socio-demographic and sex work characteristics," *Journal of Homosexuality*, 42: 29–51.

Padilla, M. (2007) "Western Union daddies and their quest for authenticity: an ethnographic study of the Dominican gay sex tourism industry," *Journal of Homosexuality*, 53: 241–275.

Phillips, J. (1999) "Tourist-oriented prostitution in Barbados: the case of the beach boy and the white female tourist," in K. Kempadoo (ed.) *Sun, Sex, and Gold: Tourism and Sex Work in the Caribbean*, Lanham, MD: Rowman & Littlefield.

Pittman, D. (1971) "The male house of prostitution," *Transaction*, 8: 21–27.

Salamon, E. (1989) "The homosexual escort agency: deviance disavowal," *British Journal of Sociology*, 40: 1–21.

Sanchez Taylor, J. (2001) "Dollars are a girl's best friend: female tourists' sexual behavior in the Caribbean," *Sociology*, 34: 749–764.

Sanchez Taylor, J. (2006) "Female sex tourism: a contradiction in terms?," *Feminist Review*, 83: 43–59.

Smith, M., Grov, C., and Seal, D. (2008) "Agency-based male sex work," *Journal of Men's Studies*, 16: 193–210.

Takeyama, A. (2005) "Commodified romance in a Tokyo host club," in M. McLelland and R. Dasgupta (eds.) *Genders, Transgenders, and Sexualities in Japan*, New York: Routledge.

Uy, J., Parsons, J., Bimbi, D., Koken, J., and Halkitis, P. (2007) "Gay and bisexual male escorts who advertise on the internet: understanding the reasons for and effects of involvement in commercial sex," *International Journal of Men's Health*, 3: 11–26.

van der Poel, S. (1992) "Professional male prostitution: a neglected phenomenon," *Crime, Law, and Social Change*, 18: 259–275.

Weinberg, M., Shaver, F., and Williams, C. (1999) "Gendered prostitution in the San Francisco Tenderloin," *Archives of Sexual Behavior*, 28: 503–521.

Weitzer, R. (1999) "New directions in research on prostitution," *Crime, Law, and Social Change*, 43: 211–235.

West, D. (1993) *Male Prostitution*, Binghamton, NY: Hayworth.

CPSIA information can be obtained
at www.ICGtesting.com
Printed in the USA
LVOW04s0121200617
538705LV00005B/11/P